RE-DIGGING ART'S FOUNDATIONS

Re-digging Art's Foundations

Essays on Gospel and Art

DAVID THISTLETHWAITE

WIPF & STOCK · Eugene, Oregon

RE-DIGGING ART'S FOUNDATIONS
Essays on Gospel and Art

Copyright © 2024 David Thistlethwaite. All rights reserved. Except for brief quotations in critical publications or reviews, no part of this book may be reproduced in any manner without prior written permission from the publisher. Write: Permissions, Wipf and Stock Publishers, 199 W. 8th Ave., Suite 3, Eugene, OR 97401.

Wipf & Stock
An Imprint of Wipf and Stock Publishers
199 W. 8th Ave., Suite 3
Eugene, OR 97401

www.wipfandstock.com

PAPERBACK ISBN: 979-8-3852-1814-1
HARDCOVER ISBN: 979-8-3852-1815-8
EBOOK ISBN: 979-8-3852-1816-5

11/18/24

Where indicated, Scripture is quoted from *Holy Bible*, New Living Translation, copyright © 1996, 2004, 2015 by Tyndale House Foundation. Used by permission of Tyndale House Publishers, Inc., Carol Stream, Illinois 60188. All rights reserved.

Where indicated, Scripture is quoted from The Holy Bible, English Standard Version. ESV® Text Edition: 2016. Copyright © 2001 by Crossway Bibles, a publishing ministry of Good News Publishers.

Where indicated, Scripture is quoted from Holy Bible, New International Version®, NIV® Copyright ©1973, 1978, 1984, 2011 by Biblica, Inc.® Used by permission. All rights reserved worldwide.

Where indicated, Scripture is quoted from New American Standard Bible®, Copyright © 1960, 1971, 1977, 1995, 2020 by The Lockman Foundation. All rights reserved.

Where indicated, Scripture is quoted from Revised Standard Version of the Bible, copyright © 1946, 1952, and 1971 the Division of Christian Education of the National Council of the Churches of Christ in the United States of America. Used by permission. All rights reserved.

Oxford University Press (© Oxford Publishing Limited)

Thomas F. Torrance, *Theological Science* (New York: Oxford University Press, 1969), quotation used by permission.

Holburne Museum (© Holburne Museum / Bridgeman Images)

Photograph of John Constable (1776-1837) *Flatford Mill from the Bridge*, Holburne Museum, Bath

Tate Publishing, London, *Mark Rothko*, Exhibition Catalogue 1987, excerpts used by permission.

To my parents,
who gave me so much more
than I realized at the time.

*For now we see through a glass, darkly; but then face to face:
now I know in part; but then shall I know even as also I am known.*

—1 Corinthians 13:12, KJV

Contents

Illustrations | ix

Preface | xi

Acknowledgments | xiii

Introduction | xv

1. Art and Reality | 1
2. A Question of Beauty (A Personal Story): Introduction | 19
3. A Question of Beauty (A Personal Story): A Process of Thinking | 26
4. Reflections on Constable's *Flatford Mill* | 78
5. Rothko, Some Questions | 88
6. Seeing the Invisible in the Visible: Towards a Theological Account of Art | 100
7. Why Art? | 113
8. Art, Time, and Eternity | 125
9. Christianity and Culture: Questions Raised by Ruskin | 140
10. Art and the Church | 149
11. The Holy Spirit in Art | 153
12. Aesthetic Certainty in an Age of Relativism: Sir Hugh Lane and the Legacy of His Beliefs | 159

Bibliography | 175

Illustrations

Figure 1. Lancing College, Sussex, Lower Quad | 28

Figure 2. Cambridge, St. John's College, *Battle of the Styles* | 49

Figure 3. Cambridge, St. John's College, The Cripps Building | 49

Figure 4. John Constable, *Flatford Lock from the Bridge* | 77

Figure 5. Sir Hugh Lane | 156

Preface

I doubt if you could have had a discussion about art with St. Paul. Art as such did not exist in Bible times, although there was plenty of what we call art to look at—statues, villa decorations, and so on. Now, of course, art is a "thing," a huge institution, so strong that it seems to have left the Bible behind. If you love both, as I do, the challenge is to discover and show that the world of art and the world of the Bible are the same world.

For some, who predominantly love art, this may seem an unnecessary exercise. But they might need to consider that art, as an institution on its own, is not without problems. It has been set up, by the art historians, to have a direction of travel. But where shall it go? Not towards truth, because we are not sure what that means. Like some spacecraft programmed with the wrong coordinates, it might spin off into a pointless orbit or lose itself in deep space. Isn't it time to call it home?

There is always the suspicion that if the Bible approaches art it will chew up its freedom. But there is no freedom as limited as that which believes life has no purpose, which creates huge ditches between the observer and meaning, and makes new rules to replace the old. The only freedom worth having is that which enables us to do things, purposefully and connectedly. The Bible, in all its tremendous variety, shows us what this freedom is.

"The Bible," here, is shorthand for the story of God and his interactions with us. You understand them by living in them. The point of publishing a set of essays, rather than a treatise, is that the essays come from life: different opportunities to speak, personal reflections on artists, even my own intellectual history. My "theory of art," such as it is, surfaces in various places and is not that well hidden; but I would be happy if it attaches itself to the reader unconsciously, as something they always knew, or once thought about, as something plainly obvious.

Woodmancote, Cirencester, Gloucestershire, July 2024

Acknowledgments

A true friend is someone who thinks better of you than you think of yourself and manages to convince you that you can and should keep going. Chief of these, of course, are my ever-supportive family, my wife Ali Thistlethwaite, our daughter Adelaide Roynel, and our son John. But there have been others who have also been in it for the long haul, and here I must especially mention two Scots, Robert T. Walker and Alan Wilson. Bob has a unique gift for being both pastoral and theological, often giving a word in season. Alan has been a constant ear for questions, ranging from practical art, Bible understanding, and art theory, and he has, supremely, the gift of encouragement.

Introduction

Many years ago, when I was a student, I had cause to write to British Rail, as it was then, about the proposed remodeling of London's Liverpool Street Station. The station had grown piecemeal and was probably a nightmare to manage, but it had beautiful gloomy vaults and some really distinguished brick arches that always gave me intense pleasure. I made the mistake of saying that the building was "of course" one of the masterpieces of London's architecture, and the company responded by giving one of their less-busy graduate staff the task of writing a patronising reply. I cannot recall all of it, but I know that he called my views "subjective." This annoyed me very much, but I could not think of a way of disproving him. That experience, and the wound to my sense that what I saw was not to be argued with, became grit in my oyster, and over many years it was the irritant that in part led to faith and in due course has, I hope, produced the odd pearl.

I wanted to know how the aesthetic sense might be more than subjective (one of the most oppressive words in the modern dictionary), because, though it is obvious people disagree, aesthetic judgment struck me as being rational and objective, in the sense of being about real features of real things. But the problem was also about more than beauty and aesthetics. I was sick of an art history tradition that shied away from discussing the very realities that art itself was concerned with. But we (the art history community) were not sure how to make the connections between the four corners of a canvas and "the real world." We could not discuss the truth of a painting. So I wanted to find a way of speaking about that.

But then there was a question about the "real world." Most of us thought of the world in material terms and somehow had got convinced that there was nothing more to life than molecules. As a student I studied Italian Baroque art, and can remember being faintly embarrassed by the "religiosity" of Bernini's sculpture of *The Ecstasy of Saint Teresa*, which we assumed was intended to conjure up or manipulate in the viewer a religio-aesthetic experience; but it never even crossed our minds that the artist was trying to convey a transcendent experience that was real. Nobody discussed with us the thought that the physical might be just a small component of the "real world." I assumed that Italian Baroque art was entirely to do with church propaganda and nothing to do with angels and heaven as having real existence. It is odd to think that it is the abstract artists of our own times who have tried to penetrate the veil, because they have not been satisfied with pure materialism.

A third preoccupation of mine has been the freedom of the viewer. Nobody, of course, wants to be merely critical, setting every work at a distance and measuring it against some predetermined schema. Neither does any of us want to be merely liberal, accepting everything put before us with wide-eyed wonder or forced appreciation. But, given that much of what happens in art viewing results from the personal chemistry in the viewer's head, it does seem to me that we ought not to neglect the viewer's contribution in "creating" the work quite as much as we do. This is not so much a theoretical as a practical concern, particularly for the modern age. We know the familiar pattern. An art movement develops outside the canon of "bourgeois" social acceptance as an "advance guard" or *avant garde*. It is rejected by society at large. Then a few bolder souls accept it, then society approves it, and then finally it is canonized as beyond criticism. The Impressionist movement has taught us what to expect. We don't want to make the same mistake twice, of course, and these days, the canny bourgeois are quick to look ahead and rush into canonization before anyone has had time to reject. But what we do not usually consider is that the viewer's new humility before the previously, or potentially, rejected work has an unseen price, which is the adaptation we make to it, maybe by discarding previously held beliefs, which were perfectly fit for purpose. This is almost inevitable. Works of art, however bizarre, are seldom destroyed, and as they rest on public display, they drag us into their orbit, challenging us to mentally create a new world in which such things have the right to exist. How much does this matter? Are we not all adults, able to look after ourselves in the presence of experimental art? Perhaps for some people it does not matter.

But we would do well to be warned by the Bible, which sees the making of religious images as the crime of crimes. But this is art, we say, and not idolatry. Yes, indeed, but where exactly is the boundary? An idol is an image that gives certain beliefs a space to exist, a public legitimacy. I am not just talking about Buddhas in garden centers. Through art, something far more subtle has taken place, the formation of a public mind. We are in the modern age, where people, worshippers of the material, treat themselves and others as objects; and we have our pervasive dehumanizing aesthetic to enforce it, or perhaps to originate it. This scenery of the mind did not come from nowhere. Artists foresaw the future, and invited us all into it.

These then are the preoccupations that will surface, in different ways, in all of the essays. I have grouped them in reverse chronological order (the latest is first), but it doesn't really matter which sequence you adopt. Some are derived from talks, usually written up afterwards, and others have been written for myself, as a means to clarify thought. The longest of these, subtitled *A Process of Thinking*, is an attempt to relate my thoughts about art to life-events, in a chronology that leaves a great deal out. When I recall ideas they are often associated with particular times and places, and I hope this coloring is helpful for explaining them.

It is clear that we live in unusual times. When I was an undergraduate, pavement-throwing and riot were what other nations did in response to political questions, but for us in Britain, the institutional consensus had rendered most contentious matters "academic." Our dons were imperturbable and witty, and any painful subject could be passed off with a joke. But today, to carry an idea is often to incur a cost. Once again, truth matters, and it is worth taking up the argument because there is such a slurry of untruth around. These essays may be found to be just nibbling at the edges of the issues that are dividing nations and even families; but if it is true that "all truth is God's truth," then those of us who are able, even the most cowardly of us, must join the battle where we find it.

I

Art and Reality[1]

INTRODUCTION

The condition of art today inevitably provokes the question, What is art? This is not because such abstract questions are appealing or easy to answer, but because when we turn from looking at the great national collections—the story of art from Duccio to the Impressionists—to somewhere like London's Tate Modern with its minimalist and conceptual work, we are bound to ask ourselves, Is this the same thing?

We have a choice here. Either we take some manifestation of art, such as Greek sculpture or Dutch seventeenth-century painting, as normative and exclude anything we cannot relate to that—or we treat art as a large tent into which almost anything can fit and accept that every "artist," just by their existence, is broadening the definition.

The current temper of our society is inclusive. We do not like to decide what is, or is not, British or American; who does, or does not, "belong" (whatever that means); what is, or is not, truth in religion. In the same way, most of us would feel uncomfortable stating that anything presented as art is actually "not art," according to some predetermined definition. And yet there is a difference between things that find their way into national collections and those that do not. There have to be some criteria. Since these seem to be ever changing, it may be more helpful, instead of trying to identify the markers of inclusion, to consider in a broad way the nature and being of art in the world, what it is, and why it can somehow invert itself.

---

1. The original version of this essay was written in 2020.

1. WHAT IS ART?

There are two ways of answering the question of what art is. The first is to focus on the preselected art object and the art experience and to try to examine them. The second is to pull back and to ask ourselves what sort of reality we are living in and to what, in that reality, art might correspond. The first method initially seems more obvious and promising, but it will be found that it leads inevitably to the second. We cannot say what art is, unless we know the sort of thing it might be; and that depends on what the universe is and what sort of beings we are.

a) Starting with the Art Object

Identifying the Art Object

Art objects are easy to find. They are in galleries, and in galleries we know what to do: we look. The objects that most readily meet our expectations are ones that are already known to be art before they enter the gallery—normally pictures in frames. The frame separates the art from the nonart environment. Somewhat confusingly, there is also a kind of object that becomes art simply by being in the gallery; it is not, we might say, intrinsically art. There is the well-known story of the cleaner in a museum who threw away a screwed up piece of paper, thinking it was rubbish, when in fact it was an exhibit. Perhaps the artist was asking the viewer to see value in what was normally discarded, or to contemplate the form in what was normally considered formless. The position of the art in the viewing space was vital to its meaning. On one side of the silk rope it would have been art and on the other side, rubbish. But, as art, does it actually have content? The artist has no means of guiding the viewer's thoughts. The screwed up ball may mean one thing, or perhaps another. In making the meaning, the viewer is doing most of the work. Why would not the cleaner's view also be valid? Without wishing to denigrate the capacity of art to surprise and innovate, in general, the work of art needs to have content and meaning before it ever gets to the gallery, and it needs to contain these things in itself.

    Before we attempt to look "at" the art object (to see what manner of thing it is) we need to repeat an obvious point. For everything that is included in the gallery, there are many things excluded. Someone does the including and excluding according to his or her own principles. The curator has become the gatekeeper, a role with considerable power, not just affecting the livelihoods of artists but also establishing the public icons of the culture.

Curators work with a view as to what should be included, and that in turn is based on a conception of the world.

To illustrate this point, we can consider a controversy in the early days of the Tate Gallery (founded in 1897). A successful Victorian sculptor, Sir Francis Chantrey (1781–1841), had left a large bequest, administered by the Council of the Royal Academy, for the purchase of the best contemporary work, and his legacy became the Tate Gallery's main purchasing fund until the 1920s. The fact that the Academicians bought only work by Royal Academicians became, when publicized, a scandal. The critic whose campaigning finally achieved reform, D. S. McColl, had a particular bugbear in the established Victorian landscape painter Benjamin Williams Leader R. A. (1831–1923), many of whose works had been bought in preference to British impressionists and other moderns. For McColl, Leader's landscapes were barely art at all, an institutionalized "art" that had lost touch with reality or society. McColl's judgment has been vindicated, and few of Leader's works are shown today, though his masterpiece *February Fill Dyke* (Birmingham Museum and Art Gallery) is still popular.

Emotions could and did run high over the question of what was "really" a work of art: is it the sort of safe and predictable landscape someone of a certain education expects to see, or is it something continually being redefined as each generation tries something new? Leader himself, we must assume, had a view as to what "proper" art was and stuck to it throughout his long life. It must not be forgotten that while a traditional painter could continue to paint churches and cottages, sunsets and reflections, the world was changing: art was in revolt, empires were breaking up, wars, revolution, and Spanish flu were leaving millions dead. There is always the question of what real art is and whether it connects to the real world or to some sanitized version of it. If the true art object is one that connects with reality, then even inside the art gallery we are faced with judgments as to what reality is.

Pleasure or Realism

Before we look at the question of reality, there is a possible objection. We have been assuming that the curatorial decision as to what to include, and what to exclude, depends on a view of the world. On the one hand we have skilled producers of pictures like Mr. Leader, whose depictions of rural scenes must be art by any objective criterion. On the other is the objection that, for a world in upheaval, to paint cottages as if nothing will ever change is to turn your back on the truth. The curator, in order to decide what is art, has to have a view as to what rings true. But what if we have been exaggerating the cognitive significance of art? What if art is essentially to do with pleasure? Perhaps we go to a gallery not to learn about life but for the pleasure of seeing things beautifully made or painted. The curator has only to judge what is most satisfying to know which art to admit.

It is true that the pleasure art gives is a large part of the reason people visit art galleries, and that this apparently has nothing to do with agreeing with artists' worldviews. For example, one could visit the Prado museum and enjoy looking successively at Bosch's vision of hell, El Greco's saints in ecstasy, Velasquez's royal family, and at Goya's paintings of insurrection and massacre; and although one might have feelings appropriate to each subject, the kind of pleasure involved is essentially the same. We only need to distil this pleasure to be able to identify valid art in the present and future. What is this mysterious pleasure of art?

Frustratingly, we cannot get outside the art experience to observe it. It is like a dream. You know it has happened, but you are no longer in it. When you are inside it, you cannot observe it. We will come out of a gallery of beautiful paintings invigorated, inspired, and enlarged, and the same works of art a month or two later can move us all over again, perhaps in different ways. So it is reasonable to consider that the foundation of art might be a certain sort of pleasure, not any cognitive strength it might have. As moderns, in fact, we have become expert in bracketing off any cognitive content a work of art might have—for example, that a picture depicts Christ and his mother—so that we might all the more enjoy the way it is painted.

There is however a difficulty in viewing art under the heading of pleasure. It is not that it is not true; it is just that it does not say enough. Pleasure, we are told, is experienced by certain alterations in brain chemistry. All we need to do is alter the brain chemistry, and sensations of pleasure are ours for the asking. Someone might conceivably make a living in Trafalgar Square selling serotonin pills to people about to spend a couple of hours in the National Gallery, saying that they could save their time and get their pleasure with far less trouble. But they, or their customers, would be missing the point. The reason for going there is to see the paintings, not to "get pleasure." Similarly, a mother might experience intense pleasure when her daughter gets married. But what does she do to get pleasure when she runs out of daughters? So the joy of a great painting must have more to it than its ability to activate our pleasure sensors.

Pure and Impure Art

However, there is something we might salvage from the idea of art as essentially pleasure. Suppose we divide art into two kinds, pure and impure. Art that is pure is art that, however it arose, still gives pleasure as art, because it is beautiful. It might be based on premises that you could not possibly agree with, like King James I's self-glorification in *The Apotheosis of James I* by Rubens (the Banqueting House ceiling). Because it is so well done, it may have the capacity to lift you out of yourself and perhaps increase your own fruitfulness. Without adhering to any "art for art's sake" theory, you could say that it does you good as art. It is possible that this is a very Protestant way of looking at art, because it ensures we can enjoy the art of many extravagantly Catholic artists, like Rubens or El Greco, without cognitive challenge.

Then there is the second kind of art, the impure, where cognitive challenge, or at least the power to persuade, is precisely the point of the art; and if you do not surrender to the idea, you have missed the value of the art. You might argue, of course, that the purpose of many of Rubens's great paintings was to persuade us to become good Catholics; nonetheless it is as art, with all its roots and ramifications in the tradition, that we most commonly receive it.

A good example of impure art is the "revolutionary" art of which we have seen much in the nineteenth and twentieth centuries, which is designed not simply to enlarge or progress the tradition but to introduce into the bloodstream of society a different understanding of the world. For example, in his time Manet was considered revolutionary, because although he clearly painted in the tradition, learning his craft from Velasquez and Goya, he introduced a new way of looking at the world, a world he saw as if without metaphysics. For example in his *Olympia* there is no Venus, or exalted female principle, there is "just" a courtesan on her bed. There is no Christ behind the dead Christ in *The Dead Christ with Angels*; in his vision, the subject is just a corpse. Following in Manet's revolution came the Impressionists, who once more left a cognitive wake behind them. For them, or at least in their work, there is no conviction about what exists, there is only vision and an agnosticism about the real nature of things. That is not necessarily how we receive their paintings. In God's providence, their vision was so embracing of reality that they could not miss the sanctity of light revealed by matter, even as they claimed to know nothing of its source. But the view that we cannot know what things are in themselves, but only as they appear to us, launched by Kant and amplified by that great artistic movement, has now become most people's starting point as they consider knowledge.

We could go on. From believing we cannot know what reality is, culture has moved on to take up the empty space. For example, Henry Moore's figures, figurative and abstract, have (as I see them) created a kind of substitute reality where humanity is, as it were, carved out of nature and is by no means separate from it. This has huge implications for ethics. If we are only nature there is really no such thing as right and wrong.

This kind of art, the "impure," is difficult to deal with. If it is well made and has artistic integrity, and if it comes from an outstanding craftsman and original thinker like Moore, you cannot just throw it out because you do not agree with it. You can, of course, put it in a museum and put a label on it apologizing for the fact that in the 1960s people like Moore had backward ideas and constructed a whole view of humanity based essentially on pantheism; but works of art, unlike statues as such, have a potency that cannot easily be restrained by labels. They address the person. They cause us to compare what we think we believe with what they suggest. They introduce doubt. "Am I really who I think myself to be? Or am I a piece of evolved slime, with no deeper identity than any other being, animal, or vegetable carrying DNA?"

The Art Side of Impure Art

If "impure" art is inherently persuasive, what about the "art" side of impure art? Art clearly is different from advertising or propaganda; there is something to enjoy in impure art even as we wrestle with the meaning and implications. Does this "art" aspect of things have no cognitive implications? Does it "just happen" to be there, like the beauty of a spider's web or the mystery of frost at dawn?

We could try to define the difference between art and propaganda like this. Propaganda is designed to shift a person from A to B, to get them to vote for X rather than Y, and as such it has one goal and one meaning. It is designed to exclude alternative readings. "If you see this, you will think that" is its aim. When it has propelled you into the goal, its work is done. If it is a statue of Lenin, it will have no complexity. It wants you to believe in him rather than to see him as a human being in the round. Likewise with advertising: You will not carry on looking at the advertisement when you have bought the shirt. You have obeyed the trigger and "you" are no longer needed. Art, however, is addressed to the person. It is multivalent—like reality itself, we can intersect with it in different ways on different occasions. Whereas propaganda leads to capture; it has only one desire, which is to have you; art leads to freedom, because with art you can see reality more fully as it is.

So let us then look further at the "art" side of art, the supposedly non-cognitive part that "just" gives pleasure. It has marked characteristics. Apart from some deliberately contrary modern work, it is designed. It has a start point and an end point. Within this boundary is "the work," and outside that boundary is our space, the public space. Within the artist's space, there is purpose and intention: everything designed has an end in view. The part contributes to the whole, and the whole, as we have said, has a boundary, a line between "art" and not-art.

The same can be said of music. There comes a moment when the conductor lays down his baton, the pianist rests her fingers, the applause breaks out, and we know that the piece is finished. But within that piece, the time is the composer's and the performer's; it belongs to them. Put in a simple and banal way, the composer or artist "makes a whole," a whole in which everything within it relates to everything else and contributes to its purpose. Every creative activity occupies this given condition: new objects are being made, and everything within the object contributes to its point or aim.

b) Form, Leading to Reality-Questions

It will be seen here that we are discussing "form." Form is one of the things we enjoy in works of art; the balancing of words in a poem, the placing of windows in a facade, the composition of figures in a canvas. But form cannot be the whole of art, enjoyable as it is, because form is conditioned by purpose. Suppose I am making an abstract painting. I decide to paint a patch of yellow. Then my eye tells me that the yellow looks "all wrong" with its neighbors. I change it to something more harmonious, assuming I am not making a deliberate discord. This seems like a pure operation of form. My rule is harmony; I work within it and make beauty. But in fact harmony is not only a rule—it is a purpose, something I desire. It is the means to make art because harmony is something believed in.

In other words, "form" is not simply a means to an end ("content"), but has meaning in itself. The existence of form is part of the arresting condition of reality.

The fact that form, or beauty as we often perceive it, is not neutral comes out clearly if we think of places of deprivation, whether accidental, like a concrete jungle, or deliberate, like a Chinese gaol. We have perhaps read the stories, of inmates of prisons, where the sight of a single leaf, or of the web of a spider, gives hope. What is it, of which people are deprived, where there is no beauty? We who have access to beauty whenever we want it may find it hard to see the difference that beauty makes. But beauty has a meaning. It speaks of wholeness, of things allowed to flourish and come to fruition; it speaks, not just of perfect design, but of that "extra" by which the Creator has made them "good." For someone in a Chinese gaol, it might tell them that there is another power apart from the State, and that the government's concept of what is right, its attempts to impose conformity, are far from the truth of how we are meant to live.[2]

This is, thankfully, an extreme situation, but one we can identify with, because we all want to know whether beauty's promise is true. Beauty may make me feel good, but does it mean that there is good? I can receive it, but can I rely on it? We can receive beauty, mindlessly, as beautiful form, but at some point we are confronted with the fact that it is there, not just as form, but as something in which our very existence is bound up.

We have, I hope, seen enough to be convinced that, in trying to say what art is, the focus on the art object still leads us inexorably to wider questions of meaning. We cannot in fact say what art is without asking ourselves the wider questions of what reality is and of who we are. Unless we have had a stab at these questions, we cannot know how art fits in to the wider picture.

2. WHAT IS REALITY?

In one sense, this is easy to answer. Reality is everything beyond our front gate; not just our gate physically, of course, but the outside boundary of our personhood. No one sentence can describe what reality is like, which is partly why we have the arts, painting, novels, music, etc. A great novel, or a great symphony, will attempt something of the whole picture.

a) What Is Reality Like?

If we ask ourselves, What is the quality of reality? there is less agreement. We can, at least, say that it has characteristics that leave us with questions. Some questions are compelling but not pressing, like, How did we get here? But others are urgent because they defy our ability to make sense of things. The chief of these is the question of good and evil. We have no leave to doubt either that there is good in the world—from the sunshine of a mother's smile to the personal sacrifice that saves nations—or evil. That is agreed on by all,

---

2. Nien Cheng's *Life and Death in Shanghai* (1986) is the memoir recalled here.

though there have been some serious attempts to warp what those opposites are. But the puzzle of good and evil is not that they are there: it is that goodness cannot actually be good if it is limited, frustrated, or compromised. In other words, reality, like a novel, sets up the need for its story to be resolved. Goodness, to be good, must triumph. But, at the moment, the battle rages, and we are not yet at the last chapter.

Reality, then, leaves us with questions, questions that cannot be answered from within their own tensions and paradoxes. Hence the divergent religions and philosophies of the world.

However all these ways of looking at the world can be summarized in three possibilities:

1. The world has no meaning.
2. The world has meaning, but we cannot know it.
3. The world has meaning, and we can know it.

The World Has No Meaning

For many moderns, this has become the religion of choice. It is believed, in this view, that reality is altogether impersonal, that the universe just happened and took on the characteristics it has, and that by no plan it brought forth life, which eventually led to us. It is believed that all the remarkable statistical coincidences that enabled a planet to be formed with just the right conditions for life were random, and it is believed that morality is just a convenient human fiction. However, believers in this scientific hypothesis seldom live in a world without meaning. If they are betrayed, in love or career, they certainly feel it; if they are robbed, they might remember "thou shalt not steal," if they fall foul of certain governments, they might wish they had their "human rights." There is a whole structure of meaning without which society cannot function, which cannot be set aside by individuals just because they choose not to believe in it. And you cannot "evolve" a metaphysic. If it is part of you, it is not over you, and if it is not over you, it has no transcendent authority.

The World Has Meaning but We Cannot Know It

This is another popular religion. If the first is rigid and austere, and not for the fearful, this religion is catholic, inclusive, creative—a net apparently open to every creature. Each of us can bring our thoughts on what reality is and add them to the mix.

In the past, this religion was known as polytheism. As in the Roman Empire, every kind of idol, every belief, however contradictory, can be accepted, provided it does not interfere with the civic religion of the state. Today we have relativism: the idea that every belief can be seen as true from its own perspective. It is axiomatic that none of them make truth claims that could come into conflict. For example, Islam is presented on the public stage as a primitive but picturesque cultural form aiding social cohesion, not unlike Morris dancing, well dressing, or carol singing. It is seldom recognized as a belief system making actual claims, which need to be accepted or refuted, chief of which are views of the character of God that have wide social implications.

Behind this amiable "Roman" system, where all beliefs rub along but none press their truth claims, lies one simple assertion. It is not precisely expressed, except by a philosopher such as Kant, but it is believed that beyond the visible world, the world of the senses, there is a kind of curtain, beyond which we cannot go. Behind this curtain is the meaning of life, the book of answers, the clue to our destiny; but what lies there we cannot know for sure. So, based on the observations we make, we are free to speculate. As when Moses went up the mountain and stayed longer than expected, we down below assume we know nothing of God and can make "gods" of our own.

Such creative agnosticism seems harmless enough, and in a tolerant society, what can be a more fascinating topic of conversation than someone's newfound dabbling in a cult or religion? But it will be noted that, despite the tolerance, there is one belief that this account of reality radically excludes. In its Jewish form, it is that Moses on the mountain had actual contact with the real God, and that the real God gave Moses his actual words. In its Christian form, it is that we can and do know the meaning of the story, because God, who made the world, manifested himself and his truth in the most perfectly communicative and accurate way he could—by taking on a human life.

We shall see later that art can adapt itself well to all three categories: sterile meaninglessness, polytheism, and the belief to which we now turn, that "Jesus Christ was manifest in the flesh."

The World Has Meaning and We Can Know It

The three views of reality are not exactly parallel. The first requires some effort to maintain. A "meaningless universe" requires constant dodging around awkward facts. You have to be fairly hard-hearted not to believe there is such a thing as love or justice, or that we, meaningless blobs of jelly, have power to assert truth. The second view needs no effort. To believe "there might be something" but "we cannot know it" offers no disturbance to the contentments of life and, if you are of a liberal cast of mind, a multiplicity of beliefs in the world offers you plenty to tolerate. The mind gravitates naturally towards polytheism because "openness" requires no actual choices. But the third view, that the world has meaning and that we can know it, is not something you drift into. It contains the answer to the conundrum of life, but it is not an idea that we could possibly arrive at unaided.

This is where, today, we have a credibility problem. If we think of the Christian religion, we will probably think of a sprinkling throughout the country of church buildings where people "go" and where, within those walls, they can practice their "beliefs." They go from neutral ground into their own sacred ground, believe what they believe there, and then come out. We might picture the City of London, for example, where there are numerous old churches tucked away in the canyons of corporate banking, where a person might find quiet and respite from the pressures outside. But few people doubt that "the reality" is the overarching system represented by the banks and traders, not the religious beliefs inhabited for a short time by visitors to a church. On a more national scale, "reality" is what is reported in the newspapers and other media. The Christian faith is, at best, a small corner of that.

However, Christianity's claim is not that it is part of a larger whole, one part in a multipart drama, but that its own story is the drama. On the face of it, this seems hard to believe, because all we see is polytheism, the forum of public life conducted between competing temples. We do not see, as much as we need to, the truth of Christ embodied in institutions—although we have churches, hospitals, welfare, law, a servant-monarchy, and standards of probity in public life, all as a consequence of the Christian faith.

But the truth is that reason and our natural sight could not have imagined anything like what Christianity claims is the reality. This is, as we know, that God's Son, the originator of everything apart from himself, should become a baby; grow up in Galilee under the Roman Empire; die bearing judgment for sin on a Roman cross; rise a couple of days later to reign, after his ascension, on the throne of heaven; and then send his Spirit on ten dozen people, the foundation of the worldwide church. We could not have thought this up, although it is the longed-for answer to that question, How can goodness still be goodness if it is too weak to succeed? For Christ is not only the beginning but the end of the story in which, as popular novels dimly reflect, goodness will triumph. Our difficulty is that so often we view the story of Christ as an event *in* history, a flickering candle that is easily blown out by the storms of history as a whole, rather than the event *of* history, which has no other valid shape, origin, and destiny.

It is evident that this is a view of reality that cannot be assimilated in a detached or academic way; we cannot think that everything Jesus did and taught is "God," that both in acts and speech he is actually and in reality supreme, without having to align ourselves personally with that truth. Just as you would not say that a man had grasped the truth that his house was burning down if he just remained in it going about his business, so we cannot "believe" that Jesus is coming back to judge and rectify the world if we do not make him paramount. This is a view of reality that cannot be contained as a possible idea, to be considered alongside other contenders. To understand it is to move towards it. It is in the very nature of "God" to be all-commanding, all-defining, the very signature on reality, and so we cannot even begin to admit God's existence without laying down our own definitions of reality and at least mentally bowing the knee.

As we move towards considering the importance of this for art, we need to note a few conditions of this God-originated reality.

1. It is partially but not fully disclosed. It originates in goodness and is headed towards goodness, but we do not yet know what it will be like. This means it is directional and dynamic. For example, we can think of a well-known work of art, Michelangelo's *The Creation of Adam* on the Sistine Chapel ceiling. Michelangelo, at a moment in history (1508–12), conceives the figures of the two most important persons in the universe, God and the first man. At our own moment in history, we can assess the appropriateness of this combined image according to our current ideas of God and man. There will be some feedback between Michelangelo's ideas and our own as we assimilate or refuse aspects of his vision. But there is also a truth beyond what we know now, which will be disclosed to us at the end of time when we meet Jesus face-to-face, and also know more fully what we are. In as far as we know Christ now, some of this future knowledge leaks into the present and gives us a confidence that we know what the truth is. But only when time concludes shall we really know.

2. This partial disclosure of reality nonetheless tells us a great deal. Because we know, at least in outline, the end of the story, which is that the goodness of God will be vindicated, we can see that goodness has reality and substance, anchored in the creation; whereas evil, despite its temporary successes, has no ultimate share in the structure of things. It gains its force by perversion, or by occupation, of the structures of goodness, but it has no creative power. Just as in a coup d'état necessary bodies such as parliaments, banks, and radio stations are occupied and seized for the new power, the

structures themselves, albeit malignly occupied, are inherently beneficial and of God. In the same way, art's place in reality is not in itself two-faced or ambiguous, although it can be occupied to broadcast partial truths or alien philosophies.

3. Personhood is directed towards a goal. This is not just the accountability of judgment (what I ought to have been) but of destiny (what I can be and am made to be). This means that what we are is lived towards what we shall be, but what we shall be can also be read back into our life now, as a plant, genetically at least, can be read back into the seed. Hence our decisions, framed by this future direction, are weighty, with real-time and eternal consequences; and our knowledge is genuine, because we were designed, with all the power of consciousness, to understand. We are not the flotsam and jetsam of a random universe but beings equipped to deputize for God in ruling the earth. For art, this means that artistic judgments—shades of color, the properties of a line—are real judgments, oriented towards truth, with an assumption of accountability; perhaps exercised too much in fearing people rather than God, but made knowing, in the privacy of the studio, that art is an occupation that matters.

4. A universe that has meaning is of course different from something that has "a meaning." Having "a meaning" signifies equivalence: we can look up the meaning of a word or understand the meaning of a painting. But a universe with meaning signifies something more like purpose, value, and destiny. It derives from the thought that everything was created through Jesus Christ, and therefore is oriented towards him, gaining the truth of its being from him, just as its very existence was uttered by him. We understand something of this through the multivalent meanings that we work with all the time. A pebble, for example, might be for us a sign of erosion, the crashing of waves; it might be the precious memory of a walk on a beach; it might be a paperweight given by a child. All these meanings are true, true of the interactions between persons and things. But behind that is "the meaning," the truth that God comprises in himself the knowledge of all that everything is and its potential in our world; and God being God, it all signifies goodness and gift. This means that art has meaning too. It goes beyond the pleasure principle. It has a place in our world that is unique, impossible to reduce to any other concept (as in "art is communication"), but must exist in reference to our origin and destiny.

3. ART IN REALITY

So can we now say what art is? Provisionally, we can deduce that all of reality derives from, and therefore refers to, its Creator (in the simple sense that a painting by Titian is fully itself but also refers back to the artist who originated it). In that art belongs to the created order, it is also good and has a function within a good creation. However, we ourselves are not living in a good creation, fresh from the hand of the maker; we know it has been compromised, and the very signals it gives are confusing and distorted. So we need to ask ourselves whether art still has a function and calling, not just "in heaven" but in reality as we know it.

The time we are in is one of warfare, when good sometimes seems uppermost, sometimes evil. But this texture of reality, that so clearly started well but is now a fight to the death, gives the agenda for art: to show in the cross-thread weaving of life both transcendent truth and the defiance of the rebel throne. We measure art by its ability to see the real activity of both. Art that errs on the side of optimism looks sentimental; art that cannot see glory is apt to become hostage to the other side. This texture of reality is everyone's life, and it does not take a Christian to observe it, but it does take Christians, I believe, to hold up the flag of the returning king and declare that good and evil will be seen exactly for what they are.

a) The Quality of Art

We have described, I think, the program of art, but what of art itself? It is not all school and sermons; it is also play and recreation. It has a quality all can recognize, but that can only have real existence in a God-spoken creation. How is this evident?

1. *Existents*. The essence of art is to make something that never existed before; out of things that already exist; and which has a referent, that is, it refers beyond itself. The art is not the destination; the referent is. Just as the art is made of preexisting materials, it is also indicative of things or truths already existing. The distinct feature of art, however, as opposed to signposts and other communications that point the way, is that the truth referred to is also embedded in the medium, in a marriage of form and content.

2. *Mind*. A work of art is not just an object; a "mind" is essential to it. The work is made physically of molecules, formed in a certain order, just as my computer screen assembles colored dots in a certain order. Neither of these arrangements mean anything without the human mind that interprets

them and gives them coherence. It is the mind that finds order and interprets it as meaning; without the mind there are just molecules and dots.

In a meaningless universe we may interpret such dots as we wish, but they do not have actual meaning. Thus, in such a universe we might identify a certain physical form as "a camel," but that would be only for our own convenience. There would be no such thing as an actual camel, since the universe (in this view) has no intention of producing such a thing. It is as if the "stuff" of life was blancmange or cement, temporarily and randomly formed into certain shapes, but those shapes have no authoritative reality. But in a universe with meaning (leaving aside for a moment the polytheistic universe), humans and animals and cabbages have real existence and so does art, because intention, understanding, communication and the joy of insight are all real. When we look at art, our minds pull together the clues that the artist has given us, and in the wholeness of the work, whole meanings are transmitted; and a union takes place between artist and viewer.

3. *Love.* It is characteristic of the creative process that while, to begin with, one may be aware of rules that are stipulated, these cease to dominate the work and may serve only to underpin it. The maker's preoccupation is not with rules but with the needs of the work. It has been remarked of C. S. Lewis that he was not careful about his personal appearance, but he was meticulous about the meaning of words and the formation of sentences. The energy behind this, we may surmise, was not that he suffered from fear of his proofreader or publisher but that he loved his work, and that it was for the work's sake that he tried to get things right. This kind of love, which goes beyond prescriptions and requirements, is characteristic of all real art, and it involves a freedom to take time, even, as we say, to "make time," to stay in engagement with the work.

4. *Grace.* Likewise, in art there is an interplay between skill and grace. The poet may have a mind stocked with words and an imagination in which they freely flow, but the mysterious availability of just the right rhyme for the sense is still something that goes beyond skill and seems to enter the area of gift. Similarly, the painter, supposedly in absolute control of the space within her canvas, learns not only to "design," but to take as gift the ideas that come in a given space of time, learning to work with what is there, either in form or in imagination. Such opportunistic freedom conveys a lightness of spirit that is absolutely characteristic of the best art. Art that does not enjoy that gift is described as "labored."

5. *Freedom.* The freedom to choose and to place things as we want is absolutely inherent in the creative process, but it is not an absolute or arbitrary freedom. It is the freedom to apply oneself to make things as they need to be. It is a freedom not against purpose but for a purpose. This is a quality

that is manifestly "in" real art but not in art that is controlled down to the last comma by the censor, by the overbearing state, by official prescription, or by an interfering patron. It is, therefore, along with ontology (real being), love, and grace, a sign of a kind of universe in which goodness exists. We know that now goodness only exists partially and is always under threat, but if it really exists, vindication is implied. It exists now as a signpost and a promise.

This is the reason, I believe, that one comes out of an art gallery invigorated. It is not so much that certain configurations of harmonious form and color appeal to certain receptors in the brain, though that may help. It is that we are affirmed that we live in a reality in which love, grace, and freedom are real, manifest in space and time, and, praise God, found sometimes in the most unpropitious places. This is why collectors collect: because the things that are good often need finding.

So, to summarize, in a world with no meaning the molecules bound together in art have no actual significance; hence art, as something that signifies beyond itself, does not actually exist. However in a world with meaning, the freedom to denote realities through art, through the blessed gift of making, is real.

4. THE WORLD AND THE SELF

We have looked at the world beyond the garden gate. What about the world within it, the world of the self? We have seen that God has entrusted all perception in the world to that most unreliable instrument, the human mind. This is baffling and frustrating. "If only America, Russia, and China could agree!" No, we actually see the world in different ways, and that goes not only for the nations but for every person in my village or street. The human mind does not only not see things the same way, it is not even oriented in the same direction. We have concluded that the world makes most sense if created; but is it not odd that at the top of the created order is a creature so unstable, so unwilling to occupy and persist in his created form? St. Paul senses the longing of the rest of nature for us to become, at last, active sons of God (Rom 8:19–22).

When we look at nature, and at human attributes like love and kindness, and at art, we find signs of the kind of existence we were called to enjoy. But when we look at "me," we find something very much less constant. The characteristic of "me" is that, far from heading direct for home along the straight path of my human destiny, I am diverted by other destinations and identities. Social beings, we are caught up in great movements; who shall say what fills us is authentic and real? Since we have no direction, we have little critique; everyone takes hold of what seems good at the time.

This feature of the self, that it is not fixed but blown around from every quarter, means that polytheism, the trial of one god after another, is its natural home. Though the self is, on the one hand, drawn to reality, because reality feeds it with a sense of existence, it is also distracted from reality, because of its own internal disposition to ignore overwhelming reality in our deluded aim of making ourselves God, without appreciating that the post is taken. For this purpose, as a means of distraction from the awkward conditions of reality, we have created idols.

We have seen that art in its nature leads towards God because it reflects his generosity, in making a means of understanding the world, and also his goodness, in making a reflection of his own creative act. But we have also seen that there is an opposing natural religion that lazily believes that every point of view, however contradictory, can be accommodated. This we have called polytheism, or, as moderns call it, relativism.

Relativism has its own art form. All it needs to do is to distract from the destination of art—which is reality, and behind reality, God the Creator and Redeemer—and its job is done. How does this work? The usurping art form does not point beyond itself but points at itself, exercising a sort of black hole gravitational pull so that its existence seems to have power. As the art becomes less, the artist becomes more, until, as with some conceptual art, it is all artist and no work. An inversion starts to take place: instead of having art that leads somewhere, we have art that leads to artists, to curators, to art historians and catalogue writers, and to critics. They become the true subject of the art. The effect of this is to diminish the existence of art as a gift in creation, intended for understanding and delight, and to create a false reality, in which understanding belongs to a certain kind of priesthood whose role it is to obscure and mystify the truth. From this there follows an inversion in the understanding of creativity, which—instead of being a gift by which we engage with delight in the world's weight and meaning—becomes a self-generated pure invention in which the least possible dependence on reality, history, or other persons is praised and which never gets beyond the artist, who in turn becomes a substitute god and absolute creator.

To cut people off from the real Creator is the point of the exercise, but this modern substitute art does not stop at that. Since the self is considered the source of art, that art becomes more and more degraded, like a stagnant pond, and a kind of death sets in: either the death of a sullied imagination, or the death of a devout negativity, in which "nothings" are supposed to be "something" because they bear the name of art. It is not surprising that contemporary art is depleted when we live in a world in which dominant voices attack the foundations of civil life—marriage, family, children, identity, nationality, birth, and death—and try to remove every sign of the grace of God.

In conclusion, we have seen what art is, a sign of God, and we have also seen what substitute art is, a sign of the opposition. The devil's work is to feed on the flesh of art, occupying the places in which art has flourished but retooling art's essential structure, from being an insight of the artist to making it an extension of the artist, and worse, giving artists the illusion that they are making art when they are only creating idols of their own creativity. But we have also seen that art is a gift of grace in creation, accessible not only to the virtuous or the earnest but to all, as the human inheritance in a created world. It is a gathering of sign gifts that explodes in the hands, with a sense of meaning that comes partly from the perceptions we put into it: but even more from what we are, in the foundations of our being.

2

A Question of Beauty (A Personal Story)

Introduction[1]

IT IS NOT VERY difficult to tell if some place is ugly. Without any artistic education you can distinguish between a place that is uplifting and beautiful and one that is joyless and soulless. However it is not easy to say what is beautiful about beauty and what is ugly about ugliness; and because it is difficult it is widely assumed that it cannot be done. And because "joyless and soulless" is much cheaper and takes much less effort to produce than "uplifting and beautiful," the freedom we enjoy in the absence of any agreed standards is often taken as a license to go for cheap and ugly.

There are many evils in the world, and aesthetic evils do not compare with oppression, injustice, slavery, and starvation, but perhaps they are of one piece with them. Ugliness, after all, is a denial that people's well-being requires any more than physical and material needs. It implies a particular view of people's humanity—or the lack of it—and it reflects back to them a refusal to grant them intrinsic worth.

In any case, it is certain that, whatever one's views of "modernity," a change has taken place in the last century, so much so that environmental beauty in cities and villages is now on the preservation list—like red squirrels or wild orchids—and the characteristic signature of the arrival of people is ugly buildings, by which I mean buildings that will never, in the future, be sought out for their quality and beauty. Cheap and ugly building has become the style of every city on earth; neighborhoods have become

---

1. The original version of this essay was written in 2023–24.

indistinguishable, and there is very little sense of place or distinction, even between one country and another.

There are all sorts of reasons for this, reasons that are obvious and excusable, such as the mechanization of building and the huge growth in population. But before considering these, it is important to note what has happened and that it represents loss. Everywhere we go, now, there is the risk of beauty being interrupted by something man-made that is careless and obtrusive. Because this fact is everywhere, we accommodate ourselves to it, and make the most of the beauty that we can find, even in places like New York or other megacities, because the sun is shining, the glass is clean, and we allow a certain awe before the display of power and wealth to substitute for real delight.

But accommodation is a form of fatalism, a general agreement that this is the modern world and that nothing can change. Indeed it is hard to imagine what kind of revolution would have to take place to enable an improvement on the ubiquity of the cheapest and ugliest standard steel and concrete building worldwide. However, almost every evil is accepted as a fact of life until it is challenged. So it is good to feel the weight of ugliness in the world, simply to ask the question of whether it is there as a form of necessity or whether it in fact represents some perverse choice.

This is a personal account and it is organized around my own story, because everyone's sense of beauty comes from somewhere, and it is easier to discount (if the reader has to) what is purely part of my artistic culture if you know what it is. It is also easier to understand the issues if they come as part of a narrative, rather than if they are presented in purely abstract form, though we shall have to do that too. In any case, the question of beauty and ugliness is about people, their loves, loathings, and choices, and if we cannot be direct about how an individual deals with the issue, we have already lost the point. It may be that peacocks and blackbirds have a sense of beauty, but it is fundamentally a human problem.

At this point, however, I would like to outline where I think I have got to and then leave the longer essay, a sort of aesthetic autobiography, to show how I got there. My story seems largely like an argument with relativism, the question of whether there are real rights and wrongs out there, or whether each island of human culture can claim its own rules. Everyone has to face this issue, implicitly or explicitly, and I was struck by it, in relation to beauty, at an early age.

My conclusions can be organized, I believe, in quite a simple form. We begin with our apprehension of reality, whether beautiful or not. Then there is the testing phase, where we put our apprehensions to trial: are they real and what do they mean? Then there is a third phase, which is the most interesting: when we test the tests. We ask ourselves what sort of world we in fact live in. That phase can only be resolved by commitment.

We begin—all of us begin—with an apprehension of reality and a perception of some things as beautiful or ugly. It does not matter at this stage whether these perceptions are learned or at least refined by thought and experience. At a level of feelings we make a response to something as "beautiful," or something else as an "eyesore," and we begin to put the experience into words. We might later discuss "which came first," the concept of the beautiful or the beautiful reality, but the principle to note is that *reality has impressed itself upon us as beautiful or ugly,* and we have responded in words. I do not see that we have a choice about this. What we see is who we are.

Then there is a second stage, which we could call the "trial" or "permissions" process. It is a kind of minefield or obstacle course, where we take our naive impressions and try to decide whether they are legitimate. We ask questions, such as, Are these judgments not just personal, but about reality? and if so, Are we permitted, equipped, and epistemologically capable of making them? By the time we have run the gauntlet of Western philosophy in all its most destructive features, we may have been intimidated into saying, "My impressions were just me and do not have the validity of statements about real states of affairs." We might then lose confidence in any statements of value or approval and eventually be willing to admit as "good" any old ugly thing that is placed before us. However we may also, thankfully, escape, still believing in our own rationality, though we might not be quite sure how. Perhaps we assert it privately or, by force of personality, universally.

Then there is a third stage in which we pull back a bit from the question of whether we can or cannot accurately apprehend reality as beautiful. Behind that can be the philosophical question of whether we can apprehend reality at all. These questions may seem purely academic, especially if we have other things to occupy ourselves with; but they have a habit of turning up when least welcome—for example, in questions of love and romance. What do my feelings mean? How seriously should I take them? But beyond these revolving internal questionings lies the much bigger question of what sort of reality we in fact live in. Is reality constructed in such a way that we do not know and cannot know what it is, except according to the devisings of our own minds? Such a place sounds hellish; but doubt as to the essential effectiveness of perception can be surprisingly popular.

At this stage, the obvious solution would be to lean on science. Science just "works," and it hides its metaphysics. Nobody needs to ask how it works. And so from science we can conclude that since reality is intelligible, the understanding we have is real. We know that everywhere the human mind penetrates there are explanations, and things make sense. When we try to go to the moon, the moon is there. The calculations for the trip work, on Monday or Friday. Reality does not change according to its mood or our mood. The devastating functionality of science is there for us day by day, night by night, whenever our subjectivity threatens to take over.

But science, for all its functionality, does have a weakness. Its metaphysical foundations are borrowed. Nobody can prove that reality is dependable and consistent. It just has to be so. There needs to be, behind the reliability and observability of the universe, some organizing principle that says it is reliable. The principle has to be there, beyond our disproving—or our experiments and theorizing could not function. We should be in a perpetual anxiety: "I know that relativity theory has been proved this time, but next time we might not be so lucky." Such a universe would be intolerable. But our belief in an organizing principle, that the world is consistent and rational—everyone knows—has to rest on God, whether we think we believe in him or not. There is either God or a vacancy. We need a personal counterpart to our activities, an affirming consciousness, to validate them. That vacancy can in fact only be filled by a being who is God. Only the reliability and consistency of God himself makes sense of what we have to believe in—that there is a reason for things—in order simply to think. We press forwards because we believe that there are answers waiting for us.

It is, nonetheless, relatively easy to think of knowledge in terms of the reliability of science, because science is practically at hand. But with beauty we are concerned with something called "the subjective," belonging to the personal realm; as is often said, "beauty is in the eye of the beholder."

In a technological society, "subjective" can be used as a derogatory term, and the temptation is to push our notion of beauty in the opposite direction and to try to tie it down mathematically. It is perfectly possible to imagine beauty being expressed by mathematical relationships—after all, face recognition technology can doubtless measure beautiful features if it needs to. But the fact that a computer could recognize beauty indicates the point. A computer could not be moved or attracted by beauty; beauty is something meant for humans. The question of beauty is inseparable from the question of what sort of world we live in. Do we live in a world of mathematical accidents in which nothing "means" anything? Or do we live in a world where beauty might signify something? Beauty speaks to the heart. Beauty can also beguile us from the truth. Is this ambiguity in the meaning of beauty just an unfortunate burden from our biology, or does it tell us something about reality as a whole?

Reality, of course, does not just sit still, like a picture. We cannot try to understand reality without seeing it in time. Our own lives make more sense—or fail to do so—as they unfold. As in music, each happening has significance in relation to what has already been and also to what it is hoped will come. We cannot expect everything to make sense all at once, even something we can grasp as good, like beauty. But we need to decide whether our lives are moving in the direction of meaning or of dissolution and meaninglessness. Granting that we do not as yet have all the clues, will there eventually be a solution?

Suppose, for example, that an individual sees something beautiful, like a rose, and in a moment of joy interprets it as a sign that there is such a thing as transcendent goodness, from which such beauty comes. When the rose withers and dies, that belief will have to be held on to, as the "evidence" is now against it. Of course, many worse things might happen to the observer of the rose than simply watching it die, which is expected, after all. Perhaps that person has had to contend with evil, evil that seems to drive all before it. Where is "transcendent goodness" now? The only way that link between beauty and truth can be maintained is if it is actually true and one can know that it is true.

One could perhaps intuit such a truth. But to be authoritatively true, there has to be a statement of truth—that this is the case—put into words. Such a statement cannot simply hang there. It has to be authoritative, connecting "both ends," so to speak, with an authority on one end and with reality on the other. If we see a station sign saying "Oxford," we assume it has been put there because it really is Oxford. Someone has authorized it, and he expects to be trusted that what his sign says is true. There is, then, complete consistency between the reality and the trustworthy and authorized sign. However we could conceive of a situation where the authority, for his own perverse reasons, has put up the sign "Northampton" on Oxford station. Perhaps he is trying to tease Oxford philosophers. But in such a case, the word "Northampton" would have no meaning. Because it does not correspond to reality (and certainly does not change the reality), the word is not functioning as a word. It is evacuated of significance and might as well be arbitrary decoration.

Similarly, the intuitions of art are called to account. Either they have authority behind them or they are arbitrary patterns. (We might recall the early Cubist pictures that incorporate words that signify nothing.) The apprehension that beauty is true, that it refers beyond itself to a real state of affairs, has to be true at both ends—real at our end, as a genuine perception, but also real as authoritatively given, from a thinking, deciding, personal being. And if it is truth founded in the Truth (the knowing that lies behind everything, which sounds very like Jesus Christ), it cannot just be a word or theory; it has to be an actuality, manifest in time—not necessarily this time but at least in time to come.

Such are the demands on us that beauty brings. If it seems to refer to goodness, we need to know that goodness is real. If goodness is transient, as beauty so often seems to be, we are apt to question its goodness. It seems a promise that cannot be backed up, a false exercise in wishful thinking, a denial of nature's creed. In this present life, we do not yet see the triumph of goodness. We see good and evil grinding against each other like tectonic plates, each, for a time, in different places, seeming to have the mastery. But the very transience of beauty, not just in nature or the beauty of youth, but in the vulnerability of works of art to loss and destruction, presses us to look beyond time. We cannot know truly what beauty is—whether it is promise or fraud—until we know which system, that of good or evil, actually owns the truth and comes out on top. Perhaps we already see that evil, which is inherently barren, parasitic, and destructive, cannot actually survive beyond its temporary triumphs. But to have the end of the story in our hands requires an advance copy, so to speak, of the final script.

In this present life there is a battle for truth—we know that. One can hardly plant the flag of truth anywhere without it being fought over. Like some World War II Pacific island subject to combat between Japanese truth and American truth, truth is not just academic—it is territorial, the possession of communities who hold it fast. The Christian church is an invisible territory of people who believe that the empty tomb of Christ means that he rose from the dead, and that in so doing he vindicated his message as being the Truth. The "might-is-right" brigade who thought they had ended his life were shown to be deficient in their understanding of ultimate reality, and of who is really in charge, and of how things will end. This Jesus, who had reversed death, which had been the final word of the old order, also promised to come back in such a way that his rule, and the rule of everything he stood for, would be manifest to everyone. If this is the case, then there is nothing of a false dawn in the beauty of a rose or in any of the good things that in human life we are moved to do.

In this brief account of my thinking and of where it has ended up, it will be seen that the argument with relativism may have solutions. Relativism in itself is incoherent and unstable, because life is impossible without a common currency of truth. There are many who understand this, and are able to bypass relativism and assert what they know is true. But although I have found their arguments and philosophical solutions important and comforting, I have come to realize that in the end they are not enough, and that we have to commit ourselves to a view of reality, a place in which we are content to live. I do not see how this is to be done if all we know is what we see. In the fog of battle, the signals are too obscure. We might easily bend or twist before this ideology or that. But if we find that he through whom everything has been made is identical with the man who died on a cross (which we could hardly agree to without it changing us), then we shall be able to identify not only the architecture of reality, but its final destiny. And if we can see that, we will know that the poverty of mind, imagination, and resources that leads to ugliness has no lasting future or any final justification.

3

A Question of Beauty (A Personal Story)
A Process of Thinking

Foundations

I grew up on stories of my great-uncle, a well-known collector and art philanthropist of his day,[1] who had absolute conviction about his artistic judgments and expected others to follow. For me, with a less intuitive and more theoretical cast of mind, this raised the following questions: Is artistic taste merely subjective? Can we know that we know that something is good? I had strong views on art and architecture. Could I justify them? The following is an account of how, over many years, I encountered and resolved this issue.

It might be asked, Does this matter? It does if we want to stop the world from getting uglier. Believing we have no access to the truth of what is good is absolutely no help when artistic decisions are being made, particularly in the public sphere.

I must have been an annoying boy. I do not see any evidence of this in the largely tolerant way I was treated. I did not like school games but nobody much minded, and I lived before the days of the ubiquitous football shirt. However there was something different about me, and that must have been, at least to some people, inconvenient. I really loved beautiful things and cared about art. I dawdled home from school so that I could look in

---

1. Sir Hugh Lane (1875–1915). See the final essay, *Aesthetic Certainty in an Age of Relativism: Sir Hugh Lane and the Legacy of His Beliefs.*

the windows of the local interior design shop, or visit a jolly antique dealer, whom I plied with questions. I remember loving the old gateposts in which Hampstead abounded and looking at the lettering of house numbers and names. Even as a child I was developing a sense of "how things should be." My mother was an artist, Slade-trained, and she fostered these discussions. Artistic judgments were as natural as breathing. Very often I was over-critical and poisoned my looking with an insistence on making things measure up. But most of my memories are of looking at art that was simply good.

My parents honored my love of art by sending me away to a school with a good art department and beautiful buildings set in the Sussex countryside. Boarding school is strange, of course. One develops all sorts of behaviors to compensate for the removal of the one thing really needed, the present love of a mother and father. In my case, this was complicated by the fact that my parents' love for each other took the strange form of constant quarrelling; hence, though I needed them, I felt ashamed of them. In turn, their need for me went a little beyond what was healthy, and I felt in a continual push-pull of wanting them and wanting to be away. The relevance of this to aesthetics is that beauty, the solace of things that are what they should be, became a much needed comfort.

It is important to note this "comfort of beauty." Much of what follows will be an attempt to rationalize appreciation of beauty by various stratagems, in a way that seems quite detached, as if one was observing oneself from outside. This habit of detachment, an ability to internalize how the group sees you, is itself a product of boarding school. But below that there is also the primal need in which art and beauty really matter, even if they are a comfort indicating deprivation somewhere else.

Primal needs, or primal loves, induce loyalties. If something matters to me, it matters absolutely, and like first love, I will defend it against all comers. It is as intrinsic to love as it is to a love of art that there is no such thing as "just my taste." Our very rationality is bound up with the judgment. For some people, a piece of music engenders the same loyalty as a football team, and there is no discussion. What I like is as hard to remove from who I am as a tattoo.

However, a primal need matures and the cold winds of self-questioning blow, in art as well as in love. And then you start arguing for what at first you felt. First love becomes pain, as you seek to justify it in the world at large. This account will show how I have attempted to deal with this issue—this primitive belief that what I see is really there—and what explanations I have found to show that what I have believed is not altogether far from the truth.

I

First of all, let us imagine our family's meal table. My father, a linguist and leather trader, was fond of the expression, *on ne discute pas les gouts*—"one does not argue about taste." This proverb, he felt, was enough to close discussion. My mother, who had the temperament to challenge most of his views, did like discussing taste. Art was her lifeblood; her uncle had been a famous collector and two of her cousins were antique dealers and collectors. But my father had a point. One person liked one thing, and another liked something else, and there was no arguing with them. My childhood was during that period when everything "Victorian" was considered taboo and "bad taste." Victorian buildings were by definition ripe for demolition; and those who defended them, such as Kenneth Clark and John Betjeman, were considered perverse. But at least one cousin loved Victorian things, and I had rather a fondness for old mahogany and florid carving. Was anyone "right" or was it all just "taste"?

Figure 1. Lancing College, Lower Quad (photo by author)

These questions came more clearly into focus at my Sussex boarding school, which comprised two quadrangles in carved stone and flint in the Victorian Gothic style and a vast chapel—then, still unfinished. The buildings' domestic scale and happy proportions met all my aesthetic needs and I was grateful for them. But there was one excrescence in the ensemble. One of the school houses had found a need for more study space, and the decision had been made to break the continuity of design (that is, the now unfashionable, very costly neo-Gothic) and build a steel, wood, and glass modern box without any obvious aesthetic ambitions. As has become commonplace today, the old and the new were juxtaposed, without apology, as if there was no philosophical explaining to do.

From the schoolboy observer's point of view, there was a dilemma as to how this building was to be seen. Was this a "sorry we can't afford any better" kind of apology for a building? Was it a "we know it looks awful but please be patient until we can find some decent money and designs" sort of building? Or was it meant to be "the latest thing," parachuted down from modernity to show us what should be done amid this benighted, fossilized remnant of Victorian sentimentality? This was the era when Nikolaus Pevsner, author of *Pioneers of Modern Design* and *An Outline of European Architecture* (our set book for A-level art), was the leading authority in matters of design. He had come up with the idea that the "real" Victorian architecture had been the muscular cast-iron skeletons of the railway stations and Crystal Palace, and that all the laborious and much fought over "styles" had been an inauthentic skin, more to do with public appearance than physical reality. If a building was steel underneath, how could it pretend to be Roman or Gothic on top? For him, modernism had simply shed this stylistic skin in order to reveal the reality of the new, utterly practical world of money translated into engineering, a world that had shed its metaphysical pretensions. From this point of view, a modernist building was more "honest" than a pseudo-medieval one, because it was what it was, purely utilitarian, without any imposed signification of medieval piety or romance.

So here we have, then, for a relatively undefended youngster, a three-way fight between beauty, honesty, and meaning, all happening in the mind as he looked at this cheap and thoroughly useful building.

The Aesthetic of Beauty

In the first place, the old buildings set the norms; they are there already and self-evidently designed and built with care. For them to look their best, their environment is important. There is an "aesthetic envelope" that cannot be broken without damage. The new building is ugly. It does not pretend to have any proportion or handling of detail or color that the eye can rest on with satisfaction. It is not a "look at" building, but a "look away from" building. So here we have, in one corner, so to speak, an argument about what is, or is not, beautiful. This relies on an imaginary construction of "what should be there." It is a kind of rationality that is not easily specified but is used to judge things that already exist. It is to some extent a metaphysical system of right and wrong, and it is seen and felt and then specified. Someone might well ask, Does this system actually exist, since we apply it without knowing what it is? That is part of its vulnerability.

The Aesthetic of Honesty

Then, in another corner, so to speak, is an argument about honesty, and styles as appropriate to eras. In this view, the Gothic stonework of the cloisters and windows is under suspicious interrogation: Why are you there? You belong to the modern era of steam trains and factories. How can you pretend to be medieval? Why would you make workmen spend time on your trefoils and carved capitals when a simple concrete post would suffice? Are you not simply covering the stench of money, which controls everything, with the perfume of a little style? Behind this interrogation, which these days we might call "deconstruction," lies a theory that styles belong to eras as do leaves to cabbages; that styles are an entirely "natural" formation. Each era, so it is said, produces its own natural style, and ours is the style of naked engineering. Honest people will follow it.

It has been well pointed out, much more recently than my schooldays, that if a style is "natural" to an era, then why did Pevsner and others so vigorously need to promote it?[2] The argument is similar to the challenge to Marxism: if the victory of the working class is inevitable, why does it have to be imposed? But for me at my age, it made sense to ask the question, Why were we building in Gothic? Our school chapel was being completed in Gothic, by medieval methods of construction—though with carving more by machine than by hand. What did this mean? Can you detach Gothic from the matrix that formed it and have it remain the same style?

The Aesthetic of Meaning

In a third corner (if a fight can be allowed three corners) is a question about meaning. Our modern building wears the airs of modernity, the idea that it is part of a great movement in architecture that has created a global style, signifying "function is everything, hang the rest." Whether you are a hotelier in Greece or Spain, or an apartment builder in Beijing or Mumbai or any of the megacities, you know that to build means to erect a concrete or steel

---

2. David Watkin's *Morality and Architecture* sees the modern movement in architecture as a self-chosen style disguised as a historical necessity, a cause pronouncing itself to be inevitable.

structure, to fill in windows and walls, and it does not matter very much how it looks. There is permission in the public space to build for utility, so that any aesthetic debt (to make things look good) is borne not by the builder but by the public at large. We forgive the modern city, because we know it has to be cheap. We forgive the modern City of London, because we know financial centers have to be like that. We are not convinced they owe us beauty. We take the debt on ourselves.

So modernism is not just "honest" to the way we are today, a product of modern economics. It has a particular philosophy. We could summarize it in a couple of statements. First, money is more important than beauty. What a person has is more important than what he spends it on. In the past, noblemen beggared themselves over beautiful buildings. The rich of today are probably more careful, because to them the numbers are more important than the product. Second, there is no metaphysics. There is a physical world, and we must deal with that alone, and any belief in aesthetic obligations is as naive as thinking there is a universal right or wrong. When we are installing a plastic window to keep out draughts and cold, and so spoiling an ancient facade, we do not need metaphysics to guide us. Architecture is shelter and comfort, and any further meanings are illusory. (When I was older, I saw that there was indeed a metaphysic in modernism, a salvation story of perfect purity and clarity, cleansing the human mess, but at this stage I saw it as purely practical, "form follows function."[3])

But if modernism had a meaning, a philosophy of life conveyed by its style, so did Gothic. This meaning could be summed up in the phrase "it's worth it." It is worth someone sitting for hour after hour splitting flints to make these glorious shimmering walls. It is worth someone carving a complicated trefoil at the head of windows. It gives a sense of value and of honor to the users. It is something for the eye to rest on with pleasure. It is worth laboring over the proportions so that the buildings "settle" into their surroundings and nothing looks out of place. Underneath this care is a reference to some higher good, to which these buildings are intended to conform. There may be a reference to the medieval "Age of Faith" (so-called); but intrinsic to this style is a sense that in this life we belong in an overarching scheme to which architecture is as much subject as any other kind of behavior. The dining hall had a hammer beam roof, like a medieval hall. This did not have to be there. It was there because conviviality could be celebrated. And if the aesthetic part of our being is acknowledged in the external world (through stained glass windows and fine paintings), then it

---

3. I saw it because I was taught it. Dr. Alan Ford, my supervisor at Cheltenham College of Higher Education School of Art, delivered many eye-opening lectures on modernism.

is clear that our aesthetic selves, and perhaps all of our selves, feel valued internally. Much of this does not only relate to Gothic architecture but to any buildings that recognize external obligations and that value the culture of dignifying and honoring people.

This kind of meaning is proof against deconstruction. Someone might argue that the Gothic style was adopted to bamboozle parents into believing that a religious style meant a religious education, and that style was therefore just a means to an end. There may well have been instances of that in Victorian times. But for the Gothic style (or any other style) to be executed well, it cannot exist on a diet of cynicism; good execution relies on an adherence to external standards and choice, as though we choose to carve a window "this way" rather than "that way," not by a rule book but for the window's sake, so to speak, according to its own language of form. Let the architect and craftsmen loose, and they will soon be wanting to work according to the job's own inner logic, probably irrespective of your budget.

So we have then a battle over beauty, a battle over honesty and authenticity, and a battle over meaning. Each of them refers to a "higher value" that is used to trump the others. But where are such values found? How can we settle and know what's right?

I have another scene from school days. I remember what I was ruminating on, and I remember the place: appropriately for rumination, it was a cow field that boys used to walk through on the way to the local town. From it we could look up to the college with its imposing buildings and immense chapel—a place of authority and a symbol of adherence to the high church movement. Schoolboys, of course, had very little idea of this, and except for the rebels, chapel services and rituals were a given. But the buildings certainly represented a kind of irresistible force "over" us. I mention this because for me aesthetics were also a kind of absolute. There was a right or a wrong in the way things were done. I used to study lettering and calligraphy, and the discipline of shaping letters shows you clearly that design has to follow certain internal principles. If we miss certain codes of design, the reader will be distracted, and not be able to see "through" the surface of the text to engage with the words intended. Within this principle, of course, there is infinite variety, as anyone who has looked through a font collection knows.

The question that preoccupied me was this: There being a great gulf between, say, what should be done in architecture, and what actually is done, what is to be done about it? Why is it, when it is so obvious that cities like Renaissance Florence look better than places like heart-scoured Birmingham, that our planners and builders seem so indifferent to how things look? We have a planning system; we have bodies like the Royal Fine Art Commission, which gives opinions on new designs. How is it that, by and large, our cities get worse rather than better to look at? In that grassy field, two solutions presented themselves. One was to put me in charge of all planning decisions. Even at that stage I realized that the idea of such aesthetic dictatorship was wrong in principle. The arts are creative, and it is a mistake to concentrate on pruning what is already there when you have done nothing to assist or guide the growth. It is pointless to pull up weeds if we do not know how to cultivate good plants. So that led me to my second thought: if only pupils at school could all have an aesthetic education—to know how to form a letter well and how to look at a building. Then we would develop an artistic culture in which bad buildings would never be accepted. Good proportion is something that can be learned, and it can become part of the common language of discussion.

My confidence that (*a*) I knew what was right and that (*b*) it could be taught may strike readers today as overly hopeful. But it hides a question that is not so easily dismissed. Truth, when you are growing up, is embodied in institutions. If we did not trust at least some of the people who teach us, we would go crazy; and they, in turn, are handing on that which they find trustworthy. In an open society, these institutions are porous to truth. An open society is one that is not so well guarded that truth cannot get in. Institutions may be rotten, distorted from their purpose, or even oppressive, but individuals can always bring something new to them, so that over time they can reform. So we do trust secondhand truth, and it is not wrong to do so. The school chapel, unfashionable as its daily regimen was in the 1960s, did represent, in stone after mortared stone, a body of belief, which surely was worth examining. It was not just a building, but a sign of what a community believed in. So I was not wrong in thinking I might have received something truthful enough with which to educate people. An inherited culture in an open society is worth paying attention to. But the real question comes in the area of conflict. What if your culture is porous, not to truth, but to whole patterns of thought which are in fact destructive? How do you carry on if the institutions you trust do not support you?

I was not particularly prescient and could not have foreseen postmodernism, but I was aware of a rumbling and shaking in our institutions. Under the pressure of left-wing mockery—very playful, but it had its effect—I could now see the school buildings in a different way. What if they now represented not an institutionalized form of the way things were—representing truth, and Christian truth in particular, as something we inherit as a given—but a shrunken body of belief that is now just one view, shrivelling under the glare of modernity? From now on, any belief in absolutes, aesthetic or otherwise, seems to be on the back foot and, instead of being part of a community's belief, has to be defended by an individual.

But that is not the half of it. The aesthetic dictator, ruminating in his cow field, has a vulnerability. What if his beliefs are purely personal? Is that not the lure of dictatorship, that other views are suppressed, in case they are right? It is quite easy to imagine that our supposedly objective categories are simply a personal program. The present British king, after all, who, as Prince of Wales, tried to exercise an artistic guardianship over the built environment, was frequently accused of imposing a personal taste that derives, in part, from the institution he represents. In another country the monarch might have more power. He might have been able to cover his nation with neo-Georgian buildings. Would that then be a personal taste or something objective? Some of us find it easier to mock than to think; but we need to see the real question at stake. Yes, we can dismiss assertions of taste as personal. Yes, we can silence the enthusiast with accusations of subjectivity. But what rule are we ourselves (if we are critics) standing on? Where is truth if King Charles, and others like him, are wrong? We have not provided a law or rule to align with reality that is demonstrably superior to his.

The issue at stake for the young person growing up—as it was at least for me, thinking in nature under a summer's day—is that of how to establish my rationality as rational. If I see things one way and others do not, do I simply back off, and say, "Sorry, I was simply born liking things of this kind—there's no meaning in it" or do I brazen it out, and say, "It looks like this to me, so that's how it is"? My taste over ice cream flavours is just that: my taste. But my taste over art is an attempt to get to grips with reality; it is a truth assertion—of how things are and how they should be. But how on earth can I establish that? "One does not discuss taste," my father repeated, but we do have to negotiate beliefs in a world where others disagree, and in doing so, we find out who we are.

So we are left here with two questions: One is whether aesthetic judgments are real-world statements, attempts to describe how the world actually is, not just in physical form, but what it signifies. That is to say, are aesthetic judgments equal to statements like "that person is good, that one is wicked"—genuine attempts to describe a state of affairs rather than simply an articulation of a personal state, like "I feel I like you"? When we assert, "That building is beautiful," that certainly sounds like a real-world statement. However when that view is opposed, such confidence can easily run into trouble, and we might wonder if we have made only a description of ourselves.

This leads to the second question: How are we to handle the rationality of those who disagree with us without undermining our own? For the young person growing up: When someone louder and stronger than me disagrees, how do I know I am not crazy?

Everyone will have an implicit answer to that question, because we have all grown up and have all had to learn to disagree. There are certain arenas, such as the political, where disagreement is organized, so that there is a space where jousting is allowed and another space (not social media) for common civility. When we meet new people, we are circumspect, because we know that at a deep base of conviction, they may differ. We explain these discrepancies in all sorts of ways—social, psychological, etc.—indeed in any way that does not compromise our own rationality or explain away our own beliefs as similarly conditioned. We know what we believe; it is the way we see. But we can sit in the same room with others who differ.

However with the arts, there is a unique combination of the personal and the rational, so that in our judgments we are simultaneously talking about "it" and about "us." We are asserting not just our own individual ability to connect with the world but the right to exist with our own flavor of perception. This belief, that what I see is what is there, is a priceless treasure. We could not engage with the world at all unless we trusted our perceptions. And yet, every day and in many ways, this belief is challenged. How do we handle this, and how does a person growing up handle this? My conclusion would seem to have been (and I am not sure I am still in the cow field thinking this), "I would like other people to believe what I believe even though I am not absolutely sure that I know that it is true. However, unless I believe my perception is true I cannot function at all." In other words, I find that, however I argue with myself, my beliefs are written into me like Brighton Rock.[4] They are part of my functioning. And, provided I stay in contact with the world, and correctable, they are a reasonable place to start.

I have pushed my questions to a conclusion, albeit a temporary one, because our minds cannot remain in suspense for long. There are other answers I arrived at later. But I never stopped encountering the issue that provoked this whole internal debate: that the world was growing uglier, year by year, but our ability to say anything about it was growing less and less. "Beauty is in the eye of the beholder, so don't tell me I can't build here," is indeed one approach. But because it is difficult to explain how aesthetic standards are really there, we seem to be in continual retreat from those for whom lack of objective values is simply a money saver. It must be possible to find a territory where we can discuss what sort of world we want and what it might look like without totally suspending our judgment. Surely we have had long enough of seeing responsible people hold their hands up in despair, declaring, "It's all so subjective."

4. For those unfamiliar with this metaphor (common in the UK), Brighton Rock is a souvenir confection—an extruded tube of sugar, which has the name of a seaside town inside, all the way down, legible wherever you break it.

II

At this point, any reader might wish to know whether, after a few more years standing in cow fields or even the learned halls of university, I think I have cracked the problem. The answer I have come up with (when I say I, I mean I and those who have helped me) is to view beauty as something that makes sense, not by following a rule book of form but as ontology, as a constituent of how things are or should be *by the nature of reality*. Beauty derives from submission to the truth of how things are; it is not "creative" but is a link between the personal and the universal. The fault of many aesthetic theories is that they start with the individual, rooting the goodness of beauty in a very unstable subject—that is, human judgment—rather than in the whole prospectus of creation. But we need to see that what is good is not just a meaningless accident of nature or of our perception but is good in the sense of really being meant to be there. To see things that way, there are choices to be made along the road. At least, that is what I found.

I resume the story. There was a point in my school career when I considered the idea of going to art school. I loved making art and would have valued a good training. However, I had somehow learned enough of the revolutionary clamor going on in art schools to fear it and so was willing to leave aside the artistic route for the academic when it was offered me. This was the era when the system of learning how to draw from ancient statuary and the life model was dismantled. The old plaster casts were thrown out, and students were expected to find art emerging from within themselves, rather than from copying nature. There had been problems with the academic system for some time. Many had been the young artist, emerging from art school equipped to draw in the classical style, who found it hard to relate their skills to the modern world. A huge cultural shift had meant that "nature," as we understood it, now seemed unsympathetic to the toils of modernity, which must now be expressed in abstract, or at least sharply symbolic form. The Victorian age—the era of my grandparents—attempted to believe that great ideas could still be expressed through images of the gods and goddesses of the ancient world, or through landscape, or the moralities of narrative paintings. But now no one did. There was a sense of artists trying to squeeze the visible world once again, and very little juice was coming out. So art fractured in different directions, always looking to express the time we are in. That seemed far too demanding for a young person who simply wanted to draw and paint, and I perhaps rightly feared being left behind. And yet the question always at the back of my mind was, How does modernity know that its foundations are secure? Are they resting in reality or in some version of reality that will turn out to be false?

III

The next arresting moment in my aesthetic memory was when, after two years at Cambridge, I changed from history to art history. My first essay required me to discuss a painting in the Fitzwilliam Museum, a Tintoretto that previously I had walked past with a glance but was now to spend hours with in study. What made it so good? How had its composition given it such an electric presence? That this kind of study was not only permissible but required gave me a new insight into knowledge. If I felt rather like a confined dog let out for a walk, it was because, in an unheard of way, my own perceptions were found to have testimonial value, alongside written sources. No wonder I suddenly felt as if I existed.

Naturally not everything I said was believed, or taken account of. But my own vision was, at least, part of the discussion. This surprising fact came home to me even more strongly when, after Cambridge, I found myself working in the art trade, in a gallery where, among the comings and goings of a dealer's stock, were some memorable paintings by great artists. In this place, there was a shorthand for personal opinion: price. I was astonished that values in the thousands could be ascribed in seconds, based on how good a painting was reckoned to be. The point here is not that individual assessments were absolute, any more than assessments of equine form on Derby Day, but that personal perception, rationally argued, provided a credible language for discussion, and that even students, with all their immaturity, were not prevented from using it. This taught me that the inner world of art perception, the pre-analytical engagement with art in which all who look at paintings are involved, did not have to be professionalized to have value. It was in fact a datum, alongside others in art history.

The memory I have just given might imply that, as students, we were not schooled. However, severe limits were placed on our subjectivity. It soon became clear to me that the story of paintings we were taught was—other paintings; the main object of study was a work of art's "family tree," the combination of influences and direct quotations from other works that had generated it. For revision for our finals, I made up a game I called "Domenichoes," based on dominoes. Cards had artists' names on either end, and could be matched up with artists they influenced. For baroque art, which had numerous threads of connection between the leaders—Caravaggio, Rubens, etc.—and the followers, this worked quite well.

However the fact that it seemed to me a game to look at paintings like this showed a degree of scepticism, even cynicism. The "content" of a work was understood to be what we can discover of its components. However, we know perfectly well from computers and other artefacts that the components of a machine do not tell us what it "does"—nor do the components of a work of art tell us what they have been combined "for." The picture has a focus and purpose, whatever its derivations. We can analyze ingredients, but at some point we might wish to eat the cake. Personally I did not object to this manner of employment—looking for sources—and took to it with relish; but neither did I think that this is what art was. But I was struck by the fact that to make art history scientific and objective, it was necessary to discuss issues of a second order—sources of a painter—rather than the meaning that the artist was after.

An example of the scholarly understanding of "meaning" was a brilliant book on Poussin by Anthony Blunt (scholar and, it became apparent, spy and traitor) we were required to read in which he attempted to enter the thought world of Rome's seventeenth-century intellectuals. The underlying assumption was that an artist can code a picture with meaning by using a symbolic language, perhaps known to the patron or a small intellectual circle. A number of Renaissance painters have left us works of which the "code" is lost and the meaning still unclear. Sometimes we are left wondering whether even the painter understood the commission. But there is also a sense in which "the meaning is not the meaning." Even if we understand the names and actions of the figures, that does not explain why the painting connects with us—why it is a work of art rather than a puzzle. The meaning that throws itself into our laps, so to speak, whether we "understand it" or not, is very hard to describe. It is sensed; it is pre-analytical; but it is near what art is about.

A tough-minded writer of an earlier period had been content to sweep all of this preoccupation with "meanings" away. I was introduced to his thinking during my first year of art history and soon developed a love-hate relationship with him. Roger Fry, who brought Post-Impressionism (a term he invented) to Britain, campaigned for a whole new way of looking at art that is subject free, mentally subtracting the story from an image, so as to be aware only of its aesthetic design. You could call it an "impressionist" way of looking, because it saw art as essentially a harmony of colored patches. Subjects and stories, for Fry, were just a peg on which art was hung. To me his view was at once outrageous and tempting. We can look at art like that; indeed it often seems preferable to scoop up the sensuous color of an artist like Veronese or Guido Reni than to delve too deeply into their martyrdoms or classical suicides, to which even the artists seemed oddly indifferent. But his ideas were also outrageous because they were dogmatic, seeming to close the door on a very human part of life—the desire to make meanings and communicate them. Fry was himself an artist, and somewhat skilled in portraiture, an area where "meaning" cannot be evaded, and it is possible that the artist's preoccupation with "how to do it" caused him to be more concerned with means (color and form) than ends. But probably more influential on him were the philosophical roots of his circle, the Cambridge Apostles, a group of sceptical intellectuals including, slightly after Fry's time but from the same mental world, the legendary philosopher and atheist Bertrand Russell. Such people were confident that of all that possibly could be known, from physics all the way to metaphysics, God cannot be and that there is a gulf beyond the sensory. Hence in art too it is not surprising that the tangible and sensory, the immediacy of color and form, which sometimes leads to quite a mystical sense of emotional capture, is cut off from knowledge of realities in depth.

It was not difficult to argue against Fry, since in his later years he learned to modify his rigid scheme, realizing that story and subject, just as they do in song, might have a part to play in art. The irony of his formalist position became apparent as the history of modern art (written by the winners, of course) gradually congealed into an accepted story. For Fry, formalism was essentially a way of looking at art. It was as if art seen abstractly, and all abstract art, was about the contrivance of emotion through form, rather like film music. But for the moderns, form was not so much a means to an end as a view of how life is. In a sense, it is a subject.

I felt cross enough with Fry to write three lectures on him (in subsequent years). In retrospect, he was hard to deal with partly because of his sense of mission and appealing simplicity but mainly because of a sense that what lay behind him was not just an argument to be refuted but the door to a void, a void where meaning simply does not exist. Fry's inability or unwillingness to look beyond the formal surface was not a "mistake." With all his love for great art and real skill, he was stepping backwards, unheeding I think, into modernity.

For modernity, form is not what is there but what *we* do, how we structure the world. At first, this had a "spiritual" sense. For Mondrian and the early abstract artists, formal designs were a stab at the essence of things. There was an unknown, and unknowable, spiritual world to which they could point. But for the true moderns, there is nothing beyond form, no metaphysic beyond our own ideals. When we ring a bell, there is no answering echo. Human life, and its intellectual devices, is all there is. Fry's formalism, in its innocence—as an "emotional" way of looking at art—was a Trojan horse for the human ceiling and empty skies of modernity.

But if Fry's theories, in a world freshly hungry for meaning in art, no longer rang true, it was much harder to say where the meaning of a painting lay. Fry's recipe had been straightforward, comprehensible, universal, and easily distilled, as it was by his disciple Clive Bell, who coined the phrase "significant form." But how do we move on from there? Whenever we visit an art gallery and take a drink, as it seems, from Goya or Velasquez or Cézanne, we know that something important, but also enjoyable, has happened. But it seems that for all our aesthetics, psychology, and science, we lack a context in which the power of aesthetic experience makes sense. Clearly it means more than stopping for an ice cream or taking a pill; but what sort of a world do we live in, which makes art both pleasurable and deep?

At the time I studied art history, the discipline was still small and finding its feet. To some extent, questions were still open and had not yet been systematized and professionalized. The teachers still loved art, and pleasure had not been banished from the lecture room. There were always those few who found new ways to make a delightful subject boring. But among fellow students there were real enthusiasts who somehow turned barren lists of baroque painters into feasts of desire. I mention this, because while some theories of art seemed to want to reduce it to an operation on the mind or a contrivance for the emotions, there were people who simply revelled, not in what art can do, but in the art itself. I felt that I learned from them that if we are to understand art, we must be thinking of actual works of art in all their physical reality rather than trying to skim off from them the means towards a sensation. In this process, we turn freshly outwards towards the actual work rather than inwards to try to observe our internal processes of reception.

The Department of Art History had a leaning towards what was then known as "connoisseurship," the Berensonian reading of pictures at close range, especially with an eye to attribution. Some of my happiest experiences were trips to the London National Gallery Restoration Department, where Titian's *Bacchus and Ariadne* was on the restorer's bench, and to a private restorer who was restoring a Claude and a Titian portrait, which he described as like working on a late Beethoven quartet. This taught me that much of what we experience in a painting is transmitted in the "handwriting" of the artist; and that there is an immediacy in the great painters being able to convey their thoughts from heart via hand to heart, without intermediaries. Even Mondrian conveys a presence, the presence of the witness, through his handwork.

At this point I was still an undergraduate and there was plenty to go on simply on the basis of sensuous pleasure. Baroque art and architecture, which at first I had found unappealing and unintelligible, were the perfect instrument for training the eye. With Rudolf Wittkower's lectures, I learned how to "read" a facade and to discover the aesthetic problems with which the great Roman architects had wrestled. It was enough to learn to care, because they cared, about strictly visual matters. I found it important to discover what you *can* do in art, how personal discernment may lead, not just to pleasure, but to understanding a work in depth. The meaning of art history, for me, was that it did not deny individuals, with all their sometimes strange tastes and quirks, but shaped them into effective perceivers of what was there.

But while there were plenty of routes to finding what you *can* do in art history, there were also some suspiciously locked doors. One such door was the notion of "truth." Art was not supposed to be a route to truth. One of the most persuasive teachers of this view was the sage of art historians, E. H. Gombrich, a scholar whose freedom and creativity had opened many doors, but not this one. A well rooted man who loved realities, he was suspicious of big metaphysics. Exiled from Vienna by the Nazis, he knew about spiritual dramas getting out of control, even in his own field.[5] In the dominant Hegelian art history, style was fully accounted for not by individual decisions but by "the spirit of the age" (*zeitgeist*). This meant that all history was shaped and predetermined (though that did not preclude dictators and other enthusiasts from helping history along). Gombrich resisted this oppressive determinism with a passion. But he did not believe the remedy had anything to do with truth, the real anchorage of art (in my opinion). Art could not be considered a route to truth (he probably did not trust "truth"); it was a place of communication of ideas, no more nor less. And because art does not make propositions (the picture does not "say" the sky was blue—it simply shows a blue sky, whether or not that was the case), art's business was no more than conveying the artist's thoughts.[6] This seemed a reasonable argument, but nonetheless I felt something was being shut down. Art too vividly gave a sense of connection with what was real. While no one could prove that Holbein had captured all of Henry VIII in person, or even part of him, it seemed to me that the sphere of truth, even of partial truth, was of the essence of the artist's project.

The other *can't* I encountered at this time was, oddly enough, from the philosopher nearly of that name. Kant's aesthetics was presented to us by a good-looking and amiable professor who claimed to have read every word of the *Critiques* in German. It is clearly my weakness that I remember his

---

5. Gombrich, *Art and Illusion*, 16–17, elaborated on in Gombrich, *In Search of Cultural History*.

6. Gombrich, *Art and Illusion*, 59. "Logicians tell us . . . that the terms 'true' and 'false' can only be applied to statements, propositions. And whatever may be the usage of critical parlance, a picture is never a statement in that sense of the term. It can be no more true or false than a statement can be blue or green. Much confusion has been caused in aesthetics by disregarding this simple fact."

body language more than the content of his lecture, but I picked up a couple of things that became important.

The first is that philosophy—which we never knew we needed—had developed a role that, once admitted, was hard to refuse. My situation seemed not dissimilar to that of a healthy man who proceeds through life eating what he pleases. But when something goes wrong, he suddenly finds a use for the medical profession. But then his health seems largely taken out of his hands. For us in art history, the majority of questions were historical and practical, and the aesthetic connection was taken for granted rather than analyzed. At our end of the building, colored slides of works of art told us most of what we wanted to know. Whereas at the other end of the building where the Kant lecture took place (actually the Department of Architecture), the questions were all to do with "whether" and "may we" and "how." Here were questions we had not had to trouble ourselves with. The aesthetic experience was now bounded by signposts and permissions. Its power, the indisputable reality of art—and yet the fact that its existence is not absolutely laid down but a truth apparently plucked out of the air—left transcendental questions hanging, both unavoidable and unapproachable.

Philosophy did not seem to be about solutions—more about signposts saying where you can and cannot go. One of the signposts was a prohibition. There is (apparently) no move from philosophy to theology. Transcendent solutions are not permitted, because they do not fit within the terms of the discussion. However deep the quagmire, reaching out to "God" for a helping hand was not playing the game. Kant had blocked that route as a form of real knowledge; although he did permit a metaphysical area as a working hypothesis. Of course, it seems self-evident that aesthetics should work from a this-worldly perspective; and that if we are dealing with sight and with form, which are preeminently physical realities, then we must be able to work out what is going on by limiting ourselves to perception, as we can observe it. If the equation is: "person + painting = aesthetic experience," why bring God into it? It seems that if we say "God," we are no longer trying to solve problems. On the other hand, if the problem cannot be solved because of the way we have framed it, then maybe we should be looking elsewhere for the cure. What if reality is shaped by God for God's purposes? What if he has not excluded himself, but we simply treat him as if he is not there? It is one thing for philosophy to chart its own boundary and to work out what can or cannot be done within its limits. It is quite another for it to declare that human life is itself confined within those limits. What we can know (and know that we know) is surely the real datum, not what we are told we are permitted to know.

My second conclusion, deriving from the first, was that if philosophy has found work to do, then there must be a brokenness in human artistic relations. We do not call the doctor unless we are ill; we do not call the plumber until the pipes are leaking. There was clearly a need in art. An attempt had to be made to regulate the passions of art, to order its disagreements, and to decide (however impossible) what was and wasn't art. This was unexpected. Moving into art history had felt, for me, like having an extended holiday, such was the pleasure of the task. We thought of the artistic life of Rubens, of Turner, of Constable and Monet as essentially innocent and of art as good to look at and good to do. But it soon became clear that the problem of the aesthetic relation—Is the art in the object or the viewer?—was only one issue in the long-running warfare between artist and reality, painter and client, innovator and public, viewer and critic, historian and historian. The "history of art," so benign when first encountered in Gombrich's *Story of Art*, was a thorny path.

IV

I forgot to mention that for someone who loved art so much, I knew very little about it. This was put to the test after Cambridge when I was taken on as a salesman by a reputed Bond Street firm, which specialized in British painting as well as in the Old Masters. You may picture a cavernous, hidden-away gallery lined with mahogany and dark red plush. I was soon brought face-to-face with my prejudices. Up to this point most of what I came to love, particularly British landscape art, I had previously disdained. I mention this to say that taste is something learned—but also something that captures you, so that what you like becomes an involuntary fact about who you are. From being someone scornful of many different areas of art, I became (aided no doubt by the fact that I had to sell a wide range of art) omnivorous, with a growing love for art wherever it flourishes. However that did not make me indiscriminate. If you love art, you cannot but dislike that which stands in the place of art but is not the real thing.

One of the effects of being in and out of Christie's and Sotheby's at sale time is that one becomes very quick at sizing up paintings. Inevitably there are few masterpieces on the walls, and most of the art that is sold is work in the tradition of, or in the manner of, the originating artists. I learned not to despise this work. If an artist does not have the talent or power of Claude but has studied him enough to imitate some of his most effective schemes, then the resulting picture, if carried out conscientiously, is a true derivative and has, at a remove, some of the qualities of the master. The true artist will also contribute something of his own, something that indicates a personal vision. The false, or "mannered" artist as Constable called him, will wish only to give an impression of good art by copying tricks, with no attention to nature, from which real art originates. All these judgments matter when one is trying to decide whether a painting will last the course for someone to own or whether its superficialities will quickly tire.

The sort of judgments that can be applied to eighteenth-century works based on nature are far harder to apply when looking at modern art, when any question as to the artist's sincerity cannot be answered in terms of the pictorial handwriting or response to nature but must be judged from something as lean as an arrangement of squares. But the issue at heart is still the same. Does the work connect only with other paintings, as some kind of clone of what has already been done, or does it represent a hard-fought perception about life and the world?

Learning how to distinguish true from false in art may seem rather a luxury, and given the fact that comparatively few people find themselves in art exhibitions, I suppose it is. But it is also a necessary form of mental housekeeping. We need to know what it is we see, and, more importantly, what we take into ourselves. In recent years we have become conscious that we cannot eat every attractive thing that takes our fancy and expect to stay healthy. But in cultural terms, openness is still the desired faculty, and we admire today not so much the person of taste—Lord Clark in a previous era would have been one such—but the infinitely plastic character who can wrap themselves around every new manifestation of art, offering it understanding and approval. If a person can dip themselves in the dye vats of modern art, it does not matter to them that they come up stained; such have voluntarily yielded up their power to criticise, let alone the willingness to say no.

It is, in principle, easy to say yes to everything, to wonder at every novelty and not to be caught saying that you do not like or understand it. But the question arises: At what point do you lose yourself? At what point do you lose that distinctiveness that likes some things and dislikes others, because you have been made that way? Or more importantly, at what point do you abandon your moral convictions because it is easier to condone than to condemn? I find it very hard to know whether the plastic person of today, who seems to like and approve everything, is a real person, a proper moral actor, or whether they have so sold themselves to like everything, such that they are no longer real, solid and robust inside. They might say, "I like this," but it is possible that the "this" has so invaded the "I" that the "I," as an independent force able to make judgments, no longer exists. One may picture this on a national scale, where a country has so admitted every kind of idea, value, and law that its distinctiveness as a nation has been lost.

This, then, for better or worse, is the filter with which I learned to approach an art exhibition. I would look not only for two kinds of art, true art (which somehow connects with nature or with reality) and false art (which only wears the clothes of such genuine art). I would also look for two kinds of true art. There is art that is a true discovery—when, like the scientist, the artist can stand aside from the work and say this is how it is, and the viewer can recognize that it is so. But there is also a true art that faithfully embodies a philosophy, a viewpoint on life, which perhaps the artist is convinced of but which so scrambles the contact with reality, so thoroughly encrypts it, that it barely brings us to reality at all. This art may be easily absorbed into the bloodstream as an idea, but it is philosophy we are imbibing, not art. The sign of this is when we are subjected to one particular stream of thought; whereas art is characteristically open, a reality with many aspects. In this case, the philosophy has so absorbed the artistic endeavour that there is very little art left.

I did not, admittedly, think all this through while pacing the streets and galleries of Mayfair; but one question was uppermost, as it would be to anyone who visits the Royal Academy Summer Exhibition, as I often did. This huge show is intended to represent all that is best in British art, and you could say, looking at it in those days, that it represented the nation very well. It included everything from the safe and traditional to the risky and radical, with a bit of compromise in between. The question that struck me was this: What has to be done to unblock the wells of art so that more of the art that arrives for consideration is genuine, and so that more of the people who love to make art are free, free to make the kind of art they probably really admire?

V

After nearly four years in Bond Street, I plunged all my resources, and no small amount of the government's, into returning to Cambridge to embark on research. I began with an intuition that embarrasses me now, of which I told no one, but which is necessary to this story, because it was a stage on the path to solutions. The vicar of a City of London church, who I never met, had founded a body called The Relaxation Society. Someone gave me one of his brief, very relaxed, printed summaries, and I often went to his church before work to lie in one of his armchairs and attempt the technique. As one of the tensest people I knew, it was a tall order to "command" my limbs and extremities to relax, but I got enough of a taste of what was being aimed at to realize what was at stake. The clergyman's theory was that if we relax enough, we will meet God. When we are tense, we are locked in ourselves; when we relax, we lose the prison of self and are open to reality, specifically, God's reality. I am not sure how I would assess the theology of that today. But the vital point for me (and the intellectual excitement was ruinous for my attempts to dial down) was that an epistemological bridge was possible between me and reality, and that it could happen, not through head knowledge, but by real person-to-Person presence—not strained, not striving, but there. This seemed to be a pointer to two issues that had concerned me with art. One was that here was a way of describing "mannered" art, art that went through all the motions of representing nature, but heartlessly, with only a head knowledge of how art was done, so without personal contact. The other (taking rather a bigger leap) was a way of seeing modernism in art. Modernism was perhaps making real-world projections (i.e., big picture views of reality) but essentially as mental constructions; and because it generally denied the existence of God, it was working more with ideas than with heart contact. In other words, it was (I surmised) working with a broken epistemological bridge, which it was trying to reconstruct from the human end. This explained for me why modern art impressed me, without resonating.

This intuition, though in some ways it seemed flimsy and eccentric, had two elements on which I could build. The first was that it saw the possibility, indeed the necessity, of placing artists on a spiritual map in order to see what they were actually doing. This idea was new to me. The art history I was used to liked to plot artists on a different road based on an idea of inevitable progress as one style led to another. Needless to say, the ultimate goal was not stated, so it was never clear whether "progress" had been made at all, though there was certainly change. But if there was a spiritual map, then we could plot artists in relation to a center, roughly called "truth," and describe their work in terms not just of their directions but of their distance from the center. But how do we judge this? How do we compare, say, Picasso's variations on Velásquez's *Las Meninas*, which are clearly original, innovative, and playful, with their weightier original? This brings out the second element of the intuition. Against any false historical objectivity that tries to describe Picasso's activity in deadpan terms (i.e., "this influenced that"), we find that it is we, the viewers, who weigh our experience, who feel for any sensation of depth and meaning, who try to register, as the ones addressed by the artists, what the truth of their contribution is. We can only do this by making comparisons between the paintings and the world as we know it. This is a personal activity, and the pictures both lie under our judgment of truth and also test our own truthfulness, because true art will also bring something to our consciousness that is new to us. My own judgment, having seen the Picassos, was that his pictures expressed not only reverence for Velásquez but a slightly squalid rivalry; and that he was denying to the seventeenth-century master the depth of view, through his Christian piety, by which he valued human being; instead Picasso imposed on him a lightweight twentieth-century nihilism. That is not a final judgment. They are still art and may have something else going on that I missed, not least, a kind of humor.

Intuitions take us directly to a new place of seeing, a vantage point from which everything looks slightly different, but they do not tell us how we got there, nor how we can explain it to others. When we find that colleagues and senior academics, with eyes and bodies like ours, can sit in equal proximity to the truth and draw very different conclusions, there is a temptation to doubt our intuitions and to write them off as simplistic or naive. This then affects our confidence in the very instrument, our perception, by which we live. But intuitions, though we may interpret them wrongly, are real footholds on the mountain and connect us to reality. We may fail when we put them into words, and perhaps try to fit them into the framework that we have, but they are indissolubly about who we are, connected to what things are.

This came home to me one day in a London square. I had been studying Constable and trying to put together two truths about him. In his letters and lectures, which I loved, he was the most purely personal of writers; his personhood is raw, undisguised, and immediately expressed in a way unusual among British writers; his passions, loves, and hates are expressed with trusting openness. His painting, too, is personal, but it is personal-objective: he is the most truthful painter of skies and landscape, but in his truth we feel a sense of exposure, without conceptual process, to what is actually there. Subjective vs. objective: these normally, to us, are contrasts, but with Constable, one seems to be a means to the other. This truth came home to me when staring up at some bare plane trees in Bloomsbury. The crisscrossed branches, the seed heads hanging down, the giraffe colored patching of bark were beautiful as only the eruption of nature in a London square can be; but what struck me forcibly was "my end" of the beauty. The beauty was there, but without me as receptor, at that place, that angle of vision, on that pavement, it would not have existed. Later on at Cambridge when I came across the work of Michael Polanyi I understood the idea of perception as bipolar, rooted both in the object and the person of the viewer. But to me at that time the meaning was more personal. It was the realization that I, as a person, had value in the whole perceptual scheme.

I must have been back at Cambridge by the time this took place, because I had bought the volumes of Constable's letters in a Cambridge bookshop. But, characteristically, another significant realization did not come from research (which I remember mainly for the number of times I fell asleep in the university library) but from something more adventitious. For some reason I got myself involved in giving a talk on the Cripps Building, St. John's, to a college society attended by some very eminent dons. This was excruciatingly difficult, as I was much more tongue-tied than expected, but the observations I made and tried to explain (and later did explain in full, in the college magazine) proved to be instrumental in showing a way forward.

The Cripps Building[7] was the modern building in St. John's. The sequence from the front gate went First Court (Tudor), Second Court (Tudor), Third Court (seventeenth-century classical), New Court (neo-Gothic), then Cripps Building (modern). In white stone and concrete, it stretched out to form two courts in a continuous ribbon, a bit like a DNA molecule. Since I was talking mainly to people who had little architectural awareness (after all, they had only commissioned the building), I focused initially on two kinds of "not looking." There is a kind of "not looking" we do when everything is in place. For example, the Second Court of St. John's, across which members of the college will walk many times a day, has everything where it should be: doorways in the middle of the ranges, symmetry of windows, some large windows to express the dining hall, a tower to give orientation, and so on. You barely need to glance at it to know where you are. Visually, it is a safe environment, without confusion. The "meanings" are clear too. Walls enclose rooms. There is an interior of rooms where life goes on in private, and there is an exterior for what is public. So we can do our academic business barely seeing where we go. You could even say that from the building we know, implicitly, how to relate to the institution. There are hidden places (for fellows) and more public places (for members) and you can work out where you belong.

But there is a second kind of "not looking," and that is the kind we do where the visual field is full of ambiguity, so that we cannot get a "fix" on it. Then we pass through it, as through a blur. I spent a lot of time looking at the Cripps Building before I realized how odd it was. There were courts that were not courts, because the building at first wrapped around them and then sheered off in another direction. There were walls that weren't walls, ambiguously load-bearing or decorative, and there were windows that might also be walls, exposing interiors to view, so that inside and outside became confused. There was an ambiguity between concrete and stone,

---

7. Designed by Powell and Moya, built 1967.

both used profusely, and of much the same color. As a result, one could not view the building as a coherent assembly and know exactly what was meant or how it fit together; the eye simply had to pass by.

Figure 2. Cambridge, St. John's College, *Battle of the Styles*; Chapel Tower, New Court (right), and the Cripps Building (left). Photo by author

Figure 3. The Cripps Building, St. John's, 1967; home for my first year (lower window, second from left). photo by author

This sounds like a critique of a bad building, but I felt something much more important was at stake. As an undergraduate I had spent my first year (and my fourth) in Cripps and had found it a disconcerting experience. Confining myself here just to the physical structure of the building, it seemed to "float" rather than be rooted (because its support system was unclear); it seemed without beginning and end (since it was a kind of strip made of staircase units that might have been continued indefinitely); and though it related brilliantly to the stream it bridged and to the views it framed, it seemed to bear no relationship to the college to which it was supposed to "belong." As a result, it was suffused by a feeling of "this could be anywhere," which is not what you want when you are looking for a home.

My talk may have included some settling of scores, but it arrived at a point that I was later to find really useful. The earlier kind of architecture, as in Second Court, we may call "natural." It has things in common with nature: symmetry, intelligibility, and the grace of beauty—simple decorative forms for their own sake. But the main thing it has is a relation of objectivity, both with respect to the institution, and to the person or persons who built it. The institution is expressed in the layout: chapel, dining hall, long gallery—a particular place for particular scholars based around worship and conviviality; but *the building is not simply the product of needs*, but is itself considered as an object that must be completed and "fulfilled," so to speak, on its own terms. It is the building that "needs" a decorative lantern on the hall and lead finials above the dormer windows. It is the building that requires a certain shape of arch and color of brick. Once every "need" has been met, the building is complete; it expresses the living institution and it can "settle," so that we can go about our business but give it no further attention. We are ourselves, and it is itself.

The modern building, however, is complete in the sense that it functions, but not complete in "thereness," in resolution as a coherent object in itself. This sounds like rather a sophisticated complaint, considering the luxury of this building compared to student accommodation almost anywhere else. But that consideration makes the point: this building is a projection of student needs, as defined rather abstractly and physically, but it could be anywhere. Its "belonging" is abstract (it meets a brief) rather than ontological, happier with an idea of student than with people in an actual institution.

It will no doubt seem unfair to pick on a building that, in its time, was a landmark achievement of design and generosity. But what this opportunity to speak gave me was a precious realization: that the kind of judgments we needed to make in architecture were not based chiefly on "what I like," but on a perception based on objective relationships. Did the building relate coherently within itself, part to part, seen as a whole? Did it relate as an object placed in its surroundings? (Or had it apparently arrived from somewhere else?) Did it relate to the institution? Did it relate to people as people and not according to some abstract definition of them? All these questions were objective, based in the object.

The "true" architectural object is not simply the projection of the architect's mind, genius though he may be, but is something perceived as belonging to a situation, with needs external to the architect. This selfless attendance to the building's character as an object allows the building to become part of its environment, and this in turn gives it what I called "location," an attachment to a particular place. As a current recipient of college publicity, I am fascinated to note that the Cripps Building very seldom features in photographs. College photographers hunting beauty, or a settled, coherent view, seem to avoid it.

It was about this time that I thought that "objects and objectivity" might make a good title for a PhD thesis. Not being trained in philosophy, I pulled back but was convinced that here was a way of tackling the problem of the so-called "subjectivity" of judgment. The idea was that it was quite "object-ive" to judge how fully a work of art or architecture succeeded in being an object—that is to say, an object separate from its maker, taking on real being in the world. For that, it would require not only formal completeness and unity but also such "content" as made it able to be at home in the world. A parallel would be that of giving birth to a child and bringing it up; success is achieved when the son or daughter is an independent person able to relate to the world. Or, if we are talking about art, a good portrait will be one that is both formally complete (it needs no further work), and is complete in content, in that it evokes an individual and, beyond that, the individual's relations with the world.

However, my account of art, satisfying as I found it, soon ran into a problem. I do not know to this day whether the formula "objects and objectivity" is simply sleight of hand, though I like the thought that if something is an object, or becomes an object, we can be objective about it. But suppose it is true? What do we do with it? Can we simply say to architects, "Go on, make objects"? The reply would be, "We did all that in the nineteenth century and look where it got us. We don't like objects any more; we like processes."

There are two issues at work here. One is the incipient moralizing in my theory. If we could only do things right, they would be all right. Just so, but if you have to persuade people or force people, then it might just come out all wrong. We have seen half-hearted Georgian, under the well-meant influence of then Prince Charles, and it is not pretty. At around this time I became fascinated with Ruskin—a danger for me. On the one hand, his conscientious and sacrificial dedication to the best of architecture—climbing ladders and walking on ledges, in places like Verona and Venice, to draw capitals and arches to illustrate his many books—made me feel I owed him attention. He was the man who had not only studied the very *Stones of Venice* with passionate care, he had also not held back the most controversial possible view of architecture, as based in the moral and spiritual culture of a nation. One culture, in his view, might be generous and free and another, greedy and sordid, and that would show up in building. This made perfect sense to me, even though it was difficult to follow him in the twists and turns of his judgment. He brooked no mercy: if Venetian Gothic was "good," then Palladio and Sansovino were "bad." On the other hand, Ruskin's moralizing approach to architecture had been sterile. It is true that Gothic Revival, partly under his influence, covered the land. But it never satisfied him, because the conditions that gave rise to Gothic and allowed it its astonishing freedom could never be reproduced in the commercial treadmill of the nineteenth century. You cannot moralize your way into freedom, and you cannot moralize your way into art. I wanted to; it seemed the simplest thing to plant "should" in front of a style I like. But people are not motivated like that. They are motivated by what they see ahead more than by a rod at their backs.

The second issue I faced was somewhat more obvious. I had picked a fight with something bigger than me. A building like Cripps does not just wither and die because someone criticizes it. It remains, and because it remains, alongside all the other buildings in the now ubiquitous, inevitable modernist style, it exercises cultural power. Like political leaders in some countries, it does not have to be liked, because it cannot be voted out. Even though it has broken the aesthetic envelope of that side of Cambridge (and one may claim, not too badly), this outrage is over a *fait accompli*; and, as when a stepfather arrives in a family, the new reality may not be loved, but it has to be lived with.

So what, then, is the purpose of criticism? I wanted an art theory that could be practical and useful. But it was clear that my mouse's squeak was not going to stop an elephant in its tracks. The movement behind the architectural movement, its powerful reach, had more behind it than a quirky and ill-considered aesthetic. There were reasons we were building like this, one of which was the failure of an alternative vision.

At the time I was in Cambridge, there was an attempt to revive the classical style. Architects such as Quinlan Terry had the courage to turn their faces against the assumptions of modernism and to build in a picturesque Palladian pastiche, which cultured people soon learned to hate but which has sometimes adorned the public space (e.g., in Richmond) in a way that architecture for years had refused to do. But the trickle has not become a tide. So what can criticism do? It wants to wring its hands, but it is better to laugh. Modernism likes being taken seriously; it likes being a cause. Its belief in itself does not appreciate laughter. It does not like being thought cheap, though it frequently is. It likes to think it cares for people, which it does, in the way a chicken farmer cares for chickens. It likes to think it is artistic because its buildings can reflect clouds. It likes to refuse space to any other style, in case it is shown up. Architecture is a "church" which claims to be doing good. So we do not hear architects taking the blame when estates turn sour or high-rises fail in their promise. They are, after all, only representatives of their culture, doing as they are bidden. Ruskin, perhaps you were right: architecture does indict a society.

I was not trying to become a critic. I mainly wanted to be free of the modernism that felt alien and all too likely to be imposed upon me without my consent. This way of looking at architecture did that, and I was thankful. But even more importantly it taught me that what I was contending with was more than just "style." There are styles that are so natural that we think nothing of them until they are threatened. But there is another style, the "International Style," which is not really a style in that sense of playful and creative expression; it is more like a philosophy, a way of being—utilitarian, materialistic, calculating, and limited—of which the core theme is "there is no alternative." The odd thing was that I had always believed that philosophy was something you studied. I never knew that it came at you, fully armed, exploiting weakness, creating doubt.

At stake in any artistic judgment are two fundamentals. One is the conviction that in what we perceive, we are making contact with reality. Our personal sense of being is bound up with this confidence. The other is that we can make sense of this belief when others do not see things our way. We have to manage both of these, the respect for our own integrity and that of other people, at the same time. It is not unusual for any academic, journalist, or politician to have to navigate this paradox—as we have said, it is what growing up is about—but I had a particular baptism in this truth when I chose to assault the mountain (so it seemed) of Ernst Gombrich's *Art and Illusion*, an immensely persuasive book I had been introduced to at school.

For me *Art and Illusion* was now in the way, painfully so, as Gombrich had been my hero. I believed I knew what I was seeing, but he was arguing not for a direct perception of truth but for a slow progress towards it, by "schema and correction," as one convention after another was refined. His friend Karl Popper had led the way in a view of science, not as a set of concepts directly impressed on our minds by nature, but as a series of theories whose chief merit was that they accounted for observations and had not yet been falsified. For Gombrich this suited art well, because it relieved the viewer of any metaphysic connecting art with an overarching "truth"; instead it frankly admitted that art, even by great artists, was one approximation after another. But it also necessitated the truth that, in order to judge what sort of "schema" you have, you must be able to get around the back of art, so to speak, and judge its reality. It is baffling that for neither Popper nor Gombrich is there any point of arrival; there is a continual evolution of truth but no destination. I took courage from several objectors to Gombrich's scheme.[8]

Gombrich was reacting against a Hegelian view of art that posited a spirit of the age as deterministically in control of style, and wanted to set art (and politics) free with a more "secular" causation, essentially of mind and will. However for me, something was missing; or worse, something important was undermined. If we can never reach the world but are always locked in to tentative theories, improving but never arriving, is not something essential to our humanity lost? In any case, as an account of art, the theory did not work; it could not explain how Duccio and Giotto, whose ability to account for reality visually is easily exceeded by a novice art student today, are still masters whom we can enjoy. I wanted to argue that there is some truth that they see directly, even if the nineteenth-century academies would have improved their drawing.

I gave a paper on this theme in which I expressed what I considered then to be the heart of the artistic experience. I believed that the human condition was "a state of disconnection from the world, the insecurity of not being able to sense where our particular cocoon is lodged," leaving us in a condition of "perennial unease, from which only our love for each other, and our love for things, releases us." I went on to say "If art is truth, then, that is another way of saying that the pleasure of art is in the joy of making connections with things outside ourselves." Art, in other words, is the bridge that overcomes our alienation from reality. I concluded:

> The issue of truth in art is only another aspect of the question of whether we can perceive truth at all, an uncertainty which is part of our state of disconnection. If art is one of the ways in which we experience the act of perception, and feel almost

---

8. For example, Paul Richter writes, "[Gombrich's] claim that perception itself follows the model of schema and correction raises the following objections: (i) The method of modification of perception cannot be called 'correction', since there is nothing to correct against; (ii) The method of modification of representational art cannot be called 'correction' unless all that is meant is bringing it into closer agreement with the shifting sands of perception." Richter, *Gombrich's Model*, 341, discussing Gombrich, *Art and Illusion*, 272.

sensuously that it is true, then it is not surprising that it appears to have at times an almost religious role in modern life; or that the thought that it is largely dead is attended with such panic.[9]

The paper was received with patience and consideration. But a friend who read it, the late Prof. Ron Lewcock, the architectural historian, said "My final feeling is that you may have an *a*typical way of relating to art! Certainly, it does not apply to me!" I do not remember finding this comment particularly painful, but it raised acutely the question, How can we be sure that when we look at art, we are seeing the same thing? If I am so convinced that I know what I see, how do I explain that my friends see differently?

To save postponing a debate on this, I do have an answer, which is probably the one we all use. In life we walk different paths, and those paths condition what we see. One person will be passionate about truth, and another not particularly interested. We find we are heading in different directions; we are ardent for different causes. But we have not chosen these things. Very often it seems we have been chosen by them, or for them. Who we are is decided way back in our history, by choices that were made for us. My art loving goes back two generations at least—not just loving it, but the ways I like it. So I do not expect others to see things my way. They have been formed differently. However, I do not simply project that past upon the present. Our perceiving comes with questions. Does what I think I see really hold up? Does what I think I saw last time remain true today? Unless we could see, we could not correct, and if we could not correct, we could not see. Perception is a matter of conviction, and conviction likes to make itself sure. This is not the same as Gombrich's "schema and correction." The more accurate your means of perception, the more you will want to confirm it. To use an example that I think Gombrich himself uses, consider that I see a red blur in the distance. Is it a bus? It gets closer. It is a bus. It really is a bus, the bus I am waiting for. At this point the perception is more than a hazard. It is a truth: I can board the bus.

However, convinced though I was that I had reached somewhere in my argument, I still felt that there was something claustrophobic in this argument with Gombrich. What was the point of my picking holes in a few of his ideas? I had a moment of glory after my paper walking down King's Parade at night, with a don who appeared to like my approach; but I had to accept that "truth" was tribal, and that I could not expect to change anything.

---

9. From an unpublished paper titled "Conventions and Conventionality: Truth in Art, and Half-Truth in Art and Illusion," delivered at the Cambridge History of Art Department Research Group, Oct. 19, 1978.

That dim sense that beliefs are culturally embodied, and that members of institutions that hold their beliefs in common have every reason not to change their views, ought to have prepared me for what was to come later. Our situation, it seems, is not so far from that of the ancient world, where invading armies would not only change the ownership of a territory but its whole truth system, and woe betide any inhabitant, new or old, who even considered thinking differently from the legally authorized belief. The problem for me was not courage. Any foolhardy person can threaten the system. The problem was internal. When I think differently from the institution, how can I be sure? My argument with Gombrich had left me with only two elements to navigate life with: myself and reality. In practical terms this sufficed, but if I wanted any appeal from my decisions, I found that I was judge and jury. Hence the sense of claustrophobia. If I imagine Gombrich and myself in a box, he believes he cannot touch the walls of the box except by ever-improving theories, while I believe I can touch them directly, but we are both still in a box. There is no outside view.

I remember an argument with a Cambridge theologian in the corner of a college courtyard. He was a sincere, clever, and kind man and a prolific author. I was saying that I found it hard to write because I was never sure I had got to the truth. He replied that none of us really has "the truth" and, if he writes, surely others will correct him if he is wrong. I envied his freedom compared to my perfectionism. But I felt outraged that he seemed to regard truth so lightly. As long as he wrote what he thought, he did not seem to worry whether it was "true." I felt we had to be aligned with the truth and arrive at it, and nothing else was worth writing. In retrospect, there was wisdom in his words, not least in respect of the freedom the writer needs. But my sense of the call to do truth, coupled with the impotent frustration that I, my mind, was my only equipment, began to work in me a comprehensive sense of doubt.

Around this time I went to America, with the object of seeing for myself the work of the abstract expressionists. This trip was notable for two changes it worked in me. One was that I began a shift from an external to an internal view of abstract art. Pollock, for example, whose work I saw straight off the plane at MOMA, made at first no sense because (my head being full of baroque art) I was looking precisely for sense, for design, for purpose, for coherence. Those things are all there, but they are not the objective and they survive by default. Gradually, after some travel and a sense of context, the "internal" view stole over me, and I came to connect his tangled skeins of paint with my own life, with the doubt area in me, with that sense of a screen, a bramble hedge, between me and truth. I longed to be able to transcend myself and "get there" (to ultimate reality, presumably), but when

I saw myself through (as I thought) Pollock's pessimistic eyes, I felt more like a fly trapped in a web. I am not sure it matters whether my estimate of Pollock and his contemporaries was "right." The key realization was not the "abstract" part but the "expressionist" part, that their own lives, their positioning of themselves in the existential frame, was not some detached philosophy but lived through their painting. They could have been mistaken about the way the world is; they might have been wrong that there is no one and nothing to hear their heart cry—when there is; but I knew that they represented something true in me, the way I felt it might be to live "as if" we have to exist alone.

The other change was not art but cinema related. I went to see Woody Allen's film *Interiors*, apparently a homage to Bergman, but I knew nothing of that. It represented a grown-up family, well to-do and aesthetically inclined. The mother, an interior designer, excelled not only in controlling her environment, to the ultimate of taste, but in controlling people. Her husband, however, unexpectedly spoilt the aesthetics of a perfect life when he announced that he wanted to "find himself" and left, finding himself very well when he ran into the arms of a lady who fed him roasts and gravy, things previously denied him. Their grown-up children also found excuses not to be around. The controlling mother was left with little to control and the prospect of a bleak existence. Only the new stepmother had a spark of generosity. I recognized myself in most of the characters and saw that the aestheticism of the mother, far from helping her humanly, had no power to save. I was the one, you will remember, who thought art salvific. But here was a body of people with everything they needed except the power to love. I felt the film was describing me. In that Boston cinema I mentally cried out with St. Paul, "Who shall deliver me from the body of this death?"[10]

I watched the film again in Cambridge. The Boston audience had watched in silence, solemnly, almost aghast. The British audience laughed, and they laughed most of the way through. They thought it a satire on America. Good to know that we British would never behave like that. But I knew I had been noticed.

VI

And now my story takes a sudden turn. I had always been a Christian, as I understood the term, and had scarcely ever, in my life, missed Sunday church. I had also known significant answers to prayer. In Cambridge I started attending an apparently moribund church near my house, where an

---

10. Rom 7:24, KJV.

elderly vicar drew me, because he spoke as if he meant and understood what he said. I went to a funeral there and could see that for him salvation and heaven were real. In all my years of churchgoing, I had never met this. I did not consider—how could I?—that it might be Christ in him that attracted me, but he had something I knew I wanted. In one sense this was an interruption to my scheme of study. Nietzschean men do not humble themselves or ask for help (my supervisor was a great proponent of Nietzsche). But I felt my efforts had run into the ground.

People who want to succeed at the PhD degree usually choose confined topics they can drill into, but I was irresistibly drawn to the big questions. These days what I attempted would not be permitted. But the overload from my questionings, although it nearly finished me off, did me good. Two moments came together. One was my humbling—never pleasant—as I accepted that my grand ambition had not succeeded. The other was that my local church had acquired a new vicar, an exceptional man of faith and study, who one day said to me, "David, have you thought about conversion?" Great was my internal squirming at the word; but a few months later, that is what happened. In a mission meeting, held in my house, an upstanding man from church told us of his fiery marriage, and for the first time I grasped the truth that I did not have to be good enough to be a Christian. With my parents' marriage in mind, I was sold. In any case, I had exhausted alternatives. As if in a very dark tunnel, I saw a tiny bead of light. If that was God, I would say yes to him. After a few days of consideration, with a young trainee vicar, I knelt and said "the sinner's prayer"—while my elderly neighbor was pounding at the door.

A lot changed. I started attending church meetings and sang choruses. My aesthetic self was often affronted but I pressed on because I was getting bread. I assumed, of course, that God would help me fulfil my ambition, to help me up my mountain, and that I would "succeed" at last. What I did not realize was that I had broken a cardinal academic rule. Our mountains are our mountains, to be climbed by us alone; if we reach the heavens, well and good, but it is by our own philosophic efforts. Transfigurations, revelations, these are excluded. The idea that God himself might set the bounds of the discussion and structure reality in an accessible way, which we could understand through Scripture—well that was a kind of blasphemy against the elevation of the human mind. Incidentally my supervisor, the ex-Christian, Nietzschean atheist, when I stopped avoiding him, was patient and not hostile. He said it was a case of the immovable object meeting the irresistible force, a mark, I felt, of respect.

Notwithstanding the academic prohibitions, God did help me. I began to want to include him in the aesthetic relationship. Art had to be less about me and my taste, and more about seeing truth through art in the real world. I spent a lot of time on my knees, on my old red turkey carpet, seeking God for answers.

The most important answer came quite unexpectedly.

VII

There was a moment, around this time in Cambridge, when I came across a photograph of a seventeenth-century statue labeled "St Jerome repenting of intellectual sins." The idea that there might be anything wrong with my mind was new to me. I remember one day realizing "my mind is not my property" and in a Cambridge church making a deliberate and formal surrender. This was no small matter because if I acknowledged God in my work I would start to test my place in the secular academy, in which up to now I had enjoyed good favor. But I felt that integrity required it.

Help came to me from an unexpected source. Our vicar (preacher and writer, Dennis Lennon) lent me a book that he had found in a Cambridge bookshop and had been enthralled by. It was *Theological Science* by T. F. Torrance (1912–2007).

In his enthusiasm, Dennis quoted one of the less demanding passages from the book and distributed it around the parish. (This was Cambridge.)

> If I may be allowed to speak personally for a moment, I find the presence and being of God bearing upon my experience and thought so powerfully that I cannot but be convinced of His overwhelming being and rationality. To doubt the existence of God would be an act of sheer irrationality, for it would mean that my reason had become unhinged from its bond with real being. Yet in knowing God I am deeply aware that my relation to Him has been damaged, that disorder has resulted in my mind, and that it is I who obstruct knowledge of God by getting in between Him and myself, as it were. But I am also aware that His presence presses unrelentingly upon me through the disorder of my mind, for He will not let himself be thwarted by it, challenging and repairing it, and requiring of me on my part to yield my thoughts to His healing and controlling revelation.[11]

In this work, and in others such as *The Ground and Grammar of Theology*, which I found slightly easier to understand, Torrance had put into words what I had dimly come to realize: that we do not understand God, or art, or science, or anything else by ordering our perceptions according to our

---

11. Torrance, *Theological Science*, ix.

own presuppositions—and more or less cutting off everything that does not fit—but by allowing the reality of what we encounter to itself mold and shape our thought. To teach this, second only to the gospel itself, seemed to be Torrance's primary mission, and he had found a great ally in the thought of Albert Einstein, who had stretched the thought of science far beyond any principle of how things seemed to be or ought to be to how they actually are. Torrance saw Einstein as having made a decisive break with the dominant worldview deriving from Kant and other enlightenment figures, the belief that we cannot know reality in itself but only according to the structures that we impose upon it; and the belief that there is a gulf between the world of the senses (the world that science can grasp) and the world of actualities. For Einstein, our own structures of thought need correcting, and it is the real world, grasped and intuited by science, that corrects them. Torrance diagnosed, behind this dispute, a long history of dualism in Western culture going back to Greek thought, in which "matter" and "spirit" were set in opposition. This emerges in different forms, from early medieval to modern thought, but there is always posited a divide, an impassible gulf, so that you never get beyond the human world to have real knowledge, either of God or of the world he has made. Torrance had not been slow to point out that such dualisms also wreaked havoc in any understanding of God becoming man in Christ. If God cannot be known, He cannot make himself known; and if the Greeks were right, we could never, as St. John describes it, touch and handle the word of life.[12] However, that writer probably knew his gospel was driving a coach and horses through Greek philosophy.

A large part of Torrance's value to me was his superb spiritual and intellectual confidence. In the Cambridge of those days, clever people were expected to be sceptics. But Torrance (who was not popular for saying so) reminded us that brains are not sacrosanct and that we need to submit our minds to the truth rather than engage in creative speculations. In a passage Torrance quotes, Jesus prays, "I thank you, Father, Lord of heaven and earth, that you have hidden these things from the wise and understanding and revealed them to little children; yes, Father, for such was your gracious will."[13] Torrance reminds us that knowledge itself is a sphere of gracious, not human devised, revelation, a message he had taken to heart.

But perhaps an even greater usefulness of Torrance's work to me was that it explained where I was on the intellectual map, why I had got so stuck in trying to understand art, and how it was that so many of my core assumptions were in fact false. For, unknown to myself, and having only a passing

---

12. 1 John 1:1.
13. Matt 11:25–26 (ESV), quoted in T. F. Torrance, *Incarnation*, 172.

A Question of Beauty (A Personal Story) 61

acquaintance with Hume, Locke, and Kant, I was a perfect product of their school, and had the greatest difficulty in overcoming the doubt that I could have real knowledge, of God or anything. This of course could be combined with the greatest possible confidence in my own judgments! Now I could begin to see the history of the art of Europe as a battlefield, in which wave after wave of artists had succumbed to one philosophical assault after another. Torrance had himself identified Impressionism as a movement fixed on the reality of "what appears to us" rather than on the confidence that we can ever know things as they are.[14] Later on, incidentally, I came to love the Impressionists, because what they see is of course a great deal more than what they believe.

Torrance's work also gave me confidence that the argument I had been having in my head with Gombrich could be solved. Gombrich had argued that "a painting is not a proposition," and "paintings don't make statements," therefore art is not as such a vehicle of truth.[15] All this sounded convincing, but though the logic seemed to hold up, everything that experience taught, of what artists try to do when they paint, was against it. For Torrance, language is a pointer to realities. We do not look for statements to be equivalents of realities, but we look through the statements to engage with realities themselves. This seemed very like our situation in art. Through a portrait of Henry VIII by Holbein, we enquire what Henry was like, not just his face but his person. Holbein never signed a document saying, "This is what Henry VIII looked like." But his portrait leads us through, in some measure, to him. Ultimately it is the reality itself, Henry VIII's being and presence, that bears down on us, and convinces us that we are right. In Gombrich's later work he came to accord art some "cognitive value," a belief that, for its time, in view of the strict philosophical rules governing art discourse, was revolutionary.

VIII

Such was my enthusiasm for Torrance, that for a short time I imagined that correct epistemology *was* the good news of Christ, as if all we needed to do was go back behind the Enlightenment and be somehow whole. But then I

---

14. "The developing disintegration of form in art . . . can be traced back to the impressionists in their desire to separate the sensuous continuum of experience from its controlling ground in the spatio-temporal structures of the world, so that it can be perceived and enjoyed in its pure and vivid sensuous impression." Torrance, *Ground and Grammar*, 32.

15. Gombrich, *Art and Illusion*, 59.

had not yet discovered that the human predicament (mine) went far beyond the twists and turns of history and certainly lay much deeper than epistemology, though that definitely had real-world consequences. Even true knowledge can be a hazard. "Somehow," said Torrance, "the more [man] comes to know, the more masterful he tries to be, and the more he imposes himself upon reality, the more he gets in the way of his own progress."[16]

In the art community of the twentieth century, there were few people more masterful than Picasso. In my studies he had not crossed my path, but one summer I had an unexpected invitation to join a summer series of talks on art at Great St. Mary's Church by delivering a sermon on an artist of my choosing. There was a big Picasso exhibition in London at the time. I wanted to see how he fitted into the faith picture. A small congregation heard me deliver my thoughts. In retrospect my argument was provocative in the extreme. But at that time (only just) there was still a question over Picasso. He had not yet eased his way, for art historians, into the position of an Old Master, and was popularly considered a radical, someone able to pick establishment culture threadbare. It was still possible to argue his status.

My study of Picasso, mainly through what I would describe as very careful and prayerful looking, was a revelation. (My later reading, especially of Gilot and Lake's *Life with Picasso*, seemed to confirm what I saw.) I became aware, much more than I had been, of the power of art. I believed that through cubism Picasso had found a lever through which to change a whole culture, but not in a helpful direction.

I began the talk with a parable of how things seemed to me. I asked people to picture a ship sinking, with survivors in the water clutching at spars. As they scramble to survive, they see a smaller vessel, Picasso's—with the artist sitting on deck smoking a cigar and drinking champagne. They call out to him, "Congratulations, Mr. Picasso. You've blown up our ship! There's still a bit left. Blow it up some more!"

The argument then got complicated, but I shall try to simplify. The artist's early work was sentimental (his beautiful, earliest work can be seen in Barcelona). In a painting of a sickbed (*Science and Charity*, 1897), the attending nun looks ineffectual, the doctor (science) looks defeated: in the face of death, there is no salvation, only sentiment. Picasso became a consummate manipulator of emotions. But he did not like himself for it. In the famous *Demoiselles D'Avignon*, we find him almost violently attacking the surface to obliterate the indulgent pity of his vision. During this period (1907–8) we find him painting eyes in a schematic way, eyes that stare out of the picture but cannot be looked in on. In a Blue Period self-portrait, he

---

16. Torrance, *Theological Science*, xiii.

gives himself blank eyes that also stare out but cannot be seen. We call eyes "the window of the soul": through the eyes a person is revealed. But not this man. He remains unseen, in the place of power, where his self is hidden. Picasso was fascinated by masks. He collected them (African and Oceanic ritual masks) and drew them. The faces in the *Demoiselles D'Avignon* are new masks. So it seems he wanted to find that place in the world that is beyond scrutiny.

We have, then, a complete reversal of that account of knowing at which Torrance arrived, where you become vulnerable as you are exposed to realities. This is not knowledge but power. The sentimentality of Picasso's work, exemplified by his *Child with a Dove*, formerly in the London National Gallery, is a token of his real lack of interest in actual people and actual situations. If we try to ask questions of such a picture, to see what is really going on with the boy and his ball, the picture crumbles. The picture, in a sense, is not meant for looking. It is a placard, advertising the artist's sentiment. So the picture becomes not about the boy but about the artist, not a shared experience of reality but one in which the artist holds all the cards. Because we cannot question the image by comparing it with reality (since image, not reality, is all it claims), the artist remains in the power position.

Before we leap to Picasso's defence—and personally I still find his work false to the roots—let us try to see how this argument concludes. There is a spiritual place beyond scrutiny. It is not in heaven, on earth, or in hell, where everything we are or do is open to God. But it is a place a man might wish to be in and might wish to create. We have seen that connecting with reality, from here to there, is not Picasso's aim. He is emotionally disconnected. Sentimentality fills the gap. He does not want to exist in the place of seeing and being seen. He would rather be hidden and looking in. He would rather construct a reality than be found in this one. But what is the name of a place where the writ of God does not run? In Bible times, this alternative reality, with a different imaginary space, where different rules apply, which is in effect a shelter from troublesome truth—this is called "an idol."

If we look closely, we will find something very clever in cubism. There is a theory, promoted by Picasso's supporters, that cubism, by abandoning one-point perspective and crushing together many different viewpoints into one flat surface (rather as you might squash a cardboard box), is giving more of reality, a sort of Platonic supra-physical, higher order of perception. It is true that Cézanne, from whom this reordering derived, really was chasing real objects from every angle and putting them together, with a baffling logic we can intuit but not explain. But we cannot bring our questions to any of Picasso's assemblages of bent and broken pipes, guitars, and newspapers, except to know that the objects once probably existed and that their appearance was too predictable to invite very close attention. However, if we begin to consider that the artist's aim is not to take us to the reality itself (in which he has only passing interest) but to create a conventional reality *that he takes us away from*, the process becomes much more interesting. When we visualize an early cubist work, where elements of subject matter are still easily seen, we find that the artist does not take you "through" to the subject, in the way we saw Holbein doing with Henry VIII. He does not really have an interest in the subject. The subject anchors the picture as being something rather than nothing, but what we see in early cubist works is not a window to reality but the taking of something from reality and assembling it together in a kind of intermediate space. This kind of space is an art space, a not-reality, a place of pure creation.

As is often said, God's creation is the only work of pure creation, where nothing existed before. People are creative, but their creations are derivative. We can only create from what is there. No one would argue with the fact that Picasso was creative. But might his drive have been to make not just second-order images but first-order creations of spaces, that take us out of this reality?

When we look carefully at cubist paintings, and I am thinking now of the latest phase when "subject matter" has almost disappeared, we find a remarkable feature. You might call it a principle of contradiction. The paintings are not abstract and they are not without depth, but whenever an area threatens to become solid or three-dimensional, another stroke or facet will contradict it and bring it (that area) again to the surface. However the "surface" is not the fictive picture surface, where it might take form simply as a design. It is a surface hovering just beyond the picture plane. The whole is manifest neither as depth, nor as surface, but as a kind of space between that we could call a "not-reality." This is why the paintings are not abstract. They need realities (subjects) in order to withdraw from them. But what are "not-realities"? They are places where God is not. There are no such places; but idols, of whatever kind, ancient or modern, make them believable.

Admittedly, the foregoing argument sounds improbable. But hiding from God has been our habit ever since Adam. Our difficulty has been to find a space to do it in. The genius of cubism is not to oppose the spacious and too-revealing world with an alternative but to create pockets of doubt, places at one remove from the physical creation with all its unnerving contingency, a no-man's land between the real world and art, where we can mentally experiment with freedom from God. We do not need to deny God; that would be far too crude. All that needs to be done is to create a kind of mental buzz that seems to deny access to the world and to leave all sorts of appealing signposts suggesting that alternative realities, through alternative religions, are there to find.

At the time I gave the sermon, people were just starting to be seen with portable CD players (the "CD Walkman") and earphones. Their ability to cut out the world and insulate their ears with sound to me seemed a fitting metaphor for the disconnected, subjective, and doubting world that Picasso and his generation had produced.

IX

Readers may note, perhaps with some discomfort, that I have slipped God into art history. In my Picasso talk I had been arguing that the painter, followed by many others, had been engaging in a spiritual exercise, creating God-free zones: spaces that were not in this nature, which unwaveringly, if controversially, points to a creator. Nor were they simply works of the imagination, which in fact always refer back to the world we have. I had concluded that from these "zones," which exist only in paintings, but hence also in the minds of some viewers, it has been possible to work aggressively to dismantle the public supremacy of God. If you believe there are spaces where God is not, then you do not in effect believe in God at all; you have found a "reality" that does not belong to him.

There was still the question of how I should handle these insights in respect of official art history. I did not know of any books that would have told me that the God-relation of artists was the most important clue to their art; but if God is God, that has to be the case. But persuading "experts" is a different matter. The congregation at Great St. Mary's, gracious and amiable, were not experts, nor was it likely they were so devoted to Picasso that they minded what I said. But the time came, eventually, when I had to stop playing grandmother's footsteps with the art historians and had to try to bring our two worlds together. There were certain decisions to be made about thesis titles—not any easier for me than for them, as I had scarcely matured in this new kind of thinking long enough to explain it.

But at this point I discovered something interesting. There was a way of dealing with "my problem" (the problem of me for them) that was superficially convincing. There were people who wrote "Marxist art history," and others, increasingly, who wrote "feminist art history." Clearly anyone who attempted to write "Christian art history" fell into the same category of people with strong opinions based on a particular philosophy, who might, in a pinch, be permitted to plough that furrow. It seemed to make sense to say to such people, "Show me what you've got, and we'll see if it illuminates the territory." Does Marxism, or feminism, or Christianity (heaven forbid) make good sense of the facts? In a way, this is right, and it is all we are asking to do. But the hidden assumption is that "we" (the central stream of received art history, embodied in academic institutions) hold the territory, the epistemological high ground, and we permit "you" to have a "perspective" on it. We have the mountain; you have the viewpoint.

The way this works, academically, is that the status quo is not disturbed, because in doing our "perspectives" we accept certain assumptions about how art history is done. God himself, of course, is not a player. He has long ago been banished from history. We can talk about what Rubens or Velasquez believed, as a condition, rather like measles, but it would be naive of us to let consciousness of those beliefs flow through us into appreciation of their paintings, so that what Rubens thought about landscape or Velásquez about the humanity of the court dwarfs became part of the ontological structuring of our own world. If we can discuss "religion" in an objective manner as a social manifestation, well and good, but if we allow it as an alignment that invites us to take sides, then we have put ourselves beyond the pale. It is as if we can look at the contents of a shop window and have any "perspective" on them that we like; but there is no way we can actually purchase the goods.

As I was processing these thoughts, I was reminded of what I had learned from Picasso about idolatry. If you have an academic landscape where many different voices and opinions are "allowed"—and one can picture the university, with its arts and science faculties, its theology faculty, its churches and many other fora of belief—then there has to be some center that "allows" them. If that center is titularly God (and in my undergraduate day, degrees were conferred in the name of the Father, Son, and Holy Spirit), then well and good, because we know that God guarantees freedom of dissent. He wants "all men to come to the knowledge of the truth,"[17] which they can only do if they are free, free to say yes or no. Coercion is definitely not knowledge. If the center is God, there can be toleration. But if the center is some secularized form of "tolerance," in which all views are "permitted," then all views exist by permission, which is not really freedom. There is, in fact, some hidden assumption about what is tolerable. Moreover, God is displaced from the center, though possibly permitted a home in the theology faculty and churches. There he can do no harm, because there is no challenge to the hegemony of the center. But if he is not God of all, but God only of certain specialist perspectives, he is not God of anywhere. So what looks like tolerance is in fact a denial of God's central claim, that he is Lord of all.

---

17. 1 Tim 2:7

A Question of Beauty (A Personal Story) 67

Paganism down the ages, in its many different forms, has erected convincing and pleasing alternatives that begin by offering God a generous place as one deity among many and end by persecuting every remnant of true faith.

Our culture has developed a strange inversion of the truth. Some of our scientists and philosophers will go to the trenches to defend the freedom of their subjects to exclude God. They think that any admission of God's existence would be tantamount to letting the priests in to govern and limit their subjects. Instead they would prefer to believe in a world that came about by pure chance and from nowhere, with no meaning, purpose or destiny, with no healing from sorrow and no redemption from evil, and they call that rational. At their hands God, whose existence makes sense of the search for truth, who underwrites all our longings for goodness and perfection, who guarantees our freedom from sheer material determinism, and satisfies personal hopes in the face of death, has been pensioned off and sent to the old people's home.

Exasperation aside, I was still left with a theoretical question. It was clear that for me there was no going back to a "secular" view of art, and no point in doing so. But that was for my own thinking, or so I thought. In pursuing this line, was I just occupying my own space, or was I treading on someone else's grass? In other words, was what I was claiming "private truth" or a universal truth that potentially affected others? There is a tidy view of academic disciplines that potentially provides a refuge; if only (imagined the coward in me) I could be convinced by it! Thus one could conceive, in a medieval way, of a hierarchy of disciplines, where those at the top, explicitly theology, require the supposition of God; next down are the sciences, which certainly require beliefs, such as belief in order and intelligibility, but can operate in an integrated way at a remove from thinking about where existence comes from; next come the arts, which can in modern times make the "absence of God" almost their raison d'etre; and finally such things as practical mechanics, which can operate very well without discussion of God, though in the workshop his name can be mentioned rather frequently!

On this view, as far as art history is "scientific" it can be managed without reference to God; as far as it is an art, it can simply accept the cultural norms of our time—i.e., practical atheism. This kind of "objectivity" in art history corresponds perfectly with the "methodological naturalism" pursued in science, where the only kind of explanations permitted to the discipline are material.

Sympathetic though I was to the idea of leaving my fellow art historians in peace, I had not failed to notice that the subject that I loved had been increasingly reduced to a sort of "going round the houses" repetition of the limited kind of things art historians are allowed to say. In a typical exhibition catalogue, all the information one could wish for was there to explain the who, what, where, and why of a painting, but little to explain why we were looking at it. It was like investigating a corpse after a murder. Every kind of forensic test was applied to work out how and why it got there, but it was no longer able to speak. We can be thankful for some excellent critics who dare to tread this territory of meaning. But we need to lift criticism beyond the subjective impulses of even the best minds. The bigger questions remain. What is art, and why are we drawn back to it again and again? The only way of answering that is to discover what sort of reality we are living in. It cannot be that something as good as art is simply a human invention, like ice cream. It is human, but any merely human analogy like "pleasure" or "communication" seems banal in comparison.

There was also another question I needed to ask, one with practical consequences. Was it necessary, for the sake of truth, to expose my Christian faith to view? In the gospel accounts, St. Peter, warming himself by the sentries' fire while Jesus was being tried, found pressing reasons to try to hide in the group and disguise his adherence to Jesus. I also could think of pressing reasons to keep quiet. Was there not an objectivist way of doing art history, handling facts with long tongs in a detached way, requiring no reference to private beliefs? It all hinged, as far as I could see it, on the "public truth" of the resurrection of Jesus.[18] I was much struck by the way the resurrected Christ made no attempt to declare himself alive in the public square before the chief priests and Pilate, who had ordered his execution. He left no "objective" path to faith in him, except the impossible science of the empty tomb, which left no evidence of who he was or where he had gone, except for a horribly empty hole in the space-time universe.

The witness of the resurrected Christ, then, provided no ladder to publicly sanctioned truth, by which his murderers could say, "Now we have a new fact in our world, something we can master with all the other facts, *but nothing changes because facts do not move us*." If this "new fact" was to be accepted, then it could only be done by completely switching sides and admitting the alarming possibility that Jesus had been all along the one he said he was, the true representation on earth of the God in whose arms the world lay, and whom it was their official profession to please. So what kind of public truth was this? Something that could not be admitted without a whole change of view, not just in theory but in personal adherence; and something that could not be categorized because none of the pieces were in place until one admitted the inadmissible.

18. This very helpful phrase comes from Lesslie Newbigin's *Truth to Tell: The Gospel as Public Truth*.

There would now seem to be, therefore, no public truth in the resurrection that affirms any kind of "business as usual" in the normal way either of doing knowledge or religion. It cannot be seen without listening to the sound of a new kind of reality—so far, so good. But, and this struck me equally strongly, the disciples of Christ did declare the resurrection, very loudly, in the public square and had no hesitation in calling to account those responsible for Christ's execution.

Nor did they make things easy by suggesting some sort of spiritual resurrection: on the contrary, they stated that Jesus had been raised out of a particular grave on a certain day and that he was now ascended into the actual place of power from which the whole cosmos hangs. This is public truth, but it is of a new kind that drags the old appearances and mental habits into a place of exposure where, so to speak, we wonder if we have ever "seen" before. However, this public truth is not discontinuous with the old truth. Instead of calling people to believe in resurrection as "miracle," an event with neither meaning nor precedent, the apostles showed the stepping stones by which, through the whole history of Israel, this new reality had come about. As the new disciples looked back they could see, through "the law and the prophets,"[19] an illuminated track, and they suddenly realized that this kind of Savior had been anticipated and prepared for all along. The public truth was already there in their own history, but most of them had missed it.

When we take this magnificent landscape of history and truth, and focus down simply to its implications for art and art history, two things at least seem clear. First, there is no coercive logic to terrify the objective observer into adopting this point of view. The empty tomb of Christ is simply that: a question mark, and as we have said, the resurrection of Christ can only be received not by force but by acceding to a whole new presentation of reality, rather like the one that grasped St. Paul on the road to Damascus. That means that we can present but not compel. We are not herded into truth but led into it as we follow. The appeal of truth is simply this: it is true.

The second is that if there is no coercive logic, then it is possible to make pictures of reality excluding God that more or less work. Laplace made the famous statement, in answer to the question of where God fitted into his mechanical cosmos, "I have no need of that hypothesis," and ever since, intellectual constructs, whether for science or the arts, have been erected on the simple foundation "explanations are to be found in what I see." There are arguments for aesthetic truth and even for morality that, in a sense, cannot fail because those things are present and unavoidable. The

---

19. See Luke 16:16 and 24:27.

least of philosophers can argue quite reasonably that they are there. Reality, the functional interconnectedness of things, is presented with many of its essentials there on the plate. There are no "gaps" to force us to believe in God. It is only when we look at it as a whole, and ask such questions as, We know how science describes it, but what is it really? that we begin to feel the need for answers from outside the system. In other words, it is when reality humbles us that we move from observing a system that we can dominate and manipulate to wondering how such beings as ourselves should have such a great inheritance and such awesome responsibilities. In effect, we move from quantity questions we can handle, to quality questions, which are much more open-ended.

Art is preeminently a place in life where such quality questions come to the fore. We do not know what it is about us as beings that makes art something that captures us even before we have thought about it, why we are so defenceless before its truth, and why it is so elusive when we try to systematize or professionalize its production. But we cannot abandon ourselves to the view that everything is mysterious and nothing can be said; for it is not possible to have any sort of commerce in art, the hand-to-hand traffic between makers, critics, teachers, viewers, and sellers that relies on trust, unless we have some idea of what art is. Therefore, the fact that we are drawn to ask the big questions about art, such as, How can an arrangement of base materials have such power? also leads us to ask the bigger questions, such as, What sort of a world do we in fact live in?

To return to my narrative, I did attempt to persuade the academic authorities of my case that in trying to describe or "place" the work of critics such as Roger Fry or Ernst Gombrich it was insufficient simply to relate them to other authors and to the history of ideas, as if my own standpoint was from some "objective" eminence outside the discussion, and that we needed to dig deeper to find an objectivity that far transcended my own, an objectivity in God. I made this case on a couple of pages, but I was, I think, not yet ready to persuade or to be persuasive; and the authorities were certainly not yet ready or willing to be persuaded. During five years of research I had, I must admit, been treated with far more latitude than would be permitted today and had pursued my own thoughts unhindered. But I suffered from the illusion that academic bodies exist to discuss ideas and bring them to the bar of truth. I can now see that ideas might well be true whether or not the hierarchy approves of them. What makes them true is not a bureaucratic seal of approval but the integrity of their correspondence to reality. If I had expected more from the academic system, I had forgotten that academics are people, and lean towards convenience, not disturbance. There were a couple of kind friends among academic staff who warned me against extremism and being overly trenchant; but by this time the Bible was becoming a strong counterweight and "compromise" is not in its language.

X

Because of my mistaken belief that truth was to be found and validated in academic institutions, it was a surprise to discover one day that I no longer wanted to live in Cambridge. It was very healing for the mind to move, with my wife (then expectant) to Essex (never a place for prolonged speculations), and from there, after another spell in the art trade, to Leicester, where I took up a post working at the heart of the evangelical world, Universities and Colleges Christian Fellowship (UCCF), where the job was to encourage a gospel witness in different professions. With my family I attended a Pentecostal church where I learned, as clearly I needed to, that there are ways other than intellectual of being a Christian.

There is one final element of autobiography I need to mention. In 1995 my mother died, and I inherited her oil paints, palette, and easel and began painting, getting some limited training in London. I also inherited some of the dilemmas of her life, dilemmas I had lived with lifelong, but which I felt a new impulse to resolve. Around this time, too, I was invited to write my book *The art of God and the Religions of Art*, and I knew that one of my motivations was filial piety towards the kind of art so deeply imprinted in me from early years. That kind of art was a very English naturalism, founded on great skill in drawing and a deep and informed love of the countryside. My mother's training had been at the Slade School of Art in the 1930s, under a fiercely rigorous regime that had the Old Masters as its model. The dilemma was this: While modernism in art has clearly undermined the practice and teaching of academic methods, has it also undermined their validity? Is a kind of art based on these things no longer authentic, and if so, by what authority?

For nearly five centuries it was understood that drawing from the life model should be at the center of artistic training; but once that tradition was overthrown, we have been forced to ask questions and look for justifications. At the heart of the matter is this issue: What kind of art can carry the freight of meaning in the modern world? It was fine for Rubens to paint the political painting *Peace and War* as a figurative allegory, and fine for Goya, Courbet, Daumier, and Picasso, with his *Guernica*, to make political paintings out of figurative means. But it seems that today the basic humanist agreement has broken down, and that those who believe the person is the story are left high and dry. It is even questioned whether nature actually has meaning, or should just be treated as some kind of economically valuable amenity that a few lingering romantics still see transcendental value in. In this time of cultural collapse, all sorts of weeds are flourishing, chief of which is the relativism that says, "It means something to me." This providentially has enabled an enormous diversity of art in every conceivable form and allowed even such figurative eccentrics as Lucian Freud and David Hockney to find a place. There is however a huge difference between making a circus ring where anyone can perform, and all are "equally valid," and believing that certain ways of doing art are normative. Indeed the only way Lucian Freud survived being such a good painter of the figure is that at the same time he undermined its meaning, with such a bleak sense (or so it seems to me) of human value.

Perhaps it would be helpful to put the problem in paradoxical form. Either the artistic tradition is wrong, because it does not fit the times. Or the times are wrong, because they do not fit the tradition.

The first statement is clearly true in the sense that, after the First World War, there was no return to the Edwardian world of fashion and luxury, bustles and parasols. The nations had been at war and everything became more functional. Art itself, at least in the hands of some of the leading war artists, became more poster-like, more focused on the message. So times can change and art adapts. A very conservative society changes slowly, but there are still unstoppable changes of mood, such as the resurgence of modernism in our own time, where, for example, steel and glass offices, with modernistic furniture and abstracts on the walls, seem to image what modern people want to identify with. So it is true: we cannot maintain that which has no conviction for our own time, that which looks "old fashioned."

What about the second statement, that the times are wrong? We know that to be true too. Sometimes it feels as if we are aboard a runaway bus, and there is a terrible acceleration of absurdity upon absurdity, crime upon crime, and immorality not even seen as immoral. I dare not mention specifics, because no one can agree on right or wrong any more. But what we do know without doubt is that there is suffering, as almost every corner of society bears the scars of broken covenants, and wounds from those who confuse license with freedom. The times are wrong and the question for artists is whether they are complicit (as most of us are) or, more rarely, critiquing the state of things.

It is normally assumed that the arts track the culture, with occasional moments of anticipating it; but what we do not so much reckon with is art's converting power, its ability to picture and, therefore, permit a new state of affairs. If there is a dominant mood that has provided in such large measure the background music for social breakdown, it is the primacy of the self, the loosened ties of obligation, the obliteration of the transcendent, the dominance of the material. It does not take an advertising campaign to promote this: artists, sucked unknowingly into the vortex, embody it in their work as radical innovation; and middle-class opinion formers goon over it in exaggerated admiration. Against such active promotion, the tradition, the absurdly faithful watercolorist who labours over trees and skies, seems to have little power. But the tradition, for all its weakness, embodies in the relics of full-blooded humanism something solid: the existence of a reality we cannot bend around ourselves; of joys to be found in "the other," whether natural or human; and of a true right and wrong we did not invent, that issues like a sword from heaven.

We can, then, have an art that is true to beliefs that were once recognized as true and perhaps will be again; and we can also have art that is true to something false, to invalid ideals, to beliefs that cannot stand the test of time. An example of the former would be any kind of art that is beautiful, well made, and gives pleasure, of which there is still plenty—although in the acid rain of modernity, the idea that value has to do with pleasure is easily dismissed. An example of the latter would be the minimalist sculpture of Donald Judd. His empty boxes do not give us much to look at, but they have proved extraordinarily potent. They not only signify a world that is empty, like a box that has nothing in it—and many people still see the universe as "empty" space in which there is no room for God—but they have also surely helped empower emptiness as a transcendent "reality" and value. In architecture the empty space is treated as an end in itself, which it feels like desecration to fill; and in personal belief, the idea has taken hold that the mind is at its best when it is empty. The brilliance of Judd's work, not a good brilliance but the brilliance of a master thief, is the way he has stretched his "art" between two worlds; it occupies the mental space of works of art, in that it attempts to encapsulate something about the world through vision, and it occupies gallery space, giving it the right to be contemplated as art. But it is not art in the sense of being in any way enriching to look at. Its real purpose is to reconfigure our thinking about what we will accept in the permitted space of culture and to convert the mind towards a supposed ideal.

I discovered a lot through writing *The art of God*, especially about the cultural power of art. What we tentatively admit soon becomes dominant, and the dominant soon becomes immovable—a supposed national treasure before which we have to bow. Traditional culture embodies through art a sense of what is good—truth, generosity, skill and so on—that from its place of respect permeates the culture; but revolutionary art movements unravel what is good by scepticism and mockery.

XI

For writing *The art of God* I adopted a standard scheme, structuring it on creation, fall, redemption, and return, and found it remarkably potent. Of course the creation part is speculative, as we were not there, and we are left looking "through" fallen art to try to suppose what is inherent in creation. But it seems clear that in all cultures in all periods there is such a thing as artistic making, not as we view it today in art galleries but as a basic fact about how life is done. It is no different from the gift of making things that have their own life, separate from the self, and in as far as they are free from their makers, they share the life of the world. In as far as they are concordant with the world, they say something true. This I called "natural" art, and it applies across the arts and crafts. We can all recognize this; but we also know "art" that defies these rules.

In addition to natural art, which is always there, even by its absence, I also argued that there is a "fallen" kind of art, which takes natural art but inverts it. Its power lies not in the way it takes us out to realities but in the way it converts us to substitute realities, realities less threatening to the human ego than the one we have. An example might be, as we have mentioned, Picasso's *Child with a Dove* (formerly in the London National Gallery), a sentimental image of childhood, but one we do not see as sentimental because it is painted in such a way that we would not think of putting it side by side with real life. It is "art" rather than nature. The artist successfully takes us down a tunnel into "Picasso world," rather than, like most of the gallery's masterpieces, putting us side by side with reality.

There is an explanation for the existence of the two kinds of "art," one which is based on creation and the other which tries to divert us from creation into a separate "art realm." It is quite a simple idea: aspects of creation have the signature of God so strongly on them that they provoke hostility. Human beings love goodness, obviously, but very close to that love is hatred for what shows us up; the desire to destroy is seldom far behind the desire to make. Sentimentality, as in the Picasso, is really disguised enmity: the false child is more lovable than the real one. St. Paul tells us in Rom 1:20 that the visible world tells us enough about God to know he is there. So visible reality is not a neutral background to life, as we sometimes like to think; it is spiritually charged and, to those who want to get along in life without God, threatening. On the other hand, the power of idols is their ability to create islands of deception, mental places where idol-consciousness draws us away from reality-consciousness and we convince ourselves that we are in a different reality to the one we have. Idols are mere physical objects, powerless, but the imagination gives them life and allows us to believe that the exalted human self has in fact got a home. I argued that some forms of art work quite well in this respect—and their trick is to be made in such a way that you never compare them to the real world.

So we have, then, a contrast between two kinds of art: one which appears to be weak because it is dependant on the real world and the other that seems strong because it is "creative." But there is in fact far more strength in the natural art that draws power from outside itself than in the idols that rely on nothing more than deception. From this point of view, we are enabled to value the weakness of what I also called "small art"—art that is focused, with all the power of the self, away from the self—and to believe that the day will come when the other kind of art, which leaves us mainly in the orbit of the artist, will dissolve away.

Given that the human heart is so easily carried off not just by idols, which do so much to frame reality in ways that convince us of our own independence, but by beauty itself, which is innocent and wonderful but so easily torn from the fabric of grace to become an object of lust—it is important to learn a painful lesson: if we continue to put ourselves at the center of our artistic judgments, we are not really free. Our own inner workings can bind us and blind us.

The book concluded with some reflections that I found cheering. Given my initial hostility towards abstract painting, it was ironic, to say the least, that my wife Ali Thistlethwaite started painting large abstracts, which were evidently Spirit-inspired. I needed to loose my hold on certain ideas, particularly the convenient notion that some styles are good and others bad. I realized that God being alive and dynamic, there is much in art that though it was formed in a crucible of bad religion and bad philosophy, has turned out well. Abstraction, for example, though formed out of the syncretist religion of Theosophy, does not have to have theosophical meanings. It can serve as an attempt to cross the threshold of that which lies beyond the visible world, which does not have to be a Platonic "real reality" but can try to express some of the invisible powers that we sense are coordinated with the reality we know. If the spirit of the artist is engaged with God, that can change the spirit of the work. Or cubism, which in my view has been sterile in terms of real perception and the capturing of the visible, has generated an extraordinary energy in, say, graphic design and released popular art from the stifling requirements of Victorian literalism.

It is also true that while artists are deliberate actors in the world, the meanings of their works are not completely under their control. Many artists have succeeded in conveying things that they did not know were true. There is a freedom in contemporary art that, bone-headedly perverse as it often seems, sometimes comes up with gems. So what we do not want from any art theory (even mine!) is something that condemns a form of work before we have even seen it. This has not been an easy lesson to learn. We live in stretching times, and we have to navigate between the desire not to be taken in and a willingness to learn. One thing we can be sure of: art is not magic—its outputs cannot exceed its inputs; if we do find good in it, that goodness must be there; and if the art causes us to look outwards, we can be assured that there is something there to be discovered.

XII

Writing the book was the most enjoyable event in my life, surpassed only by being invited to paint the book cover. For some reason, I felt indescribable joy in the handling of paint and the mystery of expressing through painting what I was given to say. If I could summarize where, I hope, all this thinking had got me to, it would be, "permission to be." There is a bad road for artists, where you are in slavery to an ideal of what has been done and to rules about what should be done. But there is also a good road, of existing not by consent of those who seem to have power in art but allowing what God has put into you to flow out, where skill becomes a means to an end. "Permission to be" means allowing yourself to be who you are, with all your limitations but entrusting yourself to this gift of art, which for all of us actually works. Originally I had believed that art was an exclusive club that few could join. Later I saw that art is a place of possibility in which all may participate. This was brought home to me when George W. Bush's efforts in his retirement suddenly found themselves online, and we saw a very engaging and humble self-portrait in the shower, not very skilled but definitely worthwhile.

I am not so liberal that I do not notice that a lot of the "art" produced by both amateurs and professionals is terrible. There is a way art works and a way it fails to work, and I have tried to explain that in this essay. But terrible is not necessarily culpable. People do what they do as part of a culture, a culture that has often let them down. Great art, and even good art, is produced in rare conditions, and the lack of great and good art is not blameworthy. But we have a resource in the enduring fabric of creation, the very matter of life that teaches us how to go.

We cannot say we aim at beauty. Beauty is a gift that comes along the way, as we engage with truth through form. Beauty as an aim can be oddly sterile, like living permanently in a hotel. Beauty in nature, in all its surprising ways, is God's signature; it is the bloom he puts upon the world. In one sense it is a necessity, because perception depends on objects being coherent and complete, the armature of beauty. But in another sense it is unnecessary.

A Question of Beauty (A Personal Story)

We, evil people that we are, can get along without beauty, can break it, bypass it, and ridicule it. Then when it comes to us, it is not by right, it is not something that we create, but it is a grace, inherent in our being and in the continual kindness of the cosmos.

Constable, *Flatford Lock from the Bridge*, 9 ½ x 7 ½ inches
ca. 1814–17, Holbourne Museum, Bath.

4

Reflections on Constable's *Flatford Mill*[1]

I

Good writers on art provide categories that enable us to see more in paintings than we would see on our own. Sometimes, however, we find our experience of a painting goes beyond the categories that any writer known to us will use, and then we are apt, perhaps, to question our own vision, as if it is suspended over a void.

I find this to be true with critics and historians who write on John Constable. His work has a profound hold on the imaginations of those who like him, but they often deploy language that does not really reach its goal. This is partly because Constable was an avowedly religious painter, and we do not have a common understanding of what that means when applied to a natural landscape. Instead we have to fall back on such categories as "objective" and "subjective," or "classical" and "romantic." These indeed will net some of the essence of Constable, but his work though natural (or, as we say, "realistic") has a shocking immediacy that seems to break through those categories; and this encourages us to seek further. Our challenge is to find terms with which to capture the vision of nature, true but unexpected, that he leads us to.

Our first handy tool from the conceptual toolbox is the common opposition between "objective" and "subjective." The author Basil Taylor calls

---

1. The original version of this essay was written in April 2019 and revised in April 2021.

Constable, in a striking paradox, "the least objective of painters."[2] He does not mean that Constable is not truthful but that his emotions were bound up with what he saw. Taylor sees Constable as having moved beyond the classical period of art, in which such painters as Claude and Ruysdael might construct a painting in a deliberate and objective way to convey a mood or moral. Such painters, though informed by a deep and instructed love of nature, did not make their own emotion their subject. But with Constable "painting is another word for feeling," and his response to nature, as an emotional person, was at one with his desire to paint nature (generally cultivated nature) as it is. Taylor beautifully narrates the temperamental change in Constable's life from the sunny period of courtship and marriage to the tragic period of loss and loneliness, expressed in the stormy weather and "tortured" handling of paint in his later years. In this sense Constable is not just subjective but a true proponent of Romanticism, to use the second of our handy tools, where personal feeling becomes the conduit of a wider expression of emotion.

To that extent, the scale marked "objective/subjective" is useful, and points us in a direction we can understand. We think of objective as controlled, scientific, and rational, giving attention to realities in a detached fashion that yields regular and repeatable results. Subjective, however, implies that neutral reality has been used to develop a personal agenda and will be adapted or even exaggerated to that end, so that the boundary between "the world" and "my world" becomes very thin.

But if we think a bit further, the subjective/objective distinction does not quite do the work we expect. It assumes that we know what we mean by the real world and that if we point the camera at it we will find it. But what is "really there" is just what we need to prove. It may be that our objectivist thinking has so contaminated our view of the world that we are unable to see it as it is, in its depth. And, at the subjective end of perception, if we find ourselves measuring what is subjective by subtracting what we think is objective, then we are always dragging a tail of objectivity behind us. The two concepts are constantly circling each other. This is not to deny that subjective and objective exist. But they are still only a lens through which we see. We still need to establish what it is we see.

It would be helpful, here, if we had taken to heart Michael Polanyi's concept of "personal knowledge."[3] Polanyi put the person in the center of knowing—surprisingly, even scientific knowing (he was a distinguished

---

2. "In spite of his determination to approach nature 'scientifically', he was one of the least objective of painters, one of those least capable of knowing objectivity or detachment as a working state." Taylor, *Constable*, 18–19.

3. See Polanyi, *Personal Knowledge*.

chemist). He knew that we see those things that are significant to us; and that opens up multidimensional reality not to a kind of "flat" objective interpretation, but to providing answers to the variety of questions we, as persons, put to it. An artist's questions will differ from a scientist's.

However, the public appreciation of how knowing works takes a while to catch up. When most of us think of the world, we probably still conceive it in classic Newtonian terms, as a series of bodies in empty space illuminated by light and of ourselves as detached observers. The task of the artist, so conceived, would not differ much from that of the camera—that is, to apply our own lenses and reproduce the objects that we see. One point perspective, as discovered by Brunelleschi, is no different from that of the camera's single lens.

But suppose that our classic Newtonian reality is not in fact "how things are," and that perception is not to be plotted on a scale of "detached" (truthful) to "attached" (biased). It might then be that Constable's emotions enabled him to actually see "what is there," because as a person, not as a camera, he was equipped to see something beyond the finite, measurable, and conventional.

A strong feature of Constable's writings (that is, his letters and lectures) is his sense that perception has a moral character. "The landscape painter must walk in the fields with a humble mind. No arrogant man was ever permitted to see nature in all her beauty."[4] A humble mind does not master what is there but is submitted to it; it sees beyond what is assumed. It sees particularities rather than generalities. Clouds in the sky are more than "background," which the apprentice painter can learn how to "do." They have their own character and natural history, a particularity that requires study and, dare we say, love. Constable's cloud studies convey the excitement of events in the heavens, happening "now." For Constable, this humble mind allowed the artist to see beyond conventions, the mannerism in which pictures always looked more like other pictures than like nature.

Constable did not object to the conventions of art as such. The landscape artists he admired most, Claude, Poussin, Ruisdael, and Gainsborough, all used conventions to record nature, some of their own devising, such as a kind of shorthand for leaves on trees. It is fascinating to observe the difference between Constable's approach and that of the critic John Ruskin. Ruskin made accuracy of representation a kind of law, and in the high-mindedness of youth (in the first volume of his *Modern Painters*) castigated Claude for the poverty of his drawing.[5] Ruskin had noticed that

---

4. Constable, *Discourses*, 71.
5. For example, he writes, "Again, take the stem of the chief tree in Claude's Narcissus.

the branches of trees do not taper but are essentially cylindrical until they divide, as anyone who has stacked logs will know. Claude was berated for neglecting this truth. But Constable loved Claude and admired him for the wholeness of his vision. "Claude is a painter whose works have given unalloyed pleasure for two centuries. In Claude's landscape all is lovely—all amiable—all amenity and repose; the calm sunshine of the heart. He carried landscape, indeed, to perfection, that is *human perfection*."[6]

What Constable did criticise, however, was "manner," as he called it, a conventional vision that was far more tied to the fashionable world than to nature and was content to produce replicas of different manners of painting because style, rather than content, was the route to commercial value. In Claude's mature painting, though conventional, everything was subsumed in a total artistic vision that did connect with nature, in the whole if not in the details; and that was something Claude had learned from close study. "It was at Rome Claude became the real student of nature. He came there a confirmed mannered painter. But he soon found it necessary to 'become as a little child', and he devoted himself to study with an ardor and patience perhaps never before equalled. He lived in the fields all day, and drew at the Academy at night, for after all art is a plant of the conservatory, not of the desert."[7] Constable was acutely aware that any artist can fall into "manner," Claude, in his later works, or indeed himself. "Manner is always seductive. It is more or less an imitation of what has been done already—therefore always plausible. It promises the short road, the near cut to present fame and emolument, by availing ourselves of the labours of others. It leads to almost immediate reputation, because it is the wonder of the ignorant world."[8] A letter to his friend Archdeacon Fisher shows how far Constable could go in self-knowledge: "My Wood [his painting *Helmingham Dell*] is liked but I suffer from want of that little completion which you always feel the regret of—and you are quite right. I have filled my head with certain notions of *freshness—sparkle*—brightness—till it has influenced my practice in no small degree, and is in fact taking the place of truth in so invidious a

---

It is a very faithful portrait of a large boa constrictor, with a handsome tail; the kind of trunk which young ladies at fashionable boarding-schools represent with nosegays at the top of them by way of forest scenery.... But the old masters are not satisfied with drawing carrots for boughs. Nature can be violated in more ways than one." Ruskin, *Modern Painters, Vol. 1*, II.VI.I.7. However, in a later section, Ruskin writes, "Nevertheless, the foliage of Claude, in his middle distances, is the finest and truest part of his pictures, and on the whole, affords the best example of good drawing to be found in ancient art. It is always false in colour [etc.]." Ruskin, *Modern Painters, Vol. 1*, II.VI.I.23.

6. Constable, *Discourses*, 52–53.
7. Constable, *Discourses*, 53.
8. Constable, *Discourses*, 58.

manner, in all things—it is a species of self-worship—which should always be combated—and we have nature (another word for moral feeling) always in our reach to do it with—if we will have the resolution to look at her."[9]

There was a difference, then, in Constable's mind, between artists who only knew how to produce pictures "in the manner of" things that were reputed and those who went to the source, nature, and had a genuine encounter. This contrast between the conventional and the personal points to a divergence in our concepts of "knowing," that we are not always aware of. Our modern view of knowing is largely conditioned by science (though not Polanyian science), and is essentially open access like code, where all observers see things in the same way. This seems to be confirmed by computers. Face-recognition technology, for example, captures the features of a face and reduces them to binary code, subsuming observation into the essentially numerical. Identifying individuals is not done by character or a sense of their presence, but purely by mathematical deductions from proportional measurements. Such a view of identity cannot be very exciting for portrait painters but might explain why there has been a resurgence of photorealism in portrait art.

But Constable's view represents a totally different stream of thinking, not optical but spiritual, exemplified by the life and teaching of Christ. In this view, people definitely do not see things the same way. This is confirmed not just by the extremes of politics but even by the different perceptions of friends side by side in an art gallery. There are reasons why seeing differs. Seeing the truth is not obvious and plain but has a moral and spiritual component. When you think you see, you may in fact be blind.

> And Jesus said, For judgment I am come into this world, that they which see might not see; and that they which see might be made blind. And some of the Pharisees which were with him heard these words, and said unto him, Are we blind also? Jesus said unto them, If ye were blind, ye should have no sin: but now ye say, We see; therefore your sin remaineth. (John 9:39–41 KJV)

The test case, of course, is whether Jesus himself is recognized—Jesus, whom the Scripture experts, who knew all the predictions, could not identify as the Christ or even as good. In such circumstances, we do not just "agree to disagree," but sides have to be taken, because what we see is an aspect of our whole being. We do have, of course, in social interaction, stratagems for dealing with differences of viewpoint, such as friendly arguments about football teams, singers, or political parties, so much so that we are almost

---

9. Constable, *Correspondence*, 258 (emphasis original). The painting referred to is *Helmingham Dell*, exhibited in the Royal Academy, 1830.

comfortable with the impossibility of objectivity in that sense. But it is also true, as Christ made clear, that we are morally implicated in how we see; it is not just an accident that some see things one way and some, another.

> In the same hour, Jesus rejoiced in the Holy Spirit and said, "I thank thee, Lord of heaven and earth, that thou hast hidden these things from the wise and understanding and revealed them to babes [i.e., to the humble], for such was thy gracious will." (Luke 10:21 KJV)

Constable is quite convinced that the mind has to be converted to see. Adam before the fall, he says, could see perfectly. In one of his lectures he contrasts the clear vision of the created Adam with the "gradual perception" that is all that we can attain to.

> We are no doubt placed in a paradise here if we choose to make it such. All of us must have felt ourselves in the same place and situation as that of our first parent, when on opening his eyes the beauty and magnificence of external nature and the material world broke on his astonished sight intensely, with this difference; he was created at once in a perfect state, in full possession of all knowledge and mental perfection, could even call things by their names, and know what it was he saw. The gradual perception of these things to us in our less perfect state, makes them have less effect upon us, but it ought not.[10]

II

But we have not yet attempted to describe what it was Constable saw. I have been looking at a little painting of *Flatford Lock from the Bridge* (9½ x 7½ inches) with the towpath and redbrick mill that make up the subject of one of Constable's best known works *Scene on a Navigable River*. One might describe the little picture as a study or sketch for the larger picture, but it seems more than that, because although it is painted in a kind of artistic shorthand (with a furious scrubbing for the fast moving clouds), it seems more than a mere note for a subject visualized as complete. It is complete in itself, carrying its own information (even though we would have to guess at many of the features, if we did not already recognize the scene). It bursts with convincing life, as if a portion of one day in one place has been distilled and captured, and we can continually enter into it.

---

10. Constable, *Discourses*, 73.

It is obviously hard to describe the sense of joy conveyed in this scene. But two features, the light and the drama, stand out, though they are not really separable. Constable "sees" light, perhaps as no artist before him (though there are great precursors). This is a paradoxical statement, because light, we are told, is invisible. We know it is there because of what it illuminates. Hence there is a reciprocity between objects and light; the light reveals the objects, and the objects the light.[11] Constable sees this, and when he paints a scene, the light, light broken by clouds, is really there; and objects are there, subject to what illuminates them. This gives his paintings extraordinary freedom; he engages with what he finds—nature not predetermined but contingent. He allows that objects do not have permanent color independent of light but have whatever color light creates, depending on the time of day, the sunshine, and shadows. Nor does he have a static system of tones or values, as would someone who does not think beyond the deliberation of the studio; he recognizes that light, as it causes different vibrations and frequencies from objects at different times of day, really is telling a different story, hour by hour, for the artist to capture. It is as if we see not one place in different lights but the light and place *together* making one scene, a moment now sealed in history.

As evidence of Constable's extraordinary preoccupation with light, we observe a variety of ways in which light in *The Lock* is conveyed to our eyes. There are sparkles and reflections on water, light diffused through clouds, direct sun on distant fields, and warm light on the sandy towpath. Each surface responds to light differently, but it is one and the same light, and the artist's skill is in unifying such a variety of instruments in his orchestra.

Light, for us of course, is a scientific fact, and to know what it is, we turn to the physicists to describe it, currently as particles or waves. But analysis does not exhaust its content, and for Constable it certainly meant a great deal more than its physical properties. A feature of his painting is a sense of wonder. Constable does not just leave us with the fact that something is there (take it or leave it), but with the wonder that something is there. It is actual reality in itself, not some second-order deduction from it, that causes in him a sense of gratitude, and it is the fact that the things he paints are as they are that moves him.

---

11. Taylor observes, "In the evolution of landscape painting a most significant stage was reached when the duality of form and light, from being an objective phenomenon and a matter of technique and style, became deeply involved in the painter's sense of reality and in the current of his feelings. The subtle and elusive union of light and form gradually gained control over Constable's work. . . . Constable's obsession drove him to methods more unconventional than any the art of landscape had yet known." Taylor, *Constable*, 27.

We were saying that the normal, Newtonian view of reality is of objects, static or moving, in a container of empty space. But Constable seems to have grasped the fact that in our world (as science since relativity has acknowledged) everything affects everything else and that the reciprocity seen between light and objects is only one such relationship in the cosmos. This little painting successfully conveys the sense of a whole world going on, in which the invisible light, the air and wind, the flow of water, and the growth of plants and trees are all one present activity of life.

It is worth noting that the wonder of sheer existence included, for Constable, the human world. His theological perspective did not exclude the beings for whom the world was made. In our picture, we can see a little boy fishing. It is his peaceful enjoyment that articulates the scene. Beauty finds its counterpart in conscious minds. If there were no humans, there would be no beauty, because beauty is an active mental response, in which we, humans, find and delight in form. Without people, form would be mute. Constable's little fisher boy no doubt reminds him of his own "careless boyhood" by the Stour.[12]

We have seen how the interactions of light, air, and objects combine to provoke a sense of wonder at existence, calling forth worship. But creation, of course, is not the only story; and as soon as we think of creation, we remember that the world is not Eden and that much is wrong. If creation and its beauties were Constable's only theme, we would call him a dreamer, a peddler of nostalgia. Sometimes his work has been criticized for telling a public, indifferent to rural poverty, a story of country life that it wanted to hear. But there is another story going on here, even in this small painting, and it is the great story that we need.

The awkward fact for those who lament Constable's lack of social realism is that beauty is there, shockingly so, even when we are angry, poor, or starving. The challenge for the artist is not to possess it, or aestheticize it, or to make it a poultice on an unhealed sore. The challenge is to find its transcendent meaning within a sinful and grieving world. Constable was acutely aware that in this life, light is not just there, but is embattled against darkness. "I live by shadows, to me shadows are realities," he wrote sorrowfully.[13] He painted what he called the "chiaroscuro" of nature, the drama of light and dark.[14] Part of the narrative of *The Hay Wain*, for example, is the sense of tension between the flood of light and the threatening storm cloud.

---

12. Constable, *Correspondence*, 78.

13. Constable, quoted in Taylor, *Constable*, 27. Taylor does not give a source for his quotation of Constable.

14. The meaning of chiaroscuro for Constable is discussed by Jonathan Clarkson (Clarkson, *Constable*, 190–91). In his 1835 prospectus to his prints, Constable writes

Constable's life, his ability to persist, year after year, in his unfashionable attempt to make a "natural" painting when the majority of professionals could not see the point, shows how deeply he had internalized the life and teaching of Christ, who "set his face" towards Jerusalem and death and called his followers to take up their cross daily and follow him.[15] But the focus of Christ's teaching is not on martyrdom but on victory and resurrection. For Constable, life very often is a storm, or storms threaten, but light breaks through. There is something about the little upright painting that, seen in a certain way, can remind us of the crucifixion. The trees blot out the sun. Light does battle with shade. The outcome is uncertain. But clouds rise up and there is a sense of hope. We cannot push this logically, as, after all, this painting is not meant as an analogy of Christ's passion; but what we cannot fail to notice in the English summer's day is a drama in which the clouds may win. We can only take Constable seriously if we allow that, for him, evil on earth is not trivial, nor does it belong. It is subject to final defeat and the vindication of truth and goodness, and we see this in many of his pictures, depicting a sea of change in which the outcome is hope.

One might ask how it comes about that nature can work as a parable of human life. Is this an accident of existence, that we can "use" nature in this way, as if we had a choice? Constable would not think so. For the fact is that most of our thought forms, the symbols through which we articulate our world, most of our metaphors and images, are drawn from nature, as if our minds are bonded to the world we know. For Constable it is no embarrassment that the world "out there" is the world "in here"; our inner world, the spiritual world, and the physical world are in a harmony of language; for him, the physical world as mere physics, has no real existence. "For man is the sole intellectual inhabitant of one vast natural landscape. His nature is congenial with the elements of the planet itself, and he cannot but sympathise with its features, its various aspects, and its phenomena in all situations."[16]

So what might these things tell us for those who are painting today? It tells us that there is far more to reality than the photographic, and that to really see, we need to cultivate a sense of wonder. Naturally we are creatures of habit and see what we see. But God has created a world infinite in interest,

---

"The Landscape Painter shall be aware that the CHIAROSCURO really does exist in NATURE (as well as tone)—and that is the medium by which the grand and varied aspects of Landscape are displayed, both in the fields and on canvass [sic]" (Clarkson, *Constable*, 190). Constable makes clear that chiaroscuro is not merely part of the science of picture making but a quality of the landscape itself.

15. See Luke 9:23.
16. Constable, *Discourses*, 72–73.

character, and meaning, and we need never be ashamed of the personal, because each of us is called to see aspects of the truth that none but us have the gift to receive.

5

Rothko, Some Questions[1]

The aesthetic sense does not lie, or so one hopes. Like falling in love, or falling off a cliff, it happens. One moment you are looking at paint and canvas, and the next you have tipped over into a "somewhere," where emotions are excited, your body quivers, and you feel a sense of recognition. From that point you witness to what you have seen, and like someone in love, you will hold your "truth" against all comers—until something happens, and you wonder if the "truth" you perceived was all the truth.

    It seems churlish, anti-aesthetic in fact, to question the experience we have of a great painter like Mark Rothko; but in viewing art we are not playing games. We are not on a roller coaster, experiencing fear and dread in a "safe" environment and returning, thus stimulated, to normality. We are open to real transactions in how we view the world, offering real changes in our commitments. Therefore it is not surprising that we view art not just once, for a thrill, but often, testing our experiences and turning them this way and that to see if they provide a sure footing, a view of the world of which we must take notice. With some art we are barely conscious of this, and a pretty picture with delicious color will be no more questioned than some sorbet on a spoon. But with Rothko, we are in the realm of what we call "the meaning of life," the big picture, "the transcendent," and on that subject there are not just the painter's views; we must all make a judgment. We have, in Rothko, the apprehension of a transcendent, an overview of "how things are." But if, and this is the question, that apprehension seems convincing and genuine to people of all faiths and none, are we permitted to

---

1. The original version of this essay was written in January 2017 and revised in 2023.

ask also whether it is actually a false transcendent? To put it another way, if there is "something there," are we not entitled to ask, What is there?

First of all, we need to be clearer about what we mean by "Rothko" or "a Rothko." Over a period of twenty years, in his arrived or developed period, Mark Rothko developed a pictorial language of great refinement and artistic rigor, seeking to control not just the output of his studio but also the gallery space and the lighting in which his pictures were hung.[2] Although some of his large later works were painted with the help of assistants, his personal touch in the way that one color overlaps another is critical to the feel and meaning of the painting. He devised a method of layering of color, using various media, such as egg, that have not fared well over the years; which shows that the absolute matter and appearance of his fields of color were integral to the meaning. What we have in our color reproductions are not fair representations of the paintings, which depend on the scintillating appearance of pigment suspended in dilute media.

Despite all this aesthetic refinement, however, Rothko insisted that his paintings were not about art, not merely aesthetic or abstract, but were meanings-paintings—that is to say, they were about something, designed to take you from somewhere to somewhere. The refinement of means is because something has to be articulately said.

It would be easy at this point to jump straight from what we know of his personal philosophy and attempt to find it in his paintings. But that would be destructive of art. If we know what the witness is expected to say, we will not bother to hear their testimony. The meaning has to be "in" the paintings and not merely used as a filter through which to view them. There is another reason for this. If an artist develops a language, it can express many things. The musician can write a dirge but also a love song. Rothko may have been himself surprised by some of the meanings his paintings disclosed. Certainly it is probably a surprise to many to learn that in the same season of life (depression leading to suicide) in which he painted his "Gray" paintings, which look like moonscapes of lifeless ground leading to a horizon of void, he was also painting a "red" series that is vastly more cheerful. The meaning "in" the paintings can be different from the meaning "in"

---

2. "My reluctance to participate [in the Whitney Museum collection], then, was based in the conviction that the real and specific meaning of the pictures was lost and distorted in these exhibitions." Tate Gallery, *Rothko*, 85–86. "A picture lives by companionship, expanding and quickening in the eyes of the sensitive observer. It dies by the same token. It is therefore a risky and unfeeling act to send it out into the world. How often it must be permanently impaired by the eyes of the vulgar and the cruelty of the impotent who would extend their affliction universally!" Tate Gallery, *Rothko*, 83.

the person.³ Presumably the artist can paint a happy picture he disagrees with.⁴ Our philosophies can be out of touch with reality, and art can reveal this to us.

So what we have to do, rather than read Rothko's beliefs straight into his work, is the rather more difficult job of asking, What do his paintings discover? And, Is it real? Here we can only go, of course, on what we think we see, correlated with the impressions of responsible critics, but that kind of subjective encounter is not out of the way; it is the whole purpose of the painting. Unless we take time with the paintings, we are merely being theorists.

What I think I see is this. In Rothko's mature work, that is, from approximately 1950–70, he developed a language in which, broadly speaking, colored oblongs of paint are placed against other colors. Artists have always known that some colors "advance" and others "recede" so that, other things being equal, red will seem nearer than blue. But what was not known until Rothko experimented with it was the enormous subtlety that could be found in these "spatial" relationships as one color appears to be "in front of" or "behind" another color. Color is not the only means by which this is achieved: the edges of the shapes also give clues as to which color was painted "on top," and these edges are touched with a uniquely sensitive handwriting of paint, which suggests that these precise relationships matter intensely. So strongly is Rothko's color vision conveyed by these softened edges of color that it becomes memorable, interpreting nature itself, as when on a misty morning sun breaks through and groups of trees, their edges softened, become visible in effulgent light.

---

3. That said, Rothko stated in 1958 that one of his work's main "ingredients" was "a clear preoccupation with death. All art deals with intimations of mortality." Tate Gallery, *Rothko*, 15. As Irving Sadler writes, "He also implied that Modern Man's tragic awareness of death freed him to *live*. This is an existentialist conception: as William Barrett, a philosopher friendly with the Abstract Expressionists wrote: 'In the face of death, life has an absolute value. The meaning of death is precisely the revelation of this value.'" Tate Gallery, *Mark Rothko*, 16. Mortality, as life affirming and as tragic, are of course two different emphases, and Rothko moved far towards the tragic view. For all the aim to make out of the condition of death something joyful, such a belief cannot be stable, because life is thought to be defined by something that is not life but is its opposite. "Tragedy" allows at least that death is an offence to hope, as something that ought not to be, but it still gives in to death as having the final word. If death has authority, existence is bleak.

4. "Rothko, despite his craft, did not know how exactly a picture would turn out when he began it. In this sense also, his pictures did not represent existent ideas or feelings but, when successful, embodied, or were themselves ideas." Tate Gallery, *Rothko*, 53.

Rothko was known in his lifetime as "obsessive." He experimented unceasingly, and not just with the materials of his art, using diluents such as raw whole egg mixed with turpentine to thin his paint and reduce its binding, so as to achieve as near pure pigment as possible. He also attempted to control the appearance of his paintings once they left the studio, prescribing precise natural lighting, so as to maintain the mysterious depth and presence of his surfaces, and also what other paintings were displayed alongside his own. The perfect context to him had the solemnity of church rather than the buzz of a fairground, and he was anxious about what dealers and museums might do to his work.

But what did all this mean? Artists before and since have been obsessed with relationships of color. That is of the essence of "abstraction." Interior designers also care very much about the effect of one color against another. But they are designers. There is a purpose in view. What was Rothko's purpose, if more than abstraction? And he insisted he was not an "abstract" artist.

The distinctive feature of Rothko's paintings is their shallow space. By this we mean that while your eye can stay on the surface and enjoy the balance of one color with another, once you start dwelling on the colored shapes and their edges, you very soon find yourself "in" the painting, seeing the blocks of colors as hovering in space. The space given by advancing and receding color is not as deep as classical art's perspectival space, which extends to infinity. If there is a "beyond" metaphorically depicted, a space beyond the picture plane, it is misty, obscure. But it is sufficiently a "place" to be a place of happenings, where the areas of color take on the presence of "things" that might be hovering or even coming towards us. The scale of the paintings, large enough for one to mentally immerse oneself in, also contributes to creating a sense of real space, which the imagination is happy to occupy.

For some reason, all this spatial activity by means of color, surface, and edge is enjoyable. But it also seems recognizable, as if we "know" these places. This "other" world seen through the canvas is at once alien and disturbingly familiar. It is probably not heaven, it is not precise enough for any nightmares we know, but if feels as though we have been there. There are stories of people seeing Rothko's pictures and bursting into tears. Others report a "religious" experience. Rothko himself thought both these reactions appropriate.[5] But would it be impertinent to ask "of which religion" are these the images?

---

5. Rothko spoke frequently of "transcendent experience" and of the challenge of evoking it in an age without "monsters or gods." Tate Gallery, *Rothko*, 84.

Or perhaps that question is premature, despite all our knowledge, gained over millennia, that religion and symbols are tied closely together. We need to work with what we know and accept what we do not know. What we know is that "religious" experiences (from Rothko's paintings) arise unbidden; people find themselves tipped into them, having left behind the surface of the works and "entering" the fictive space of emergent and receding color. People are touched deeply and sometimes tears come. They are not in control; if anything, they are taken over. All sorts of words have been given to this phenomenon, "sublime" (from eighteenth-century aesthetics)[6] being the favorite, but at its heart is a sense of awed encounter, as of a greater "other." What of course we do not know is how this "works."

But perhaps we can speculate, based on some things we do know. It seems to me that Rothko's shallow space has tapped into the sense of that horizon of eternity from which all life is lived. Lest that sound preposterous, let me explain. Death is our end in this life but not necessarily our destiny. For most of our forefathers, there was something beyond—Sheol, Hades, the Egyptian afterlife, Valhalla, and so on. The wisdom of today is that there is "nothing." Rothko's late gray paintings seem to express this horizon of "nothing" forcefully, where the darkness is such a void that it has eaten up all life preceding it as well. Perhaps I am reading something into these images that only deep pessimism can see! But, even those who believe in extinction, obliteration, nihil, the void, and so on, as their prospect after death cannot avoid living their lives from the perspective of their decease. What is life all about? What is significance? There are few people who would wish their *Times* obituary to show that they had lived as nihilists, believing nothing, serving no one, living without purpose and direction. Very many convinced atheists live cheerful lives of constant service, because that is what they find life to be about. It works that way. So that horizon of eternity may, for some people, be an actual space and destination; but for others it will be certain "eternal" principles that call forth the best in them, and by which they try to live. These are, in a sense, their "gods."

What all this signifies is that most of us live under a "big picture" scheme of what we think life is about; but we do not necessarily depict it or even attempt to enter into the space where the levers are pulled, where the code is written, where our drivers are to be found. Why would we think that Rothko's solitary musings in his studio gave him the privilege of finding this door? Or, perhaps we should say at this stage, of finding what seemed to be a door?

---

6. Rothko read Edmund Burke's 1757 work *Philosophical Enquiry into the Origin of Our Ideas of the Sublime and Beautiful* before 1948.

The desire to do "big picture" paintings seems to have been with Rothko from the first, and he learned to explain that his paintings were not abstract—that is, merely formal relationships of shape and color—he wanted them to be seen as "about" something.[7] This is easier to understand when we remember that before he was American he was a European, and Europe is not short of religious art. His native Russia had an almost unbroken icon tradition, which with its gold backgrounds attempted to signify "the heavenly space" behind earthly space—in other words, to depict life as a whole but from eternity towards life on earth. Looking at an icon it is absolutely normal to be seeing "through" a painting, hanging in our earthly space, into the beyond of eternity. That double level of thought is simply how such paintings work, and if you refuse the notion of heaven, you miss the painting. But even the Catholic tradition (particularly of baroque religious art) seems confident that three-dimensional earthly space can have a heavenly dimension and is happy to show clouds of glory and angelic presences breaking through, as if heaven is just a veil away. In such paintings, the martyrs who look up to receive heavenly crowns and palms are simply seeing reality ahead of the rest of us.

It could, and probably should, be argued that all art is big picture art, in that the slightest mark may give a hint as to what we find life to be "about." But not all art has the ability to tip us into tears. Many people assume that all eternities are the same, that every door opens into the same space. But is it possible that Rothko's particular vision can be both recognizable and wrong? I am trying to give due weight to a duality in his work. Taken seriously, it is very serious indeed but, as we come away from it, it can seem oddly irrelevant to the life that we know. It is as if you need to be under its spell to be really convinced, a bit like listening to a lonely man in a bar, whose story holds you, until you get away. So what is it that Rothko finds and shows us, and is it true or false?

At this point we need to remind ourselves that Rothko's pictures are not one thing, or even variations on one thing. The language is unitary, but the things spoken in it are not. Pictures have different timbres, some somber, some elegiac, some more apparently life-affirming; and one might compare this variety with a painter such as Poussin, who deliberately

---

7. "Rothko considered his rectangular forms to be actual objects that he positioned on a stained field. His paintings are not arrangements of flat geometric forms that divide the picture plane, nor are they vast atmospheric backdrops. On the contrary, as he explained to Seitz, 'My new areas of color are things. I put them on the surface. They do not run to the edge.... These new shapes say ... what the symbols said.' He further commented 'I never was interested in cubism.... Abstract art never interested me; I have always painted realistically. My present paintings [his color-field paintings] are realistic.'" Tate Gallery, *Rothko*, 73.

mastered different poetic moods. But this variety also corresponds to what we know of the abstract expressionists' "religious" views. There is no creed or dogma to give coherence to their life view. At most, they were fascinated by the primal forces expressed by Native American art (e.g., Pollock)[8] or by the "tragic" view of life of the Greeks (e.g., Rothko). They did not see any definite form or reason beyond the boundary of sense, but they believed that art, if reduced to its primitive power, might help access a "something there."[9] In other words, they were not just moderns, in that they could not have been pinned down to any definite belief that there is a beyond or a hereafter, but they were also romantics, who in their freedom from belief found latitude to dream and ponder that there might be "something there." Rothko himself guarded this priestcraft with solemn reverence, creating a "chapel" in which no doctrine is celebrated except the value of his art[10] and the possibility that it gives, to open-minded believers, of access to a deeper knowledge of the world.

I have not seen the Rothko Chapel, Houston, and I fear that if I did I might miss the measure and weight of a tragic interpretation of the world

---

8. Rothko, in 1943 (i.e., in the period of his surrealist mythological painting), speaking in an interview, said, "If our titles recall the known myths of antiquity, we have used them again because they are the eternal symbols upon which we must fall back to express basic psychological ideas. They are the symbols of man's primitive fears and motivations, no matter in which land or what time, changing only in detail but never in substance, be they Greek, Aztec, Icelandic, or Egyptian. And modern psychology finds them persisting still in our dreams, our vernacular, and our art, for all the changes in the outward conditions of life.... The myth holds us ... because it expresses to us something real and existing in ourselves." His friend Gottlieb added, in the same interview, "All primitive expression reveals the constant awareness of powerful forces, the immediate presence of terror and fear ... that these feelings are being experienced by many people throughout the world today is an unfortunate fact, and to us an art that glosses over or evades these feelings, is superficial or meaningless." Tate Gallery, *Rothko*, 80–81. The interview was given during the war, when artists were trying to make some sense of the terrifying rupture of Hitlerism, and, it seems, they found intellectual refuge in Jung's theory of archetypes. "Humanity was primitive and is still primitive" seemed a good answer. However, a moment's reflection will show that the label "primitive" functions as a kind of excuse, because what is primal is certainly not culpable. It is notable that in this language about "primeval and predatory passions" (Rothko), nothing is said about good and evil.

9. Gottlieb (in the same interview) said, "All primitive expression reveals the constant awareness of powerful forces." Tate Gallery, *Rothko*, 80–81. This statement hardly seems to amount to "something there," until we consider what a "force" might mean. A wind or a storm are powerful forces, but they do not lead to murder. What sort of "force" leads to tribal butchery or genocide? The phrase "forces" cannot in fact mean something other than some sort of personal agency.

10. The Rothko Chapel, Houston, originally Catholic, is interdenominational but appears not to display Christian symbols.

transmitted by those admittedly beautiful veils of deep-toned color; just as I have failed to be moved by Michelangelo's Medici Chapel and Laurentian Library, which are said to have something of the same mood. But even from photographs, we can be definite about one thing. If Rothko's paintings take us behind the scenes to the gathering place of the rulership of this world, whatever "it" is, it is not personal. It is not the Jewish God of Rothko's forefathers, who rules by mercy and justice and who knows each one of us. It is more the hand of fate, and not a hand either, but the ceaseless mechanics of impersonal forces. A "tragic" view of life, of which term Rothko was fond,[11] says that life goes downhill, things do not work out, virtue is not rewarded, and chaos has as much right to exist as justice. It is, to a large extent, an accurate view of life—when we do not know the end of the story and when we fail to pick out "the scarlet thread" of redemption that has come down to us.

We asked ourselves, somewhat impertinently, what religion Rothko's images might represent, and here I think we have the answer. It is the religion of agnosticism. It does not have the grand reach, the reach too far, of atheism, which tries to assert as truth something that no one can be sure of, at least not until it is probably too late to backtrack. It is a more comforting religion than the Great Nothing, because it credits life as having some meaning, just not a meaning we can know. There is a Presence, there is a metaphysical space over and against us, in which the truth of existence is logged; but it is not personal enough to make demands. It does not know what I had for breakfast, lunch, and tea, call me by my name, or wake me with a word. It is part of the furniture of life, like a distant parent, looming but removed. It gives freedom without regret, because a "force" cannot attack my conscience. And yet, for those who thought there was Nothing, it is at least a Something.

I mentioned before there is a duality in Rothko, that these are paintings you can dip in and out of. Their sincerity and rigor of execution command attention. It does not take much effort to see that Rothko is a master, who has taken the path of solitude and immersed himself in the truth of color, finding things never before seen. There is a world to be explored in Rothko's work. But there is also a world outside Rothko, and, apart from that evocation of misty dawns, Rothko has little part in it. There are those who report a cleansing catharsis from his work, from which one can reenter daily life, re-centered and reassured. I can understand how, in a world that is so tawdry, where images are so cheap, so contaminated by lust and pride, it does us good to climb the Rothko mountain and receive as "tablets of the

---

11. "Only that subject matter is valid which is tragic and timeless." Tate Gallery, *Rothko*, 15.

law" his deep seriousness and rigorous artistic conscience.[12] There is such a thing as a right way of doing things, and Rothko participates in that, when so many around him fail. Also, we have to say (lest we sound critical), we would not wish his pictures other than they are. Yet the treasures within Rothko do not spread far. Though his work has authority, it is oddly ignorable when we leave it behind. When we are "in" Rothko, all is well, but when we look back at his work from being around classical art, his rule seems much more limited.

Perhaps what we are aware of is a modern gnosticism.[13] The actual law, the "ten words" that Moses went up the mountain to receive (and that we

---

12. A letter of 1954 reveals some of Rothko's inner self before a canvas: "I think I can say with some degree of truth that in the presence of the pictures my preoccupations are primarily moral and there is nothing in which they seem involved less than aesthetics, history or technology. . . . If I must place my trust somewhere, I would invest it in the psyche of sensitive observers who are free of the conventions of understanding. I would have no apprehensions about the use they would make of the pictures for the needs of their own spirit. For if there is both need and spirit, there is bound to be a real transaction." Tate Gallery, *Rothko*, 58. This author is not sure whether he is free of "the conventions of understanding"—probably not—but the idea that picture viewing involves real transactions does take seriously art's power as a catalyst. However Rothko's beautiful statement comes to the heart of my question: If you are a priest of the spirit (as Rothko seems to have believed himself to be), you either believe that all true art is authentic to transcendent truth, or you ask yourself, What experience am I priesting people into?

13. Rothko actually resisted gnosticism, as far as his statements are concerned. This, from 1945: "I adhere to the material reality of the world and the substance of things. I merely enlarge the extent of this reality, extending to it coequal attributes with experiences in our more familiar environment. I insist upon the equal existence of the world engendered in the mind and the world engendered by God outside of it. If I have faltered in the use of familiar objects, it is because I refuse to mutilate their appearance for the sake of an action which they are too old to serve; or for which, perhaps, they had never been intended." Tate Gallery, *Rothko*, 82. Here Rothko seems to be replying to an accusation (either in print or in his own head) that his paintings dematerialize reality or deny its existence, but he realizes, on the contrary, that the reality of his ideas is tied to a referent in the real world. He has simply come to the conclusion that the visible world can no longer function in a general and symbolic sense and that he has to develop a thought language in paint by which to refer to the real world. One could liken this effort to that of the pure mathematician, dealing with abstractions that nonetheless have real-world repercussions (as a student, Rothko had excelled in mathematics). However the fact that Rothko needed to defend himself from at least a misunderstanding of his work shows that it could be seen that way. He wanted it to be known that his paintings were not abstract in the sense of being insubstantial, but that they were ideas with real-world weight. However there was no getting away from the fact that he was working in a world that had been dematerialized, so to speak; where the familiar world had come to seem merely technical and practical, without ontological depth, so that objects had to be "mutilated," in his words, to convey anything. "In the 1930s," writes Michael Compton, "Rothko was already speaking about the problem presented by the modern world of objects and symbols stripped of transcendence to the degree that they could no longer

find reflected in Rothko's moral rigor), does not stand apart from daily life, as if the mountain offered authentic existence away from it all. On the contrary, the law is a pattern for practical living in a fallen world. But Rothko, in common with other moderns such as Mondrian, is looking for the drivers behind life, for the essence of existence, for a big picture that will explain everything, as if we can get behind the scenes—and the difficulty of this view is not that there is no access to heaven but that this "beyond" is seen in such a way that it diminishes the weight of the world we have. I do not see that Rothko intended to do this, but his particular prophetic, tragic message about the world could not but leave ordinary vision behind. Gnosticism, in all its varieties, creates a false hierarchy, in which a superior knowledge beyond appearances can be accessed but only at the expense of discarding space and time. But of course we are, of necessity, attached to this world, and we can in fact only play at leaving it behind. Therefore we need an art that acknowledges the reality we have. This is why, though we can drop into Rothko, we also find ourselves dropping out again.

But what of "big picture" art, the need to create an integral view of the world, not just "earth," but "heaven and earth"? Do we have to oscillate between an earthly style or a heavenly? Because surely if there is no heaven, earth is, if not "without form and void," at least void of significance, as cheap as its images in a digital age. And surely if there is no reality in earth, then heaven itself is formless, insubstantial, and without consequence. But the artists of the premodern, pre-gnostic era saw things differently. The key thought, unspoken but certainly embedded in Western art, is the reciprocity of earth and heaven. When God spoke, worlds existed. The world is a reflection of the Word. The world exists because God is good. He patterns his mind in earth. Things are his idea. We do not see him, but we see his works, works that are not empty but purposed. The invisibility of God is the counterpart to the visibility of creation. So to "find God" we do not need to leave creation behind, because God and creation are not far apart. One is the product of the other. Sheer existence has a glory.

---

be used in paintings that aimed at universality. . . . He had aimed, accordingly, at a generalised sense of myth and eventually saw that references to actual phenomena had to be 'pulverised' (i.e. abstracted)." Compton, "The Subjects of the Artist," Tate Gallery, *Rothko*, 52. De-mythology is the air Rothko breathed, and abstracted "things" was his response. However, surely there is a gap, greater than Rothko realized, between believing in the "material reality of the world and the substance of things" (a reality he is still willing to "pulverize") and believing that the actual value of particular things is inherent in them, that trees, rocks, people, and so on carry their own theological weight and do not have to be spoken for. Contrary to what we often think in an art gallery, it is not the label that makes the picture. It is the picture that controls the label. Depth is inherent in reality, not ascribed by the artist's language.

It is true that besides God, there is an "active invisible world," of angels and demons, of which most of us know nothing. But it would be wrong to think that this invisible realm (which is occasionally glimpsed at certain points) corresponds to the fates, to the drivers, to the puppeteer pulling the strings. No, life is given, it is in our hands. That is what makes us dangerous! The created world is a completely given world, and the angels do not rule—they "serve." The theatre of life is here. There is a Ruler, but he rules by rules. The cards are on the table.

The reciprocity between visible and invisible,[14] the frame of meaning that gives rise to what we see, is what makes art interesting, but you cannot have one without the other. There is no such thing as pure "word," without what that word creates. There is no word "apple" without actual apples—otherwise "apple" would be an empty sound—and when God said, "Let there be light," actual light gave meaning to the word. We do not have to look beyond creation for meaning, as if it were something "other." The secret of the world is here.

Where does this leave "religious art"? Can we access the divine through what is wholly secular? In a sense this has to be so. What is more secular than a baby's flesh, laid in straw? Can we get more secular than the crosses of Rome for the refuse of Israel? And yet, we are tempted to say, Is there no specialist knowledge, nothing the religious person can contribute by way of insight in art? Seek and you shall find, says Jesus. There must be something to be said for a spiritually focused art. Surely there are pictures that "find," that find more meaning in the world than others, because they are "religiously focused." And yet, the world we have is divinely open. It is not a specialist field. Anyone can find sense in it, because the sense is there. That is the fascination of art, that the most surprising people, from all eras and nations, have found what they were looking for, a sense at the heart of things. It is not for nothing that, as Rothko found, there is a language of color, to be discovered, not made. But what we cannot do is compress it into a particular philosophy or try to control too far what we think it says. Its givenness, the fact that it "works," is bigger than the painter, an unexpected rapture of the senses; and the fact that it is found, not controlled, is a large part of its meaning.

---

14. "Through faith we understand that the worlds were framed by the word of God, so that things which are seen were not made of things which do appear" (Heb 11:3 KJV). What is seen is intimately connected with what is not seen; it has invisible coordinates, so to speak, a call, a voice, a language behind it that is integral to it. That is why the artistic language of "things" is so powerful; they speak to us not just as inert matter but with the integrating Voice behind them.

So, to conclude, have we explained the tears? Have we found out what it is we encounter when we allow a Rothko to become "our space"?

On the one hand, we have found in Rothko a sense of access to the life that is behind life, to the place of meanings, to the world that holds the direction of our world, and all this through his discovery of that mysterious indefinite space created by color. We have seen that these mysterious spaces are abstract but also concrete, misty but not formless, suggestive but also substantial; they are spiritual spaces in which we can have the run around, with no ethical demands. Who would not want a god like that? Well, people who long to be loved and known, for a start.

Hence the duality in Rothko's art. His paintings give us a strong sense of recognition, that they know what we believe. This is none other, I suggested, than the universal religion of agnosticism ("meaning but no meaning"), the pervasive conviction that something indefinable might be there, something dignified and commanding, which never has to come into focus. In modern terms we could describe this religion as "pro-choice," since it genuinely believes that there is no such thing as ultimate reality, there to be discovered like Mars—only an infinite number of choices that we personally can make, according to how we want reality to be. Do you want to make up your own ethics? Be our guest. The fact that this is patently absurd, that there is in fact one earth, one sky, one reality, and therefore not hundreds of gods according to our own choices, does not in any way diminish its appeal. Rothko can brilliantly echo "our truth," but it can still fail the test of reality. Hence a strange irrelevance when we withdraw from the experience.

But, on the other hand, we have also found Rothko to be right. The man who studied color, who found a language that works, who laboured with unsurpassed sensitivity to find exact relationships, was at his workbench discovering something holy, just like the physicist or chemist who penetrates to the heart of things. There is a glory in how things are. There seems little doubt that our spiritual experts of today are offended by reality, embarrassed that God should turn his hand to making snails and puddles and storms; and Rothko was to some extent of that number. But what he found, and what we find as we immerse ourselves in his fields of color, is a rigorous truth, a kind of justice, that echoes within and attunes us to the whole righteously made scope of reality.

6

Seeing the Invisible in the Visible
Towards a Theological Account of Art[1]

I

Introduction

It is not at all obvious how theology touches art. I am guessing that, in practical terms, when theologians look at art, they enjoy it and look at what they like but essentially take a break from theology. When called upon to link the two, the safe strategy is to offer a theological blessing to something they already approve of, rather as they might bless mountain climbing or bird watching. Theology, in such circumstances, is not given any real work.

There is a reason for this that is not blameworthy. It is next to impossible to get inside the art experience. When you are in a moment of attachment to a work of art, you cannot simultaneously be outside yourself observing the process. It is quite speculative to decide what is going on. So theologians go off and enjoy their art, without knowing precisely why. However we cannot abandon the field to the hopeless cry, "It's all so subjective," as many do; because there is real work to be done. The question is, Can theology do that work?

I am going to speak autobiographically, for a moment, to explain what needs doing in art, which art cannot do for itself. Picture, if you can, two contrasting worlds that I was engaged with, that of university art history and

1. An earlier version of this paper was given to Worcester Theological Society, Sept. 2016.

London art dealing. In the world of art history where I studied, you have a body of people who are drawn to art, presumably because of its beauty, and the restorative satisfaction that it gives. But beauty is something they cannot talk about, because it is "subjective" and therefore unworthy of an academic subject, which has to be built around areas of uniform observation. So effectively, discussion is confined to all the things a painting is "about," except for the life in it that makes it interesting. Catalogue entries will tell you all about context and subject—which I admit I like to know—but will not discuss what makes art more than archaeology. This is the discipline I left behind to work as a salesman in Bond Street. What a contrast! In Mayfair, the word "beautiful" was frequently used. The language of art sometimes had an academic tinge but was closer to that of gourmets at a meal. There was no fear of the subjective. Subjectivity was the tool by which paintings were assessed and, more importantly, priced. There was a mutuality of understanding in the trade about what was good and what was bad (with inevitable differences, as fashions changed), and no one was embarrassed by the practice of evaluation. Instead, it was understood that the eye can be trained and subjectivity improved.

In the art trade I came to the conclusion that there was something we knew about art ("we" being the art buying and selling community) that could not be expressed within academia's language. Armed with little more than a sense of frustration and indignation, I returned to Cambridge to try to tease this out. As you will see, I am still thinking about it. Why was there such a gap between the commerce of art and theory? What was the grip of philosophy and academic tradition on art that made it so difficult to speak of real things?

In case it is not immediately obvious why the gap between London and Cambridge matters—and should matter in Buenos Aires or Beijing—perhaps we could try to spell it out. Suppose we take a statement like "Michelangelo began the Sistine Ceiling in 1508." We would find ourselves in safe territory. Suppose we then went on to discuss his "God" and his "Adam," not just in relation to prior examples, but in relation to God and Adam themselves (Is Michelangelo's "God" like *God*?), this would be much less safe ground, as it would also expose us in a relation of faith, or the lack of it, towards those beings. But the latter engagement has much more to do with Michelangelo's aims than the mere fact that he painted it. If we are going to speak of art as it is, we will have to speak also of things outside art and expose our own commitments in the process. Why does this matter? Because whatever we believe about art will give birth to more art.

If I believe that whatever the artist signs off as art is art, then whatever is signed off *is* art. The artist authenticates the work. But if I believe that art has a power of connection with external, and possibly metaphysical realities, then truth to those things authenticates the work. Art has a boundary between itself and not-art, which each generation redraws; but if certain parts of art cannot be discussed, will we not have a deceptive boundary? And if we are not clear what art is, how shall we evaluate it? This matters not just for the small community of people who discuss art but for the wider community of people who have beliefs about art imposed on them and who need to have an art language they can trust. For example, today we have to deal with the spread of urban graffiti, and decide whether it is a nuisance or an art form. If a nuisance, it has to be removed; if it is art, it is considered sacred; can it be both? We need to know what makes public space good. Or consider a topical example, which some might think of as vandalism officially sanctioned: a new apartment building in Docklands, in being awarded *Building Design's* "Carbuncle Cup," was described as a "brain-numbing jumble of discordant shapes, materials and colours."[2] Presumably, the planners were persuaded otherwise. And cleverly, the developers responded, "Architectural design is art, and like all art, a matter of personal tastes."[3] In other words, there are no objective standards, and we can build what we like. There is no "truth" about art, so no one has the right to complain.

The problem, then, is clear: if we do not know what art is, we have no way of closing the door to anything that might be not-art. In public space this matters; but even in private spaces, the doors we open, and things we admit, have surprisingly long-term consequences downstream. The habit of saying yes to things which, if we were honest with ourselves would evoke a strong "no" begins to create in us a habit of compromise and, indeed, hypocrisy. One would think this was a problem of some urgency. But if you go to a good art bookshop, you will see that there are hundreds of intelligent books on art that ignore the fundamental issue. Perhaps there are one or two little-known books out there that have the answers. But what is the difficulty? To put it simply, we are expecting a sacred output with no sacred input; we are asking for the strength of meaning in art to be accounted for, somehow, in naturalistic and materialistic terms. The result is a gap between a severely factual approach to art's content, in as far as we can tie it down, and a foggy mysticism about questions of meaning.

If we look briefly at the self-imposed boundaries of aesthetics, we will understand the problem. For normal purposes of thought, most of us think in Newtonian terms, of the world as composed of various objects connected by forces such as gravity but essentially separate. To understand an object,

---

2. *Building Design* quoted in "Carbuncle Cup," para. 3.
3. Galliard Homes quoted in "Carbuncle Cup," para. 12.

we disconnect it from its surroundings and study it—it might be a butterfly, a tree, or a "work of art." The closer we get, the stronger our microscopes, the more we know what the thing is. The modern obsession asserting that DNA somehow "is" the person is a case in point. When we study a work of art, we shall then look for the "artness" of art "in" the work; and the more we study it, the more we shall expect to find it. But the terms in which we find, and describe it, must of course be material, because that is the boundary we have.

But how do we know which objects are works of art in the first place? Is our study not already assuming what we wish to find? Here we find the great paradox of the public art gallery. The gallery is there to display art. But what is art? That which is in the gallery. The "art gallery" is a product of eighteenth-century aesthetics. Before that time there were galleries that were chiefly princely collections. For example, Charles I distracted himself, in his otherwise troubled reign, by purchasing the collection of the bankrupt dukes of Mantua. The Mantegna cycle, which effectively bankrupted him also, is still to be found at Hampton Court. From a modern perspective, we would think Charles was collecting "art." But the focus of the royal collection was not on such an abstract notion. It was on Charles's ownership of any work of quality, such as masterpieces by Titian and Caravaggio, that would add glory to the king. Today, however, we have the concept "art," and when we leave, say, the National Portrait Gallery in London, and walk a few paces down to the National Gallery, we switch our concept of viewing from the practical one of portraiture, that is, pictures of people, to the more abstract designation "art." That is how eighteenth-century aesthetics works. We arrive with a predetermined attitude of art contemplation, in which selected objects are abstracted from the circumstances that brought them into being and treated as one thing, "art." Where you have much to contemplate, as in eighteenth-century painting, with its works of fine observation, thought, and craftsmanship, the problem inherent in this approach is suppressed; but come to our own day, where anything laid on the floor of a gallery, such as rows of bricks, is subjected to the same contemplation, the fact that our concept of art has wandered from reality becomes obvious.

It may be asked how we have passed so quickly from a strictly Newtonian sense of the work of art as discrete material object to the use of such an object for semimystical contemplation. But this also is a legacy of eighteenth-century aesthetics, where, following Kant, we make a radical distinction between the phenomenal world, of which we can have knowledge (in the case of art, a picture as, say, an image made of oil paint on poplar wood), and the less-accessible noumenal world into which we put everything else, such as beliefs and values, those things with which art is usually concerned.

Of these, it is thought, we can have no real knowledge, but we can have substantial commerce in them, so to speak, for our enjoyment. All this goes back to a mind-matter dualism, which is familiar in our culture, but very unhelpful in art, because it divides the unity of the art object.

Today mind-matter dualism takes a slightly different form, due to the dominance of psychology. The boundary of the work of art is extended to include the psyche of the author and that of the viewer, as if art was circulating "stuff" between one and the other. In a sense, both psyches are considered material objects, so it is as if the same washing was moving from washer to dryer and back, with no real exit. Even if a work of art appears to touch reality, that also is a material event, for perception bounces back, from world to artist to viewer, with no real knowing.

A slightly more elegant image than the washer-dryer image was developed by my Cambridge supervisor, the late Dr. Michael Tanner, which he termed "The Tanner Triangle" (still memorable after forty-six years). Dr. Tanner's diagram was designed to include all aspects of aesthetic theory; in fact, it was designed to show that there is nowhere else to go. This inclusive triangle had three points, which he labeled "expressive" (artist related), "affective" (audience related), and "mimetic" (world related). There was one more in the middle, "autotelic." These points describe where each theory believes the real "art action" takes place, though in tension with the other points. It will be found that the different theories each suit different kinds of art. For example, Van Gogh is perfect for the "expressive" theory. In his art, Van Gogh expresses his feelings, and we read them through the work. Constable would suit the "mimetic" theory. The action of the painting is in what it describes—*The Hay Wain's* focus is on a Suffolk summer's day, Constable's "careless boyhood scenes." The third theory, the "affective," sees the real action as happening in the viewer's emotions. The artist is like a technician who can induce feelings without needing to have feelings. Op art is a calculated device of this kind. Finally, "autotelic," the word written in the center of the triangle, signifies a class of theories that believe it is the canvas (*tela* in Italian), the picture itself, that does all the work, and we do not need to know what is "behind" it.

The purpose of the Triangle is not just to simplify aesthetics. It is to suggest that this is the whole picture. There is nothing outside artist, viewer, world, and work relations, and every theory must fit here. And we will not have to look far to find this model, apparently, trapping us inside. For example, here are the words of a Royal Academy PR person, writing about abstract expressionism: "Abstract Expressionism invites artist and viewer to meet. While the artist expresses their emotions and conveys a sense of their presence in the work, the viewer's perception is the final component to the mix." It seems to be true, but it fails to say why the artist's emotions, as opposed to anyone else's, are of interest; nor why we wish to have their presence; or how we validate the viewer's perception. In other words, it could apply to people in a room, but it says nothing about art.

But this "absence of art" gives the clue to the model. It may seem complete; but it is not really about art. The elusive art quality escapes it. For example, art is *expressive*. So what? Acts of violence are also expressive. What distinguishes Van Gogh's ear from his painting? Or art *represents*. Photography does that job, obviously. And there are many *affective* ways of creating experiences in the mind—not all of them legal. The fascinating thing about the Tanner Triangle is that it really does seem like a complete world, into which all art must fit. But it misses out one important component, even in secular terms: the observer, the giver of meaning, the maker of sense. We think of ourselves as outside the Triangle, surveying the scene, like farmers checking their fences. We have the lordly view and the right to rule; we would not put up with being trapped inside. Art must surely be part of a bigger dimension.

But how shall we find that bigger dimension? Can we find it through art, as it were, or must we reach up for theological rescue? If the task seems hard, we need to remind ourselves that art already exists; we are describing it, not inventing it! People will go on enjoying Monet with or without our help. The solution, it seems to me, is to ask some slightly different questions to the usual, What is art? If we ask ourselves how art operates, and what sort of world it operates in, we shall discover that art is already to be found in a theological world—*and that we knew it all along.*

II

How?

Our first question concerns the "how" of art. How does it connect with other things? Immediately we can make an observation that is in plain sight. Art is not so much a "thing" as a "node" in a set of relationships. It is an instrument that connects things. It may connect us to the artist. Sometimes that's a benefit! But principally it takes us from somewhere to somewhere.

The "from" gathers up and affirms my culture, language, and understanding; it joins me in a community of the familiar, and from there I set off. For example, I am reading a Dickens novel. A description of London at dawn contains elements, such as steeples, that I need to be familiar with. They already evoke resonance in my history and culture. Dickens gathers his readers together in their common language. But then he takes them somewhere. He takes them to characters, places, and atmospheres they have never been to before. He stretches the common into the uncommon, until the uncommon becomes familiar. When you look at his text, you cannot see the point at which this happens. In fact, when you are "there," in the places he describes, you cannot see the text at all. You are either "in text," maybe marvelling at its elaborate construction, or you are in the place described, but you cannot be in both at once. The "work of art" in fact becomes lost to view in the very moment that it takes you somewhere.

It is less obvious that this is happening with visual works of art, except in a banal way, because we think of figurative art as copying. Goya's *The Duke of Wellington* could almost be used for a passport photo. And yet, less noticed by us, a similar process is taking place. Goya's portraits take us "from" somewhere, a shared culture in which we understand concepts such as truth, authority, and integrity, and bring us "to" the unveiling of a person, in which the biometrics of their features are but a means to an end. We want to look "through" the portrait to be "with" the person; to know what it is like, so to speak, to be with Goya in Wellington's presence.

If we are still chasing "the object," we might want to ask where the work of art is—it is simultaneously on the canvas, in our heads, and in the shared place that the artist takes us to. It is the same with a symphony. A piece of music is at the same time in the score, in the sound waves, in our ears and minds, and "in" the composer—it does not have a fixed address. The work of art has a form that connects these things.

Alongside this truth, is a second observation: although it is a node, the work of art is still a thing made. It is not an object, but, paradoxically, it is still an object. The connections we have spoken about are made "through" single objects, finished things. This symphony ends, another begins; this building finishes, another starts alongside it. There is a boundary between art and not-art. Even a child knows the creative mystery, that a thing can be made that never existed before. Even if it is destroyed, it can never fully be nonexistent.

However, if art is an object, it is not just any object, and it is more than simply an action. Art has to have a deliberate coherence. A splash on a wall would not be art, but a splash in relation to the wall, or to another splash, might be. In other words, works of art are distinguished by "thing-thing" relations. The artist, or child, becomes concerned not just with the relation of the object to herself, but with thing-thing relationships within the object. When the object is made, it "contains" completed relationships, so the artist and viewer stand towards it side by side. The work is separated from its creator, like a baby born.

This principle goes for art in general, in whatever medium: in order to be complete the work of art contains its own content, without reference back to the artist. This principle holds good generally, but it is also normative. It should, but does not always, happen. For example, I remember hearing from a builder's foreman that he had once had to query a distinguished architect's piece of design, which did not make sense. "Oh, that must have been one of my off days," was the reply. The building's design did not make sense in terms of its own coherence; only the architect knew the reason.

This making of things that are of the self but outside the self, having their own self-contained "thing-thing" relations, is key to how art functions in the world. When a work is transferred from the mind to the world, it takes its place there. It is a new thing-in-the-world, holding its own in the world as real. If it belongs, the object is "object-ive," valid. If it belongs only to the artist, we see it as action, not art.

When the new work is set down in the world, we have an "epistemological moment" where something is perceived or unveiled. I see the work between me and the world; and I see the work through the world and the world through the work. The work "tests" my apprehension of the world. I ask myself if people are really as evil as Dickens sometimes depicts them—but the world also "tests" my appreciation of Dickens. The work of art is objectifying; as it makes objects, it aims to make truth. The made object may have a bias; but through it we apprehend the world.

At this point we may be wondering how our two observations about the "how" of art fit together. We noticed that art is nodal, it takes us from somewhere to somewhere, in a set of relationships that includes artist, viewer, and world. It is not an object. But then we started looking at art as an object, as a made thing in the world. These ideas do not appear to fit, until we realize that they correspond to those strangely interconnected principles, form and content. The form of a work of art represents the aspect of making, very often a physical form; but the form of a work is not complete until the content is in place. The content is both "inside" the form, and a referent beyond it. Take a simple form, the preacher's alliteration. By the time the preacher has captured seven points beginning with *R*, he will have discovered more about reality than he knew before; he fills out his list by thinking about things. The perception is integral to the form. Those points will be contained "within" the form as a list; but their reference, of course, is to the world outside. Content has two poles: it is conceptualized or imaged within the form but refers to reality beyond. If the form and content are convincing, the work of art will "rest" and seem to belong in the world.

But this leaves us with a question. What sort of perceptions are required to make the content of a work? If I am a landscape or a portrait painter, the perceptions are surely visual. But then they may show us no more than we already know. Can art really see beyond material form?

I grew up in a world where art was predominantly figurative and content was assumed to be visual. Abstract art was really abstract, to be enveloped in, more than understood. In 1960, E. H. Gombrich wrote a work called *Art and Illusion*, in which he likened art to science and saw its movement, by a process of "making and matching," as that of getting closer and closer to reality—understood as visual reality. The climax was Impressionism. Then, around 1900, when a fully representational art had been achieved, art somehow fell off the cliff into abstraction and other movements, and its shattered fragments have never really been reassembled since. This, I think, was Gombrich's lament. But the mistake, I think, has been to allow nineteenth-century materialistic realism to set the agenda for the whole of art, which has seldom been attached only to visible reality. The truth is that the real subject of art is *invisible* reality.

Where?

The second question is the "where" of art. The clue to art is not just how it is but where it is. It exists in a world not just visible but invisible. This makes sense, because art itself has a physical and mental counterpart: it is mind—the artist's thoughts—embodied in matter. So it is not surprising that the world itself, on all sides, shows us idea in form. This is true of any manufactured thing: a car or a ketchup bottle embodies an idea, not just a function but a feeling. But even in nature we can see this principle. A tree, product of complex biology as it is, also seems to contain an idea, its total concept in form. Every feature of it, from its beauty to its complex hydraulics, contributes to that single idea of "tree." We do not have to be Platonic here, as if the main thing was the idea. The reality is one. There is a unity of thought and matter. Or take a portrait of Charles I. We see the features of the man. But we also engage with invisible concepts, such as authority and majesty. Authority is the reason (quite invisible) we do what a mere man tells us; majesty is the glory that goes with the authority. We know that invisible authority comes from God. He has directed certain people, from Nebuchadnezzar to Tony Blair to Theresa May, to rule armies. The portraitist tries to convey not mere man but man invested with the right to rule. The picture is full of idea, from personhood and humanity to royal power.

Once we admit of what the Creed calls "all things, visible and invisible," art opens up wondrously. "Invisible" does not just refer to the world of angels. It refers to all the hidden coordinates by which this world operates, such as the invisible relationships that hold families and nations together or love in its remarkable power. It also refers to that sustaining will that guarantees the reality of a tree, with real existence as a tree, rather than as a collocation of atoms. Our "naming" puts the seal on real being. When a painter such as Constable or Monet paint a tree, they paint not just sight but knowledge of what it is.

This is why it is important to see that art straddles the invisible and visible worlds. As spiritual beings, we stand on the earth with the capacity to say what things are. We do not just come at life with our measuring instruments and say, "This looks like an object twenty-five metres tall," but we say, "This is a tree." Our position is one of authority to name things according to their nature, because we have been given a governing position to see their nature. We know this from Genesis, but we also see it as a fact of life. We cannot help ruling and governing; even the stars must be named and numbered as we extend our rule. This activity seems intellectual, but it is in fact spiritual, because it derives from an authority over matter that we assume by right. In art we approach this ability to say "what" things are, alongside science's "how" things are, and we do it not in a detached, tabulating sort of way but in the sense of knowing as you would know a person. This is why a few apples from Cézanne's hand are so powerful. He seems to "know" them. As I have said, we cannot watch ourselves enjoying a work of art, but we can know who we are in the process; and I believe this placing of ourselves in the world is a source of joy.

We perhaps need to remind ourselves that the world that art bridges is also a contested world. Knowing what things are does not guarantee an honest response, nor are the "invisibles" always friendly.

Why?

Finally, we look at our third question, Why art? What is the purpose of art? Only the most battle-hardened evolutionist, for whom creation is only sex and tears, would deny that art seems to have a reason for being. And when we ask ourselves what it is that drives art, the familiar secondary causes, such as money, lust, and power, are never enough. We need to picture art within the human plan. Art—we can now see—enables us to express our identity and our value. Without art we would not know what we were. In a parallel way, the tabernacle and temple, artistic outpourings of Israel, expressed the identity and worth of God. Doing the best possible for God expressed the best possible about God. Art also shows us something of our own human glory.

Art is also, as we have seen, a gift of truth in creation. Form works in its power to excavate truth. It does not automatically lead to vain fantasies or byways of nonsense. St. Paul found Greek poetry reliable enough in discerning truth to quote it in public. We ourselves are not mistaken when we turn to novels and films for truth. Art works because it is testable against the real thing. It is outward turned; it validates itself. But it comes so close to "dis-covering" the invisible, the metaphysical realm, that it tempts to *gnosis*. It takes on the appearance of religion, of a knowing that can be operated independently of God. Art is now, in the West, along with music, the place people go for meaning. But if we look at our own Western art, it is essentially Christian. It is not what humans have discovered for themselves, but what we have been shown about ourselves. Art is something discovered rather than meaning we made.

And when we are tempted to make art a religion, we must remember the cross of Christ. The cross of Christ establishes us poor penitents in objective forgiveness, faultless before the Father. Art cannot do that. It gives us a temporary experience of integration, of being the humans connected with nature and truth that we were designed to be. It makes us recipients of good but not good in ourselves, even though a visit to a gallery may make us feel "as if" we are good.

III

Conclusion

We have travelled some distance. We began with the thought that a materialist theory of art had some significant dead ends. It deals with a mystery, which it considers sacred, and yet it cannot describe it in more than earthbound ways. Today the theory may be getting the art it deserves. So we looked at art in other ways, considering our spiritual destiny and art's place in that. In the process, we found that it has the whole invisible world to play with. Born from earth and endowed with spirit, our height is such we can reach the toys on the top shelf. We can call things into life by naming them; and we can make new things that themselves have meaning and purpose.

But I want to end with two questions; the first is about beauty. Beauty, like creation, is suffering. It was, for century after century, in every place, the primary quality of art and building. If we look at creation, or read the Scriptures, we know it is God's "house style." Heaven will not be ugly. When we see the high-rise cities of Asia and realize that the only beauty people see is from their TVs, our hearts break. Beauty is preeminently about idea in form and the fullness of grace; it teaches us that we live in a world thought, planned, and sustained. As such it has a price on its head. It knows too much. The question is this. If our public institutions are not on the side of beauty—and by all accounts, the new Tate Modern extension did not spend £260 million to house beautiful things—then which side are they on?

The second question is this: Suppose we want to be on God's side, and make the world a better place—visually—can we do it? What depth of redemption is needed to turn us from idolatry, love of self, obsession with death, and other ills that permeate our art today?

Coda

At the outset, we asked ourselves whether theology has any work to do in art. We have understood implicitly that art "works," that is to say art of the traditional eras, because it carries its meanings with it. The Sistine Chapel ceiling contains its biblical content without requiring anyone to personally believe it. The art, attached to its meanings, functions. However, our contemporary theory of art, how we understand art to work, is implicitly materialistic, and that theory is sterile when it comes to producing new art. We have the art we deserve. Much of it is not art as we would have understood it; it does not "contain" its meanings, rather, it continually refers us back to the artist and his or her personal ideology for explanation, and it is lacking the beauty that comes from seeing the world as significant.

So we looked again at art, not under the old perspective of aesthetics, which is essentially viewer centered and fixated on experience, but under the canopy of theology. The critical point is that the "how" of art requires us to think about the "where" of art—what sort of created world we in fact inhabit, and where art fits into that. When we see who we are and how God designed us to think, we are better equipped to look at the "why" of art. The "why" is, in very large part, to help us articulate life in the invisible realm.

None of this, of course, gets us near the center of theology, the incarnation of the Son of God and his death and resurrection. But it should do. In ancient times, artists were kept busy making idols. There was no need for art, no expectation that artists might contribute their own view of the world. The idol makers' images themselves, without any thoughtful veracity, were believed to have power. Then the image of God in Christ became known. What sudden redundancy! The fake gods were no longer needed. Image makers now took on the task of reminding people that God had once walked on earth. Earth itself took on dignity and splendor. There was a freedom in art because perception itself was free. Now, in modern times, reality has not changed. Jesus has not retired. There is still forgiveness through the cross, leading to joy. There is still a world lovingly made, to which Christ will return. But people need reminding; they have lost the way. They believe the world has no meaning, so they must make meanings. Artists do not know it, but they have become idol makers again. And do their idols have power? They probably do have at least the power of misdirection. That is why theologians need to remind people of the significant, redeemed world that they in fact live in; and Christian artists need to find the freedom to do what their hearts tell them to do.

7

Why Art?[1]

Art is a whole world of thinking and activity that we can enter into, as practitioners and viewers; either dipping our toe into it or going for a swim. But art can also be ignored. It is necessary but also expendable, essential and a distraction. So the question, Why art? is different from the question, Why food? Food really is essential to life, but art is essential only in quite a different sense. What kind of "necessity" could it be, that people are also so happy to dispose of or destroy it? The question goes to the heart of what it is to be human in the world.

Art is an act of human being and a way of thinking about human being. But it has two apparent competitors. Today its main competitor is science, and in the past, and to some extent today, it has been the Bible. Both give accounts of the meaning of life that are so total that we can live "in them" to the exclusion of other sources of meaning.

Take science first: to be a source of meaning is not what science seeks to do; but meaning, and our search for meaning, attaches itself to science. For example, a certain tree may be fifty feet high. Everything else in it can be measured too, its cells examined, DNA revealed, and in the end we might have, in theory, complete information about the tree. This information, the analysis, is not the tree, and we know that. But it has become almost automatic to think that the tree "is" a certain combination of cells, that our scientific analysis of the parts can stand for the whole. There then follows the common but illegitimate inference that the tree is nothing but the elements that we have identified. Science has, apparently, given it its meaning. But in reality applying our numbers to the tree is entirely our business, for

[1] The following essay is a recollection and expansion of a talk given to Cheltenham Christian Arts Festival, C3 Church, Apr. 10, 2016.

our purposes. The tree in itself does not know (if trees could know) inches and feet; it has nothing to do with them. We analyze because we want to, but the tree carries on being a tree, in all the mystery of its own existence and purpose.

On a larger scale, science has (controversially but confidently), sketched in a biography of the whole universe from cradle to grave, including the rather astonishing arrival of consciousness by unguided evolution. Because the tools of science are impersonal, the universe is described impersonally. This is legitimate as far as it goes, because much can be netted by this means. But when the account switches into meaning, to the question of what and who we are, it is assumed that the source and continuation of the world actually is impersonal. If we put a red filter over everything, everything will look red. As the old saying goes, if we have a hammer, everything will be a nail. Impersonality is the method but should not be the result. But there is no need to give science a job it is not trying to do and was never designed for.

The appeal of the scientific account of reality goes back to the seventeenth- and eighteenth-century Enlightenment, when it was believed that the light of reason would dispel the darkness of superstition and of anything that could not be proved. While none of us doubts the benefits of this operation, for viewing reality as a whole it fails. It takes for granted that the only darkness is that caused by ignorance. But there is such a thing as evil, which science cannot explain or banish, or even identify. Science assumes, by faith, that there are no limits to what we can understand and, by inference, that what we cannot grasp with our conceptual tools does not exist. And it thinks that human consciousness is the supreme arbiter of truth and that the tools we apply to the world somehow are the world. We can study our brains, but our own ego, and its right to judge, is not examined. It is rather like the investigative journalist who sees every name brought into the light of public truth but his own.

This strong, confident "light of knowing" has a strangely emasculating effect on art. If science deals with the world, what does art do? It has a place, but we turn to psychological language to describe it. Art safely occupies the "expressive" side of life, "subjectively" processing the world at large and addressing the scientific given with feelings. It is like a traditional marriage from the industrial age: the scientist is a husband who goes out to work and deals with the world, while his artist wife stays at home, doing creative things and expressing emotions.

What then of the Bible, so much neglected today? The Bible, of course, does contain a lot of history and gives, from different angles, an account of reality. But, reading it with Enlightenment eyes, we somehow expect it to be complete. We want it to be a book that shines light into every area of ignorance, telling us, not just beginnings and endings, but everything in between. It is no wonder that the Bible and science come into conflict, because, while they can safely eject art from the discussion, they are both seen as trying to fight over the same territory: safe, impersonal knowledge. But as we shall see, the Bible does not take us down that route. The distillation of facts from the Bible is not the speaking Bible that is God's word.

The Bible describes, in its unique way, where we are, and it is not a place as completely open to light as the Enlightenment would have us believe. In its most famous chapter, St. Paul, having described love in a way that is utterly clear and transparent, goes on to say, "Now we know in part," and "now we see in a mirror dimly,"[2] or as the old version puts it, "through a glass darkly."[3] Our vision is darkened and there is a lot we can neither see nor understand. It is only "then," at the end of time, that we shall see "face to face."

There is a gap, a gap between what we can see and know now and the knowledge that we will have. Note that St. Paul did not say, as we moderns would do, looking at ourselves in a less-than-flat mirror from the ancient world, "Just get a better mirror." The gap is not to be bridged with technology, rather, it is an intrinsic part of being in the unfulfilled world we have. In another place, St. Paul says that the whole creation is "subject to futility," or "vanity" (Rom 8:20)—it does not fully function or bear fruit in the way it was intended to. The philosopher Francis Bacon saw science as part of the redemptive plan to make creation work, and certainly it has done so in terms of healing, safety, and comfort; but there is a gap that science cannot bridge. Apart from the gap we have mentioned, that science does not mitigate the presence of evil, there is another less obvious one, the one of greatest importance to the arts, the gap of meaning. We live in a world that seems to have meaning but sometimes seems meaningless. Art seems to live in this gap where meaning is to be found, tentatively, but not proved, recognized but not asserted.

What Do We Mean by Meaning?

It is not easy to describe what meaning is. First of all, it can easily be misplaced. We are often tempted to try to describe meaning in a one-to-one way, like a translation: "this means that." "The black cat crossed the road, therefore I am going to have a bad day." Events have a one-to-one meaning,

---

2. 1 Cor 13:12, ESV.
3. 1 Cor 13:12, KJV.

and all we need is the code. The difficulty here (or at least one of many difficulties) is that the translation actually deprives the event of meaning. No one cares about the cat. It has a walk on, walk off part, and its only role is to be a symbol. But why is the black cat there? What is it doing in its own life? We miss the particularity of meaning, just as in translating a word into another language we may miss its resonance. Meaning is the weight of a thing itself, not what we can interpret it into. A better approach is to ask what we mean by "meaninglessness." When we say something is "meaningless," what is it we think is missing? People may say, for example, that the world is meaningless, just a planet in vast space that happens to be there by cosmic accident. Even "accident" is a form of meaning. But what they really mean is that it is devoid of purpose or destiny and that there is no creator for whom it has value. To find what we mean by meaning, we should look in the area of "personal being guaranteeing significance."

But first, just to remind ourselves of how sharp the frustration is, of living "in the gap," it is worth thinking about a few pressing areas where we do not know the meaning. Innocent suffering is one, pleasure another, and the third will have to be love. Then we will see how art looks for meaning and, to some extent, finds it.

– *Innocent Suffering*

When tragedy strikes (the word "tragedy" is itself an attempt at meaning) and a child dies, we look for meaning. A person who intends well, trying to give comfort, might say, "Jesus needed her in heaven." This is a one-to-one translation, substituting one event for another, providing perhaps brief mental comfort. It does not weigh the actual meaning, the life of promise cut short, the on-going relationships broken, the hopes and plans suddenly ended, although it is true that a word of faith might change that view. A child did die recently in a nearby village, kicked in the chest by a horse, and a not so well-intentioned person ascribed it to "karma," an impersonal punishment because the child was at a fox hunt. This, again, is one-to-one translation, requiring no thought; it does not weigh loss or grief or who a child is. It tries, somewhat cruelly, to create meaning but misses it. Another "meaning" was offered by the hunt member who said, truthfully, "These things happen." Such statements try to make accidents part of normality, a stoic form of comfort; but to weigh something impersonal in the balance with a person does not really work. We still cry out for meaning in such circumstances, but every attempt we make to "find meaning" seems to trivialize the actual event, to rob it of its actual quality of injustice and pain.

– Pleasure

Another elusive meaning is that of pleasure, so central to life that we almost miss it. I watched a pigeon taking flight and landing on the pylon near our house, perfectly judging the arc of flight and, it would appear, taking pleasure in it. We who have had pet dogs know how much pleasure they take in the good things of life, walks, discoveries, scents, food. We ourselves shop, cook, and eat with an eye to beauty and flavour and when we have had one delicious and beautiful meal, almost immediately start preparing another. What does this mean? Science might suggest we keep topping up the pleasure-inducing chemicals in our brain—but why so creatively? Would not a pill do just as well?

– Romantic Love

A third elusive meaning is that of love. Falling in love is a tremendous event when it happens, but we struggle to know what to do with it. Is it real, we ask ourselves, and if so, how do we act? The singer's question, Is this love? may one day be answered with a brain scan. But what we need to know—how to take responsible action—is beyond brain chemistry. Love seems to key into something bigger than us and for its sake we will cross oceans; but we do not know what it is we are dealing with.

How Art Helps

Art does not tell us "what" meaning is, but it does come alongside it, and help us recognize that it is there. It does not give us answers, because, as we have seen, answers are unsatisfying. It does help us to "be human" in the face of life's conundrums, even when meaning gives you a blank stare or hides her face.

– Innocent Suffering

It is particularly art's strength to avoid one-to-one explanations, to not try to say "this is that," but to weigh the quality of the event or experience. We can see this in a classic painting of innocent suffering, Goya's *The Third of May*. The painting depicts a reprisal carried out by French troops who have rounded up a number of Madrid citizens to kill by firing squad. At the center we see the terrified features of the victim about to die. Facing the impersonal line of shooters, we can identify with this man, maybe dragged out of bed, forced into sudden death with little comfort from the old monk who stands next to him; and he stands for all whose lives are viciously and randomly assaulted.

Does the artist "explain" the meaning of the man's death, perhaps by making him heroic or a martyr willing to die? Not at all. That would rob it of its very quality of futility, the pointless and cruel waste of life. We are meant to weigh the awfulness of it and not even to take sides (the faces of the perpetrators are unseen). But, and this is the point, this tragic loss of life is set in a moral framework where the awfulness of it really is awful. The meaning of the picture is to carry the meaning of the event: that murder is murder, a crime is a crime, and that politics is not exempt from the moral law. The picture points beyond itself to a framework in a moral universe.

But I hope we have not explained too much. Suffering like this is mute because we do not know, except by faith, that such morality really exists or that innocent suffering will ever really be put right. To work, the picture cannot "read to the end of the story," like some of those great Veronese paintings of martyrdoms, where the invisible angel is already preparing a crown for the victim about to die. This picture carries the sense of innocent suffering by living in the gap where the end is not seen; but we know, as best we can, that right is right and wrong is wrong.

– *Pleasure*

What about pleasure? Art is acutely and consistently about pleasure but in rather surprising ways. Imagine looking at a Vermeer. A maid is pouring milk; a loaf is on the table. The painting is a sumptuous depiction of light, objects, and a young woman in an interior. The beauty of the painting, the harmony of light and color, and the painter's appreciation of form give great pleasure. Ever since it was painted the work has been valuable beyond price. And yet, the beauty of the painted loaf, which is priceless, is also the beauty of the actual loaf that Vermeer saw and bought, which cost next to nothing. The beauty of Vermeer's loaf is the beauty of every loaf, pleasant to the eye and touch. Pleasure runs like a river over everything we see and everything we do; and though sometimes we are aware of it, and sometimes not, it is usually, like a hot coffee, there for the asking.

The prevalence of pleasure means that we live in a very strange world, a world supplied endlessly with good things, for which we have somehow lost the receipts. They are just "there." They do not connect with anything we have done or who we are except in our mysterious capacity to enjoy them, and they do not seem particularly fitting in a world so beset with evil. It is as if we have stumbled like beggars into a mansion filled with fine art and laid splendidly for dinner, which the owners have left for us to eat. In our ignorance some of us trash the place; but we are also filled with wonder. Art registers and meets this capacity for pleasure, but it cannot explain it. There is art that denies pleasure or its appropriateness, and we have the bitterly austere works of the modern-day artistic puritan. But even such works are a testimony, by their denial, to the outrageous generosity implied not just in the natural world but in the fact that mere pigments, clay, stone, whatever, can come together to make something so much greater than the sum of the parts.

– *Romantic Love*

A third place where art can show us the "meaning of meaning" is in the depiction of love. Here we need to tread lightly because each of us is part of the story of love, sometimes the lack of it. We are not only observers! The history of art shows some quite contrary messages, and each one has its influence on us. As in a visit to the optician, when two or three lenses are placed over the eyes at once, we do not just see "a Titian," but we see a Manet, a Picasso, and a Titian, "through" each other. Our images of "love," "man," and "woman" are composite images, and we look from the present through to the past, and back again.

Looking first at Picasso, then, there would be many striking images to draw from. But none is more famous or assertive than *Les Demoiselles D'Avignon*, a title that is ironic, referring to the red light district of Barcelona. Here Picasso adapts a classic image of European art, known for example from Rubens's *The Judgment of Paris*, of standing female nudes, traditionally a scene of respect and admiration. But the play between men and women in the Picasso (the man that was originally in the picture was painted out but is still present in the implied observer) is anything but amicable. The women stare out with mask-like faces that cannot be engaged with, and two of them have heads reminiscent of African fetishes. It seems there is aggression on both sides. This is not surprising—since the relationship is based on cash. If we are looking here for "the meaning of love," we will find it mainly by its absence. Picasso, it seems, is destroying a romance he does not believe in but nonetheless it is there, because anger and aggression are at root a demand for justice. Something is not right and Picasso is going to say so.

Looking back "through" Picasso, we come to another uncomfortable scene: Manet's famous *Le Déjeuner sur l'herbe*. Here are two young gentlemen, dressed warmly, one gesturing rather idly, in the company of a naked woman, while a clothed figure in the background makes up the foursome and a picnic is ready on the grass. Here there is no explanation for the nakedness or hint as to whether cash has parted hands, though the scene is hardly real enough for that question to arise. We are still in "classic art" territory. We are no doubt supposed to know that Titian painted a similar subject of clothed men and a nude in a landscape (his celebrated *Fête Champêtre* in the Louvre) and even that Raphael had designed a composition from which this is drawn. But though the composition and setting are classic, something is missing. As far as romance is concerned, there is none of it: the nude girl looks out at us, with a somewhat complacent stare. The men appear to feel nothing. It is as if "the Enlightenment" has finally caught up with "love" and found nothing there except bodies on the grass. Love is dead; it was only sex. This rather dismal view was probably not uncommon in the Paris of Manet's time, but, true artist as he is, he cannot avoid presenting it as a deficiency. Here, after all, are real human beings in springtime and something is not quite working.

Finally, we come back to a more classic statement about love. The Titian in the Louvre to which we referred, is a mysterious painting. We are not sure if the nude is real or simply an idea that the music of the singer has made real. What we do know is that for the artist, romantic love is real. Another Titian painting, in Edinburgh, shows *The Three Ages of Man*. On the right, babies mark the beginning of life, three of them—and the third, with wings, might be Cupid. To their left is a young couple who have certainly felt Cupid's arrow, because they are in love. Here the man is nearly unclothed, and, in contrast to the Manet, he seems to bare his heart. In the background is an old man contemplating a skull. Is the skull that of his beloved? We see here the whole cycle of life; and love, warm affection and delight, is at the heart of the process. The artist refuses to make love meaningless, even when death takes it away, because love is there. "Meaning," here, does not descend to explanation, which would destroy it; instead it comes alongside the truth and holds it, so that we can recognize it and say, "Yes, this is how it is."

How Much Can We Know?

When we think of art "finding" the meaning that is there, it does not of course do so unaided. It is the Bible which has authenticated experience, and told us that what we think is real is really there. Western art, as we know it, has been saturated in the Bible. Even non-believing artists of our own generation have been fascinated by the cross and think of it as the center that somehow tells the heart of the human story. But it would be a mistake to think the Bible "gives the answer," as if the trials and searches of art were somehow unneeded.

Even at the center of meaning, the cross and resurrection of Christ, where, so to speak, God shows his hand, the Scriptures are curiously reticent about the kind of explanation we would like. Christ's sermon to the pair of travellers to Emmaus, in which he explained "the things" concerning himself (Luke 24:27) is not reported. Christ does not give us an information packet we can take away but determines to give us himself. What we do see, when we look, is the summation of meaning in Christ's acts—if we wondered whether there is such a thing as innocent suffering, we see it here; if we wondered if love is real, this is where we go to be sure.

What we do not know is "the meaning" of things, but we do know that they have meaning. Today much of the story is hidden, but to think there is a God who knows is enough to make meaning real. If the world as given is like one of those adult coloring books that are popular today, full of outlines, artists are those who color it in—probably not with the "right" colors but between them an image takes shape. When we look at artists' work, we look past its awkwardness and refraction to a reality that has meaning. Fra Angelico is coordinated towards the kindness and grace of Jesus, Jackson Pollock expresses his humanity in a kind of rage, and neither of them can stop being human and giving us some sense of what it is to be one of us. We cannot step outside reality to look down on it—we have to be human in the middle of it.

God's Phone Call

An image that may be helpful for this time of "comprehending incomprehension" is the experience of overhearing someone having a phone conversation. Though you cannot hear the other speaker, you cannot help yourself imagining the things they might be saying. Animated sounds of joy, surprise, concern, and so on—suggest a picture in your mind, although you never hear the other voice firsthand. Art is somewhat like that. We never hear the "original voice" the artist hears from reality, where God is speaking through everything that exists ("The heavens declare the glory of God," Ps 19:1 KJV), but that voice is refracted through, say, Picasso's women with a fixed stare, and Manet's nude, who looks us in the face, and Titian's innocent babes. We never hear God's voice precisely, but we do hear the artist's response, that which they speak back to God. It may be an antagonistic and rebellious response, but through it we can still hear the divine call. So art is immersed in meaning; but sometimes the original signal can get, as in the game Telephone, distorted into something else. Ideally, of course, if we are artists, we want to respond faithfully, and when God says hello to us (with a subject that appeals), our painting is a hello back to him—an imperfect response but a response that is still a yes.

Truth in the Physical

At this point, those who love to hear God speak directly through Scripture will wonder, not for the first time, whether there is any necessity for art. Sermons are, after all, usually drawn from the Bible, not paintings. But art is not in competition here. There is no such thing as "Art" that stands over against the Bible and reality as an independent source of truth. Art is the physical response, in a physical world of physical beings, to reality as we find it—it is our arms and legs; we can no more deny art than we can deny running or walking. It is not a set of new ideas; it is "who we are" in the world. That is not to say that "art is physical, the Bible is mental," because the Bible is itself as tied into the physical world as speech is to act. God spoke "light," and there was light. Jesus speaks and things happen; for example, dead bodies rise up. Of course we have no concepts to handle this. The Bible teaches us things we do not know, and through this word, taken by faith, God himself acts to recreate the world.

It seems provocative to be told that Truth is a person, who spoke in a physical body. Like good Greeks, we keep trying to turn truth into a proposition. Detached knowledge seems easier to handle and less threatening. But if we consider reality as a whole and truth as that which can be truthfully said about it (like a parallel reality of cognition), then it is clear that truth-telling, the apprehension of what is there, has to be located in a person. No one can state truth except persons; and none of us can honestly say what things are except Jesus Christ. Art perhaps helps us to appreciate truth as something we apprehend, before even we understand it, and perhaps from there it is not so hard to jump to truth as a person. This will not be fully seen until the eschatological moment when the world system is wrapped up, when Jesus Christ appears as the head of everything, and turns everything the right way up; he will rectify all our bent ideas and show us things as they really are. Rulers and bosses will be confronted by something as insignificant as a child, possibly a child who has been killed, and Christ will say, "This is where the kingdom of God is—don't miss it." Sometimes art, in the way it sees right order in the world, can spot this kind of truth before we see it.

Art as Justice

Another name for "right order," the kind of order that art sees and foresees, if it is not yet present, is "justice." Justice is giving everything its due. In Velasquez's portraits of his monarch, the artist gives to Philip IV his due: respect without servility. In his portraits of the court dwarfs, he gives what was due to them: humanity, empathy, and compassion. To the Inquisition, however (through the eyes of Goya), was due suspicion and exposure, and to war was due (also in Goya) horror and repugnance. Justice is a single fabric that looks forward to the end of time when every secret will be proclaimed from the rooftops and each persecuted person will be vindicated. This is a kind of justice that makes us observant of truth and lies in art, that makes us impatient with propaganda or with the superficial and sentimental. We keep a watch on the artist, willing them to be honest but aware that they might not be.

But if justice is a single fabric, there is another kind of justice from which art is cut, not only justice in treating the world but justice in the creative act. The created world has much to teach us, and always has taught us, about things being made well and beautifully made, even when no one is looking. Art used to care about craft in this sense; now the rough, spontaneous, impulsive and even crude are allowed expressive space. But we need to consider what is of importance to God. The tabernacle was, by any standard, an expensive worship space. Not only is its making described in chapter after chapter, in Exodus, but also its specific prescription is ascribed to God himself. We know the temptation to save money, cut corners, and rush a job, but this is not what happened here; in fact, every last detail was believed to be important. This says something about God and his due, and also something about how we are to be, not with just one good side towards God, like stage scenery, with a back that no one is supposed to see. But, we may protest, where's economy, functionality, speed of building?

This, we must remind ourselves, is the tabernacle of a different kingdom to ours, with different rules. In this regime we make things that "look right" in a created sense—we give them their due. We work until they are as they are meant to be. We do not look at them in terms of the money we were not made to spend, but by a strange rule we make sure they have everything they need. This can make art expensive! Good things take time, or rather, time is forgotten when attention is given to making something well.

Why art? Let us just say, ambitiously, that art is the cloak of justice around the world. It gives the world its due not only in how we see it but in making art that is fit. In this age, the cloak is tattered, meaning is often scrambled, and true moments of art are brief and rare; but art is a sign that the intelligent, personal goodness of God can take physical form and that we can participate in his mind and heart towards what he has made.

8

Art, Time, and Eternity[1]

INTRODUCTION

Consider this statement: *art* is a waste of *time* and contributes nothing to *eternity*. Imagine standing by the graveside of someone who loved art but perhaps did little evangelism. Were his cultured interests a waste of the *time* given him? Could art have contributed anything to *treasure in heaven*? Perhaps we might feel sorrow that he did not do anything more *useful*.

Such thoughts arise naturally and inevitably from the way we, in both Christian and secular culture, think of time, art, and eternity, and of course they have huge practical consequences as to how we occupy our time. In this short essay I aim to remind us that the attitudes to art, time, and eternity that we may think are in the Bible are often imposed by us on the Bible, mainly from Western culture's inheritance from the Enlightenment and its antecedents long before.

Briefly, moderns typically think of art as a luxury, an extra to the practical business of life, an option for busy people if they have time and wealth. Time, as in the adage "time is money," is considered a resource, which may be used for profit, evangelism, pastoral care, or bringing up children, according to our values. We think of eternity as a cessation of the activity of time, when all that is physical will cease, a kind of white space absolutely disconnected from time and matter. If we are evangelical Christians, we think of eternity as absolutely provided by God for us by grace through faith in Christ; therefore (we are inclined to think), nothing we do in the flesh, let

1. The original version of this essay was written in September 2012.

alone any cultural activity, has any impact on it. I lay up treasure in heaven by being rich in faith, not rich in art.

Such views are so settled that it is hard to overturn them, not least in oneself, but there is an alternative view, which I believe makes life more of a whole, both in the wholeness of ourselves and in a wholeness between now and eternity. But first we need to be clear about the weakness of the current view. For art does not sit well with the notion of time as segments of useful resource; most art we value has taken hours, if not years, to produce, and it is common for creative people to forget time altogether when they are working and for art lovers to forget time when they are looking. It is as if, when we look at art, we have already entered a different zone in which the clock is not ticking and mental and spiritual transactions, potentially of a permanent nature, are being made. Art intercepts us in the "who" we are, addresses us, and sometimes uncovers us, and it is this "who" that addresses God and finds reality in His grace.

I

I would like to state from the outset what I understand by art. Art is meaning embodied in form. The job of the artist is to so work with form that it will carry the meaning when he or she is no longer there to explain it. The work of art, like a grown child, is able to be independent and have its own voice; its parents have begotten it but it is also free. This is how I see art,[2] and it seems to apply to any art form (although in some of the newer kinds of art, works seem to be less self-sufficient and more explanation-dependent). Why does this matter? Because the making of form, separate from the maker, is also an existential statement. If I am to make something separate from me that becomes an object in the world, it cannot join the world without belonging to it—that is to say, without being congruent with, in effect a truthful statement about, the world. If it is not truthful, it either does not belong (and comes from Mars) or it is all about me. But if it is a statement about the world, then it is a statement about what the world is, in itself, a picture of life from here to eternity.

---

2. This is an observation rather than a definition. Art is a whole, and in a short statement one can only point out certain relevant features. What you "see" in a work of art will depend on all the other coordinates you believe in, e.g., personhood, a real world, and so forth. Dorothy L. Sayers gives a brilliantly elaborated account of the freedom of art from its maker. She writes, "The business of the creator is not to escape from his material medium or to bully it, but to serve it; but to serve it, he must love it. If he does so, he will realize that its service is perfect freedom." Sayers, *Mind of the Maker*, 53.

The early Christian paintings of the Byzantines had gold backgrounds; they tried to express materiality situated in eternity. The Dutch Protestant painters of the seventeenth century painted cloudy skies with shafts of sunlight in their landscape paintings; they tried to express materiality penetrated by the grace of eternity. The Impressionists painted pictures of packets of light entering our eyes; they expressed what can be known by the senses, but of eternity, they professed ignorance. Every kind of art is a net thrown out to catch what is thought to be there. By making form you are committing yourself to what you think is real. If you make beautiful decoration, and nothing more than that, you are still stating, "This joy, this time spent, this beautiful form, is valid in reality."

This, I find, is a good way to understand art. It describes the "parent-child" relation of art to those who make it, because it is a thing made, "object-ive," not just a message. But it also describes the object-world relation, the relationship of art with truth. Art is not a statement, validated by the honesty of the speaker; art is a thing-in-the-world, validated by its fittingness in the world. If it belongs, it is true; if it does not belong, it is neither true nor art; it is just something that happens to be there. In my opinion, that is true of many modern buildings. They are not art; they just happen to be there. Accountants, speculators, and builders have put them there, but they do not "belong." Art, incidentally, does not have to be a likeness of the world; humans have been given creative gifts that allow us to make things that have never existed before, but these things are still fitting, appropriate to human life in God's world.

It hardly needs to be said that, though art is recognizable in the way I have described it, it is not how it is usually understood. So I will briefly lay out the cultural map as we have received it since the Enlightenment.

Whether we are Christians or just plain secular people, the way we normally receive art today is as an option. In front of us is the world (for example, the view from our window), and we can choose how we see it. I may look at it scientifically, I may look at it theologically, or I may look at it artistically. The most obvious contrast is between science (seeing a tree "biologically") and art (seeing "form, emotion, and color"). So I have a choice.

It is also true, in this way of thinking, that what I may choose to do (e.g., look at the world artistically), I may also choose not to do. I may "need" to look at the tree scientifically (e.g., if it is old or diseased) but not "need" to look at the tree artistically at all, especially when I am busy. The artistic view of life is easily sidelined, because, in the last resort, it is just an option, of no practical value. If I am a Christian I might add, "and of little value in eternity."

It will be seen that there is a strong utilitarian thrust in this kind of thinking, and we find that it is not there by accident. At the source of Enlightenment thinking were the objectives of practical science. This has left us, in culture, a kind of grading in durability applied to all knowledge, from "hard science" to "soft science," and in the arts, to a kind of knowing that is not considered knowledge at all. For example, if Dickens had presented his profound understanding of Victorian London statistically, it would be "knowledge" but, as it is presented as fiction, it is "art." This split in the frame of knowledge goes back, as is well known, to Francis Bacon, who believed knowledge should be verified by experiment, and to René Descartes, who sought to place the whole of knowledge, including knowledge of God, on a basis as certain as that of mathematics. He needed "God" as the centerpiece of his system; but even God's existence he submitted to proof, reaching back to the "ontological proof" of St. Anselm. If God was his keystone, the foundation of everything was his one certainty: that the self knows itself as knowing; "I think, therefore I am."[3] Ever since Descartes, philosophers have hammered away at this edifice with the chisel of proof, demolishing first his "God," and finishing with the demolition of the self, until in postmodernism we know neither God nor who we are.

But what has remained is a presumption that mathematics and science "work." Manipulations of material still bring results. Art, however, remains far behind as a source of knowledge; indeed it is not usually considered "knowledge" at all. Does this matter? Since art is concerned with what can be directly apprehended (by the see-er or "seer" in biblical parlance), it does indeed matter if such apprehension is undermined as a source of understanding in favor of "what can be proved." Thus in art we have seen a steady decline from the confident knowing of the Renaissance, when, in Leonardo, science and art were inseparable, or the fullness of observation of Rubens and Rembrandt in the seventeenth century, or of Turner and Constable in

---

3. "The very foundation of Cartesian philosophy was the search for some absolutely certain and indisputable truth or truths, upon which the whole structure of knowledge could be subsequently erected, some pellucidly clear and distinct idea which would carry its own authentication. Such truths Descartes believed he had discovered in the affirmation of his own existence and of the existence of God, the former being based on the famous *cogito ergo sum* and the latter upon the ontological argument; and on the basis of these two truths he proceeded to argue, as is well known, for the existence of an external world as a real counterpart of the world of ideas which he found in his own mind. It was easy for Descartes's critics to point out that the most which the *cogito* could prove was the existence of a momentary subject of a momentary experience; and when in addition the shakiness of the ontological argument had been made manifest, both the mind as a persisting substance and the external world as a real existent vanished and all that remained of Descartes's system was the ideas." Mascall, *Words and Images*, 65–66.

the eighteenth and nineteenth centuries, to the relative agnosticism of modernity, where with, say, Mondrian, everything beyond the painted grids is mystery. In contrast to the enjoyment of the world of earlier ages that believed in the power of direct apprehension, today we often find a puritan abstinence of blank or nearly blank canvases, which reflect a sense that the world cannot be known and even personhood is nothing.

However there are certain problems, which might have told us that this road would prove a dead end. Perhaps the most obvious is that the question defines the answer. If you want knowledge to be based entirely on what can be proved, and if mathematics is your standard, then every foot that does not fit that particular slipper will have to be trimmed. If you define the world by mathematics, than necessarily, not just accidentally, you will leave out art. More importantly, if you define God by what can be known of him logically, what kind of a God can you have? Only an abstraction. You may create a logical space for a "God" to inhabit; but you have no means of knowing him as a person, no more than to logically establish that the late Queen existed would be a step towards knowing what she was like. We know the monarch's throne is occupied, but that takes us nowhere towards knowing her person. We have seen the flag flying but not entered the door. It is not the knowledge of contact.

There are perhaps two or three forks in the road we might wish had not been taken. It was unfortunate that "knowing" was identified with "indubitable knowing." Knowing by direct apprehension, which is how we know in practical and artistic life, is different from proof; they are two different operations (and in scientific discovery, as Polanyi tells us, direct intuitive apprehension normally, not just occasionally, comes first).[4] But the attempt to tie knowledge to proof exalts empirical knowledge above every other. What can be proved involves operations on matter, carried out impersonally. That leads down the road of giving matter priority in existence. Still further down the road, matter is the only thing that seems to exist. This leads directly to utilitarianism, in which happiness is measured on an axis of pleasure or pain. If the terms in which pleasure is seen are material (in a materialist world they will be), we are led inexorably, if reluctantly, to the one, universal, hard, and numerical measure for almost everything: money.

Another fork in the road I might wish untrod is the invention of "Art" and aesthetics. The creation of this separate area is considered a triumph of eighteenth-century thought, especially through Kant's attempt to show that artistic judgment is rational. It resulted in the creation of museums,

---

4. For a helpful introduction to Polanyi's influential *Personal Knowledge*, see Drusilla Scott's *Everyman Revived*.

which remove objects from the places that give them meaning, and then try to restore that meaning through labels. The main meaning they are given, of course, is "Art," which succeeds in abstracting from, say, religious works their secondary quality of beauty, making it primary, while somehow draining out the original reference to the object to religious truth (if it is truth). I love museums; but the unfortunate assumption of aesthetics is that it puts its major emphasis on me-art relations, rather than on me-art-world relations, let alone me-art-world-God relations. Undoubtedly there is a strange chemical exchange between us and works of art as art, which aesthetics might want to analyze; but to cut art off from the world of knowledge is to leave it separated from reality in an art-o-sphere of its own. Today what is safely in museums can be ignored, which is why artists have been ever more assertively trying to get noticed in the public space.

Further back, the fork in the road that led to the detachment of aesthetics from knowledge was an assumption that we can deal with knowing in terms of two points only: me and the thing known. The Bible states that "by two or three witnesses" shall a thing be known,[5] because when we are dealing with I-it relations, we have little assurance without a third party. We very often do not know what is of us and what is of the object. The subject invades the object and the object is present in the subject and we cannot always see clearly what is what. When the subject is "God" we have no leverage whatsoever; we can know him but cannot stand outside ourselves to "prove" him. St. Paul recounts, obliquely, an experience of heaven that impacted him so deeply he hardly dared speak of it; but whether it was "in the body or out of the body," he could not tell (2 Cor 12:1–4 KJV). He could not tell if his body was present, nor did he need to know. I-it relations can be confusing on their own, and without external leverage it is difficult to erect an edifice of proof. This must be why the Scriptures emphasize the "witness of the Spirit." ("And there are three that bear witness in earth, the Spirit, and the water, and the blood: and these three agree in one. If we receive the witness of men, the witness of God is greater," 1 John 5:7–9 KJV.) We are not expected to operate solo in the apprehension of truth.

But the first fork in the road that was wrongly taken was one that we all took "in Adam," which was to try to make ourselves independent centers of knowledge apart from God. The tower of Babel is a picture of what it is to try to throw up knowledge and proof from ourselves towards God. Descartes's intellectual project, which started with the worthy objective of proof of the existence of God, had built into it the fatal assumption that knowledge starts with us, the knowing subject. Alienation from God is already built-in, and

---

5. Deut 17:6; see also John 5:31, 8:17, etc.

from that there is no escape towards him, and at length, no escape towards knowledge of the world either. But we do not build towards God. Apprehension of reality, and of God, are gifts. We do not choose God, but God chooses us. "Now that you have come to know God, or rather, to be known by God" (Gal 4:9 ESV). God's knowing of us precedes our knowing of him, and we find ourselves in his knowing of us.

There is a paradox here. In our culture, choice is central, and we appear to have much to choose from. Knowledge of everything starts with us, and we choose whichever lens we want with which to view the world—scientific, artistic, humanistic, Buddhist, Hindu, and so on. I am on a pivot and can turn whichever way I choose. But as I travel on each path in turn, I find that, from a center in myself, nothing can be validated, and without contact and reciprocation (as with a living God who answers), nothing known. I can have experiences, but I cannot know what they are. I really do not know whether the "God" of science, Hinduism, Islam, or Christianity is the same or different, because centered in myself, I have no measure, no means of triangulation. It has taken three hundred years to realize that, in making ourselves the center of knowledge in order to have secure knowledge about everything, of that which we most want to know, the purpose and origin of existence, we know nothing. It is a deeply held belief in our culture that beyond the horizon of the material world is a tract that is in principle unknowable, a white sheet of emptiness. As Wittgenstein famously said, "Whereof one cannot speak, thereof one must be silent."[6]

So we can be rich in choice and own nothing. Or we can be apparently poor in choice, putting the whole system of knowledge on its head, and end up having everything. As St. Paul said, "All things are yours . . . and you are Christ's, and Christ is God's" (1 Cor 3:2–3 ESV). All things are ours because we have been given them, and we have been given them because first we have been born. Choice does not begin with us. Conceived by the choice of others, we are placed in families, nations, languages, philosophies, and religions we did not choose, in a world we did not create, with talents we did not weigh out. In everything we know, we start from a given position and we reach a position that is limited by time, talent, and opportunity. And yet, if we will receive and allow God's person, God's word, and God's world to be disclosed to us, we can have "everything." Knowledge that is based on proof can leave us with nothing, as represented in much of the emptiness of contemporary art; knowledge that is based on reception can be endlessly

---

6. Wittgenstein, *Tractatus Logico-Philosophicus*, 188–89, quoted in Mascall, *Words and Images*, 45.

full. There is a kind of instinctive trust in the world that becomes an open door for art.

It would seem, then, that in our culture we have taken scientific knowledge to be the paradigm for knowing in general, forcing us to put the pressure of proof on every other area of knowledge. Art, which is a form of direct apprehension of reality, is therefore sidelined as not knowledge. But our situation is not such that we can rely on proof and know what we need to know. We need to go beyond the limitations of science and reconstruct the idea of knowledge as a gift to be enjoyed long before it is validated. Only then can we see if it has any relation to eternity.

II

In this second section, I want to look at a type of knowing that relates to art, one that is eternity based or "future proofed," and contrast it with a type of knowledge that is time based. Normal knowledge as we think of it (the accumulation of information) is achieved in time, and also (sadly) reduced by time. We "know" what we put into an exam paper one day; the next day we may have forgotten it and hence no longer "know" it. There is also knowledge that has been acquired by others, that can be accessed without memory, online or in books; but that also can be gained and lost. St. Paul tells us that knowledge (one assumes, a kind of head knowledge) is ephemeral: "Knowledge will pass away" (1 Cor 13:8 ESV). A friend of ours who knew a lot about butterflies went to be with the Lord two summers ago. His knowledge was a delight to him and to others while he lived on earth. Will the same knowledge, with English and Latin names, attach to him in heaven? It is hard to imagine it would; but that part of himself that he, so to speak, grew into, with its love of classification and joy in nature, will surely be with him forever.

These are speculations, but we can see that St. Paul is not at all threatened by the passing of knowledge. He looks forward to a different time-scale where he will "know fully," even as he is "fully known." This is surely a kind of knowledge that St. Paul has already experienced by being "fully known." This is different from the encyclopedic; it relies on being *in* a different place, where he can see what things are, in their depth of being as God sees them, and on being known *from* a different place, by God who can see who he is.

This other kind of knowing is the opposite of that which you can possess or independently operate. It depends on where you are and it involves being changed by where you are; you know "from" a new position. Before we even consider eternity, we find this commonly understood on the earthly plane. For example, a soldier who has been in battle knows what battle is like. Through contact with that reality he is no longer in the same "place" he was in before. In relation to the rest of reality, he has changed position. In history, it may be relevant that Hitler and Churchill (but not Chamberlain) both had experience on the battlefield; they were not just men, for better or worse, but warriors. More pacifically (we hope!), marriage is also a form of knowledge. Though outsiders can observe it, this knowing cannot exactly be had except from the inside (though Pope John Paul II did write a very perceptive play about marriage titled *The Jeweler's Shop* [1960]). To get married is to "know," by changing position, and from that position there is no reversion. Such knowledge is built into our characters. From "where we are," this knowing changes "who we are."

This does not yet take us to art, because art does not change us like war or marriage, but it does help us see how this kind of "positional" knowledge can survive time. We are who we have become through knowing. From a humanist perspective, of course, no part of us survives time except the works we leave behind. But in the New Testament the situation is reversed: death is not the full stop; it is not even the boundary because, in a real practical sense, eternity invades the present. St. Paul's thinking on this doubtless pervades all his teaching but in certain places it surfaces with particular clarity—one such is 2 Cor 4. In the context of present troubles, St. Paul writes,

> "That is why we never give up. Though our bodies are dying, our spirits are [literally, our "inner being is"][7] being renewed every day. For our present troubles are small and won't last very long. Yet they produce a glory that vastly outweighs them and will last forever! So we don't look at the troubles we can see now: rather we fix our eyes on things that cannot be seen. For the things we see now will soon be gone, but the things we cannot see will last forever" (2 Cor 4:16–18 NLT).

The "outer man" is decaying, but the "inner man" is being renewed, and it is the inner man that lasts. So something is being developed within—or is it through?—our bodies for eternity now. Not only that, but even our troubles can "produce a glory" in the life to come. There is a strong connection between life in the body and future life. It is not a direct translation of present life into future life but some kind of exchange, an exchange of the small coin of our troubles for the weighty currency of glory. St. Paul also goes on to talk, paradoxically, of seeing, of "fixing our eyes on," things that cannot be seen. In some way he is taking hold of ("seeing") things in eternity

---

7. 2 Cor 4:16, NLT, translator note.

and pulling them down to frame his life in time. So it is apparently possible to carry on valid operations drawing down the truths of eternity into time, presumably also with consequences in eternity. It is like a currency trader managing huge transactions overseas while seated with his phone at a café table. After all, Jesus told us to "lay up treasure in heaven" (Matt 6:20).

This is not, in some way, to deny our physical life here and now. Lest we should believe that the physical is somehow being denied in favor of the spiritual (which would certainly affect art), St. Paul goes on in the following chapter (2 Cor 5) to speak about our future bodies. "For we know that if the tent that is our earthly home is destroyed, we have a building from God, a house not made with hands, eternal in the heavens. For in this tent we groan, longing to put on our heavenly dwelling . . . so that what is mortal may be swallowed up by life" (2 Cor 5:1–4 ESV). As a traveller and tentmaker, Paul knew all too well what it was to live in a worn and possibly leaky tent and to look forward to staying in a house with solid walls; and as he looks at his own bodily infirmities and the transience of physical life, he looks forward in the same way to the *more* solid reality that is to come, "a building from God," a new body to dwell in. What is mortal (physical but subject to death) is to be "swallowed up" by life, perhaps rather as we put away a tent after a camping holiday and relax in solid furniture under a sound roof. What is remarkable about this passage is how strongly it counters the somewhat patronising and conceited assumption that our present physical world has some sort of priority in weight, reality, solidity, and materiality. For Paul, as he contemplates the life to come, the present reality is barely holding together.

This is not unimportant as we contemplate the survival of art, not just in eternity but also now. Art in the last fifty years has moved in a more and more gnostic direction, embarrassed by its own materiality and keen to shed it in favor of pure ideas. But if art is, as we have suggested, meaning embodied in form, as in the human body we understand spirit to be embodied in flesh, then it matters a great deal that physicality has a future. It is no doubt hard for us to grasp that we could be headed for a world that is still physical but will seem more real because it is not transient or subject to decay; but this is the world that invades St. Paul's present and utterly relativizes his present troubles and bodily afflictions. From our point of view these were hardly trivial! But Paul's strength is that he can dwell "from eternity" towards time and so allow a crossover of future reality into the present.

So, if knowledge "passes away," is there a kind of knowing that survives time? It would seem from Paul's account that, while factual knowledge may well pass, the knowledge of who he is, of "being known," with a "solid" future, not only survives into eternity but originates from eternity.

It is a crossover into time-based life of our eternal identity as known by God. If that is the case, we may have to find ourselves looking differently at the purpose of knowledge. If the purpose of our lives, and the purpose of redemption, is restored fellowship with God, then it matters a great deal in that relationship if we are aware not just of our real situation (in time, impregnated with eternity) but also of our true identity. How is it that art, from a platform on earth, can help with that?

III

The main assumption I want to make, in promoting the value of art, is that in our fallen, alienated condition, our identity is relatively weak and ill-formed. From this point of view, art could be a trap, holding up to us images that divert us from the truth and fixating us on false identities. What impresses on earth (the glory of man and woman, seen in art) may well not impress in heaven. But can we do without art? The arts also orient us and help us find our voice. For example, it matters how we address God because we must be genuine; but for this (unless we are to pray "with [our] spirit[s]" 1 Cor 14:15 ESV) we need language. Language, to be at all expressive, requires form. Coming to God in the deepest reality of our being ("a broken and a contrite heart, O God, you will not despise," Ps 51:17 ESV) means being broken hearted, but it also involves finding who we really are. Books, dramas, and paintings can all help us see ourselves in the truth.

An example can be found near at hand in almost any Psalm. The Psalms can give us a voice in every circumstance. Take just one verse as illustration: "Yet for your sake we are killed all the day long; we are regarded as sheep to be slaughtered" (Ps 44:22)—a scripture recollected by Paul in Rom 8:36, where he makes it a description of the normal life of Christ's followers. On the face of it, it is an extraordinary image. In the field outside our house we sometimes see lambs being loaded onto a truck for a final journey in which they have no say. It is not a great advertisement for the Christian life! And yet, if we treat it as a "situational" metaphor (that is, giving a situation we can think ourselves into and use as a lens by which to see life) it is remarkable how much of experience it articulates. Paul uses this picture to show us something of our Christian identity—the architecture of Christian existence, as it were—and from that vantage point we can see that certain experiences are neither random nor pointless.

When we address God, we need to "gather ourselves up," that is to stay, to situate ourselves honestly in our lives, selves, and circumstances and draw ourselves in, as if before our own hearth, from all the false identities and misleading influences into which we may have wandered. Reading a Psalm can tell us "this is who I am and where I am, and this is who God is," so that I may talk with him. In this instance, the message is "for your sake we are killed all the day long" and this imaginatively links the cause of Christ, for whose sake we die, with the "slaughter" that has come upon us. As St. Paul says in 1 Corinthians, "I die daily" (1 Cor 15:31 NASB). Whenever we are living for Christ, there is a death going on, either imposed from outside or internally towards our own self-will. A Psalm like this helps us "own" where we really are, without self-pity; and all because the Holy Spirit, through the author, chose to identify us with sheep.

I chose this image from Scripture because we expect the Bible to be transparent to the Spirit and to enable two-way communication with God. The Bible's stories and images "place" us: with Job we are troubled, with David in Ps 51 we are penitent, with Elijah at the brook we are exhausted and defeated, with Peter at Christ's trial we are fearful and ashamed—and all these positions allow us to find who we are at any time in relation to God. But in fact the same principles can be seen in our relationship with art. I say "can be" because first we should look at ways in which art can be anything but transparent to God.

The critical point is whether we use images, in the broadest sense, as transparent to the voice of God or whether we use them as a mirror. That is to say, we can use images as part of a three-way conversation or only for a two-way conversation; and in the latter lies the dangers of distortion. When we see a film, for example, we are aware that murder, adultery, betrayal, and theft may not be quite as glamorous as portrayed, however magnetically they are imaged for us. And yet, as we commune with the Spirit, we may find solid rock in underlying truths in a story, such as self-sacrifice and justice, which are seldom absent as filmmakers struggle to make their stories real.

But to see truth as "from God," and not something I simply absorb by osmosis through art, is a conscious act. Another art form with a strong message of identity is architecture. Today, for example, it is often possible to visit palaces and mansions made in the past for monarchs and the rich. It can be very pleasant to walk through ordered, spacious rooms filled with valuable paintings and furniture. So what do we do with this experience? If I am in a two-way conversation with the building, I might be tempted to envy, to think, "I am rather a fine fellow and this is the sort of environment I deserve," and, "How nice it would be to have hundreds of servants!" The building would act as a mirror of pride in my heart and could act as a symbol of a false identity. However, if I am in a three-way conversation that includes God, the very same building and experience could be a blessing. I could sense some of the worth that God has given me, the "spacious place"

(Ps 18:19 NIV) to which he has brought me, and know that for everyone to whom Christ has called, the Father has prepared a place that is perfectly fitting. "In my father's house are many mansions" (John 14:2 KJV). The point is not that we have any sense of entitlement to a heavenly palace, or even that we would want one. But it is that good architecture stirs up in us a sense of longing for places that "fit" us and to which we would belong; and for this our imaginations can take us far beyond our cramped homes, far beyond any mansion on earth, to the place that the Father has prepared for us. So, far from having envy towards the monarch who had so many builders to pay and servants to manage, our three-way conversation gives us a breath from God of a future state in which everything will be beautiful and good, and in that moment, we have taken a step inside eternity.

It will be noted that this is a physical experience, in space and time, coordinated with biblical truth. It is the actual sensations offered our sight and bodies that arouse the longing to which the Spirit of God, through the Scriptures, responds. We are not "just anywhere" having a spiritual experience, but it is a particular environment that forms a particular feeling that becomes a question, Does God know me in this way?

In certain spaces we feel more fully ourselves and in these our imaginations can be stirred to see ourselves as God sees us. This has always been known in the natural environment and many Christians find it necessary from time to time to retreat from disordered, ugly, or chaotic environments to gardens, open nature, and mountains to meet with God and pray, following the example of Christ. But it is also striking how much space the Scriptures give to the beauty of the man-made environment in the construction of the tabernacle and temple. To Protestant minds, the laborious detail spread over many chapters describing woven curtains, garments, and bronze instruments can be tedious because we have to make such an effort of imagination to value things that, in our own church buildings, would undoubtedly be considered a "waste of money." It is true that, in Israel's history, there was no inevitable, instrumental relationship between beauty of form and worship from the heart; and Christ himself dismissed his disciples' admiration of Herod's temple with the abrupt prophecy, "There shall not be left one stone upon another" (Mark 13:1–2 KJV). Beauty can only designate God's presence, if God's presence also has a human home. Nonetheless, if we fully understand what it means that the design and beauty of the tabernacle and temple came from God, not just through the design given to Moses (Heb 8:5) but by the Spirit given to Bezalel (Exod 31:3)—we will see that all beauty and culture is meant to be from God, about God. In as far as it is created by people, it represents an apprehension by inspired making of divine truth that is already there.

At this point, we may well have drawn the conclusion that if we will attach ourselves to what is clearly divinely inspired, such as the art in the Scriptures, or to the best of art and architecture, and to nature, we may well through dialogue with God find our voice, and be more established in who we are. We trust and believe that experiences of this kind—of mountains, or cathedrals, or inspired verse—will act like a key and unlock different parts of ourselves in God's presence.

No one will fault us, I think, for being this selective, for God's word itself commands us to "come out from them . . . be separate . . . touch nothing unclean" (2 Cor 6:17 RSV) and "keep yourselves from idols" (1 John 5:21 RSV). And it is true that secular culture has tried to explore everything except what St. Paul recommends as our focus in Phil 4:8: "whatever is true, whatever is honorable, whatever is just, whatever is pure, whatever is lovely" (ESV). However it is important not to deceive ourselves, thinking we can avoid art. When we looked at the Enlightenment inheritance, we saw that art can seem an option, an addition to normal, neutral viewing. It is very easy for Christians to step back into thinking, "Culture is complex, let us just leave it alone." But the place of neutral judgment is an illusion. We are in culture, whether we like it or not. The only question is, Does it master us, or is it part of the "all things" under our feet (Ps 8:6)?

I must admit, if I may speak personally, that I myself do not adopt the "immersive" approach to culture as much as perhaps I might. I am too aware that the membrane between the world and my soul is thin. However, true art makes epistemological bridges that are open to all to cross. And with the "three-way conversation" that I have spoken of, I do not need to be as selective as I once was because I am learning to see things in their place.

I am intrigued by two statements in Scripture, both describing an "immersive" education in pagan culture. Moses, Stephen tells us, "was instructed in all the wisdom of the Egyptians" (Acts 7:22 ESV). And to Daniel, put to study with Babylonian astrologers and wise men, "God gave . . . learning and skill in all literature and wisdom" (Dan 1:17 ESV). This pattern has been seen since in the education of many Christian leaders, of which Augustine, deeply educated in pagan philosophy and culture before his conversion, would be a noted example, or C. S. Lewis, in our own time. What is so striking in the Scripture passages is that this education in the wealth of pagan learning is clearly understood not as a terrible mistake to be cleansed from the body like drugs but as the gift of God. And yet Moses and Daniel were men who both knew God in an especially direct way. Where was the need for this education and culture?

Reviewing the path of intellectual history and culture, with its false religions, idolatries, heresies, and misleading byways in philosophy, all of them manifested in art, it is hard not to wish to retreat into cave-like simplicity with the word of God alone. But that, sadly, is to start in the wrong place, because the world and the word are inseparable. We cannot sheer off "word" from the world it refers to. This also works the other way. We cannot draw off the world's wisdom without the Word to guide us. As we said earlier, if we try to use education to reach God, we will never do it, and it is better not to try.

But if we see education and art as from God, we find ourselves in a very different story. We need to go back to St. Paul's vision of eternity. For him, future reality is more solid (that is, more material, in a sense) than this present age, which is subject to decay. Since that is the case, and matter, in eternity, is still something we shall be dealing with, then the question still remains, How shall we fashion it? How can we make what is there speak more of the glory of God? If God, who is unchanging, has given us now on this earth minds to understand, abilities—through art and language—to articulate ideas, and bodies to fashion matter, how much more in this new world he has prepared for us? But we can also read that back into this life. However deeply misled were the educators in Egypt and Babylon, their knowledge came through study of the world. Moses and Daniel were taught to think and to articulate knowledge through the best teachers of their day, and this was the gift of God. Understanding, perceiving, and embodying ideas, through all the arts, is a gift that makes us more fully who we are. The focus is on God, who, in bringing many sons to glory (Heb 2:10), has equipped us to lead authentic lives. We do not see what we are laying up in eternity, but we do know that if understanding and beauty are from God, these gifts from him, even if accessed through all the trials of earthly arts and education, may make us just a little bit more like himself.

9

Christianity and Culture
Questions Raised by Ruskin[1]

The Barrier

There is a famous autobiographical essay by Ruskin recounting his visit to an ugly[2] little Waldensian church outside Turin, where the minister, preaching

---

1. The original version of this essay was written in February 2012.

2. On reviewing Ruskin's account, I realize that "ugly" is what is implied, rather than stated; it is what one sees in one's mind's eye. The full passage reads,

> There [Turin], one Sunday morning, I made my way in the south suburb to a little chapel which, by a dusty roadside, gathered to its unobserved door the few sheep of the old Waldensian faith who had wandered from their own pastures under Monte Viso into the worldly capital of Piedmont [that is, Turin].
>
> The assembled congregation numbered in all some three or four and twenty, of whom fifteen or sixteen were grey-haired women. Their solitary and clerkless preacher, a somewhat stunted figure in a plain black coat, with a cracked voice, after leading them through the languid forms of prayer which are all that in truth are possible to people whose present life is dull and its terrestrial future unchangeable, put his utmost zeal into a consolatory discourse on the wickedness of the wide world, more especially of the plain of Piedmont and the city of Turin, and on the exclusive favour with God, enjoyed by the between nineteen and twenty-four elect members of his congregation, in the streets of Admah and Zeboim [cities adjacent to Sodom and Gomorrah, see Genesis 10:19].
>
> Myself neither cheered nor greatly alarmed by this doctrine, I walked back into the condemned city, and up into the gallery where Paul Veronese's Solomon and the Queen of Sheba glowed in full afternoon light. The gallery windows being open, there came in with the warm air, floating swells and falls of military music, from the courtyard before the palace, which seemed to me more devotional, in their perfect art, tune, and discipline, than anything I remembered of evangelical hymns. And as the perfect colour and sound gradually asserted

CHRISTIANITY AND CULTURE

to his small and elderly congregation, vilified the practices and lifestyle (in a word, the culture) of the city, and magnified the virtues of the elect, his own gathered adherents. This was a tipping point for Ruskin. Later in the day he looked at the glorious color of Veronese in the Turin gallery and heard the joyful sounds of a band playing outside; and, reflecting that according to Protestant theology both painter and bandsmen were destined for hell, something in him broke. He realized that art was transparently more on the side of life—at least of any sort of life he was committed to—than was the church: that is to say, his church, the right church, the Protestant church, with the right doctrine and the right to say who was saved and who was damned. From that moment, he determined to have nothing to do with it.

This life-changing fork in the road was to do with aesthetics, a steady build up of revulsion towards everything ugly and life denying, and with the realization for him that ugly and life-denying religion could not claim to be "better than" the world of the senses represented by Veronese, just because it believed it owned a patent on the method of salvation. The judgment he made was that what did not look and feel like life could not honestly be said to have the door to life.

This experience of Ruskin's is bothersome because it is so recognizable. Let me add some reminiscences of my own, more than a hundred years later. A sermon I heard, in a not-so-pretty Victorian church building, recalled a holiday in Switzerland where our evangelical vicar had visited two churches. One had been Protestant, plain and white, the other Catholic, gilded, carved, and painted with scenes of heaven and angels. There was something wistful in his account, for as a theologian, he could not think of any objection to depicting the things of heaven in church, even though his senses and traditions might have been offended. On the contrary, the notion of a space where heaven and earth were shown as flowing together intrigued him greatly. His sermon described these scenes so vividly that thirty years later I can still picture them. He did not deny the virtues of the white church,

---

their power over me, they seemed finally to fasten in me the old article of Jewish faith, that things done delightfully and rightly, were always done by the help and in the Spirit of God.

Of course that hour's meditation in the gallery of Turin only concluded the courses of thought which had been leading me to such end through many years. There was no sudden conversion possible to me, either by preacher, picture, or dulcimer. But that day, my evangelical beliefs were put away, to be debated of no more. Ruskin, *Praeterita*, 36–38.

I am reminded of Bishop Lesslie Newbigin's words: "There is something deeply repulsive in the attitude, sometimes found among Christians, which makes only grudging acknowledgement of the faith, the godliness, and the nobility to be found in the lives of non-Christians." Newbigin, *Pluralist Society*, 180.

for it was, in its own plain way, elegant. But though it had some positive virtues, to do with purity and absence of distraction, its main meaning was negative. Simplicity carried a meaning of what it was not—not florid, therefore, not Catholic. The plainness was an investment in "not-ness." But negativity in art, though quite common (like Loos's "ornament is crime"),[3] is also strangely deficient. It entirely avoids answering the question: What should the house of God look like in a positive way?

Another church, in a small Essex town, is our next scene. Unlike Ruskin's experience, here the preaching was entirely generous. But to hear it was to surmount a considerable barrier. The outside of the church in prefabricated concrete required a very special sort of person to enter—someone completely desperate! No shop or home would present you with such an unlovely exterior: tidy and painted, it is true, but poor, loveless, and crude. Like some army boot camp, it seemed designed to filter out all but the toughest. We still happily went to it for two years. The inside, incidentally, was clean, bright, and cheerful.

Our next scene is a church I elected not to go to. This was an evangelical church in a prosperous Midlands city, well funded, with a long shiny wooden cross, colored windows, and the sort of curtains you stare at just wishing there was something else to think about. Its style was modernist church-y; that is to say, it was not in a style you would build anything else in, at least, not anything that you would hope to like; it had things like exaggeratedly long windows and a thin spire and pieces of slate embedded in the exterior that were supposed to look artistic, climaxing in a crazy-paving-effect wall backing the sanctuary area. The church people were a thoroughly decent lot, with pleasant homes, furnished and friendly, but on Sundays they braved their way through this battlefield bleakness for the joy of hearing something of God's word.

What is true of these buildings could be multiplied hundreds of times: the "true gospel," countrywide, is associated with ugly, crude, or neglected buildings. If you are a believer, you are one who has learned to find the treasure in the earthen vessel, the nobility of the people behind their depleted culture, and life beyond the crude posters and peeling paint; or perhaps you are a little proud that none but the hardiest would think of entering. But undoubtedly a barrier has been created, deliberately or unintentionally. Is it not unmannerly to create secret havens, appealing only to the initiated?

---

3. Adolph Loos wrote an article "Ornament and Crime" (1908), published in *Trotzdem, 1900–1930* (Pevsner, *Pioneers of Modern Design*, 222). The popular phrase deriving from Loos is reflected in the book title *Ornament Is Crime: Modernist Architecture*, written by Matt Gibberd and Albert Hill.

Why would we not take Ruskin's course and simply abandon the whole style and all its theology as foolishness?

The Defense

In Britain, at least, taste is a very sensitive matter. Rich people have choice and delight in discrimination. Poor people have little choice and their churches show it. Poor materials often disguise great thankfulness for something rather than nothing. Poverty can be a proudly worn badge, when seen alongside the favor of God, as it shows how willingly God adopts the meek. We cannot judge individual cases. People do the best they can, often with very little, but sometimes with much. I recently visited a Jesuit church in Poland, the epitome of baroque excess with one of the largest painted ceilings in Europe. "Who paid for it?" I asked. "The Emperor of Austria." Not many churches have imperial wealth behind them.

However, the conditions of poverty most people understand well. Ruskin, of all people, was no snob; he who delighted in the primitive art of primitive ages would never have demanded the impossible from uneducated people. What aroused his ire was something else: the suspicion that ugliness was a style, a taste, something adopted out of conviction and held to with determination.

It is possible, of course, that ugliness is merely the external face of a heart of love. We have known many churches where such is the preoccupation with the things of the Spirit and the care for the poor that externals of style and building are simply not noticed. Does a shabby overcoat matter if it keeps you warm?

But it is also possible, given that the tradition of aesthetic neglect is perhaps a couple of centuries old, that there is something less accidental at its heart. Either we have then a true gospel with a false face, or, as Ruskin seems to have thought, the true face of a doctrine that is so hideous that it cannot be the gospel. What might the black heart of this doctrine be?

The simplest way to see what could be at stake is to imagine what the world would be like if these churchmen were in charge. Suppose the festive, brightly colored, and artistic life available as a "temptation" in the world simply did not exist because the church had extended its rule right across society. Suppose the "godly" had so promoted lack of imagination and joyful freedom that only their brand of somber conformity was allowed to exist. We do know of societies where such rigor has been promulgated—the England of Cromwell or the Afghanistan of the Taliban. The point at issue, of course, is not the fashion for black but the exercise of power. The root of negativity is not neglect or poverty but control. This is not complicated to understand: limits are put on freedom because of fear of what freedom might produce. It is not just bad things that need limiting but also good; because it is the good things that culture generates—humor, the arts, acts of mercy—that show up the poverty of spirit of those in control. Unrecognized by them, their instinct to shut down on freedom, the kind of unpredictable flowering that we call "creativity," is exactly contrary to the gospel. The gospel is a restoration of creativity—that is to say, a bringing of the world back to the life it might have if evil did not have it by the neck.

So there may very well be a false gospel hidden in the heart of supposed doctrinal correctness. Quite possibly there was, in the chapel Ruskin visited, and in others like it, a subtle slander on God, that he does not really like people outside the elect and that even his friends need to be kept under strict control. But these things are inevitably difficult to assess; impressions can be false, people can be misunderstood, and judgment must often be suspended. What we cannot doubt, however, is that culture and preaching, the form in which the message comes, cannot be detached from each other. Whatever people hear will be modified by what they see, the manner in which it is given. There is no exit from culture. Choices have to be made. The prime minister (at the time of writing, David Cameron) apparently used to dress in country tweeds (aligning with a certain group of people) and now dresses more plainly and anonymously; he cannot do both at once, but he must wear something—and every costume conveys a signal. Christians are no different. What they do is "read." If religious people go for "plain culture," this may be read advantageously, and people might think that "not decorative = not worldly = spiritual." But then they might not. They may simply read "plain and ugly" as plain and ugly.

Sadly, wrong decoding can also happen in reverse. A church building that has had every attention lavished on its design, whether a gilded baroque chapel or a Victorian re-creation of Gothic, can easily be "read" not in spiritual terms at all but as some kind of manipulation practised on the viewer or as a lavish expense in a time of poverty. Cultural signals are invariably ambiguous.

So we are left with a dilemma. Efforts to convey positive messages within a culture may well be misunderstood, but to do nothing also conveys a message—of cultural apathy at the very least. However, if we are not to misrepresent Christ by our appearance and habits, then the question of culture must be approached. This cannot be done prescriptively, because every circumstance is different. For example, some Christians are rich and almost cannot help making money. For them to dress in cheap clothes would risk the appearance of meanness. Others are poor, and their beauty may be in character rather than in cut and weave. But however we live, cultural choices are being made, and are part of the whole message of our lives.

Renouncing, Consuming, Making

We could look at the Christian's interaction with culture in three areas. There are the things we renounce (the films we do not watch, the luxuries we can manage without). The value of these is mostly between us and God and can be very confusing to outsiders. Some renunciations they will admire, while others may frustrate or annoy them. Sometimes those outsiders will keep our conscience better than we can ourselves and be fully aware of what we should not be doing. But the main impact of lives will be by what we do, rather than what we do not do.

Second, there are the things we consume. This is the culture we do not make but go along with. Here again our choices may confuse. An obscene film may be very instructive or even of spiritual value but, to someone else, inexcusable as a form of entertainment. The issue here is that we have no control over the cultural product, only over how we receive it. In architectural history, the classical style might be for one person Roman and pagan and for another a sign of Christ's victory over Rome. The original was not Christian, but by reception (some think) it may become so. It is wonderful to have the freedom to enjoy and ingest cultural products of all kinds, from kitsch to popular to high art; but if we see and understand them under the banner of the cross but do not explain it, no one is to know.

So that leaves the third interaction with culture: the culture we make. People are not necessarily aware that they make culture. A meal is very quickly eaten and washed up; but the love and care in the selection and preparation of food leaves a lasting sense of well-being. Likewise with the care we bring into our homes: it is something we are scarcely conscious of in the daily tidying but it adds up and can make a welcoming place of joy.

But there is also a directly made culture that is the work of specialists, people who have special gifts and training to be writers, musicians, and artists, which can be embraced by Christians. In all communities there are specialists in the arts, of course; but it is notable that the Bible also takes particular account of certain trained and gifted people. To this training something is also added. In Exodus we read that these individuals were given, in order to make the tabernacle, a particular endowment of wisdom and of God's own spirit (Exod 35). To put that another way: it is seen in the Bible that to take an artist of exceptional merit and skill and apply him to a work of God *without an endowment of God's Spirit* would be to invite failure, work that was lacking in essentials.

Possibly this is more important than we normally realize. So far we have seen that "bad culture," the culture of lack, crudeness or insulting ugliness, can turn people away from Christ or at least signal something other than his Spirit. But we have also seen that cultural signals are often ambiguous and that the best efforts may have unexpected results, as in the harsh reactions that people have to Victorian church restorations, despite the pious motives behind them. We cannot directly "do culture" for the sake of other people.

Culture Towards God

It seems to me there is something we miss in our discussions of culture, and that is the vertical dimension. If it is true that "bad culture" puts people off Christ, how are we to be sure that the "good culture" we attempt to replace it with is not itself "bad culture"? In any case, we do not want to become actors on a stage, trying to have the right "look" for our audience. If we are hypocrites (actors), and perpetrate anything that does not come from the inside, we are at the very least in danger of bad art, and at the worst, of manipulation by appearances. Others' likes and dislikes are also ephemeral and a poor guide for making real art. For that we need something deeper and stronger. But claims to work "vertically" under the inspiration of God are surely inviting self-deception. How can we make this notion have practical meaning?

At present I have only the hint of a thought about this, but it is something to start with. Where the gospel can go sour is when we think of it as a "thing," a message, a baton which we take and run with; this idea is not wrong but it is incomplete, because it misses God in, through, and with us. It leaves us with a sense of "doing," and of ways and means, all of which may be good, but their emphasis is horizontal and we can easily neglect the heart, the love, the reason we are doing it all. That approach might well be termed "functional": the emphasis is on whether it "works." It can be blind to grace, to the activity of God in redemption, working with us or even despite what we do. It goes well with functional building and a functionalist aesthetic. Though Ruskin's Waldensian chapel long predated functionalism, there is a kind of coldness represented by what it stood for, which could be part of the stream leading to modernism, in which everything is calculated according to "need."

But there is also a place of healing for this functionalism, and that is when we begin to connect Christ as Redeemer, of whom we are sure, with Christ as Creator, who is perhaps less understood. From him, we are told, flows everything that is good in the world. It follows that if our "direction" is not just horizontal, to obey his commands towards our fellow humans, but vertical, to be like him, then we shall be much more openhearted to the profuse and diverse life that the Creator originated. Better still, we shall be actually in touch with his Spirit when we work creatively. It is of course costly to care about good and fine things, because it is to wear your heart on your sleeve. The woman who bathed Jesus' feet with expensive perfume[4] endured much hostility for that simple act because it broke all the boundaries of what was considered appropriate worship. It was too "costly" and "unnecessary." But her display of faith, by contrast with the frigid religiosity of those who thought they lived by the rules, was warmly human, original, fearless, and affectionate, a pattern for the creative act.

We need to keep in mind Christ's goal of restoration of the whole creation. We have got very good at treating the creation as a resource and subjugating it under what is man made, so that even nature starts to look industrial; but in making everything "useful" we easily forget to ask, For what? What is the totality of life meant to be? Human beings have been placed in the creation with astonishing gifts of making the world even more beautiful, of ordering it by buildings, gardens, and art, with a visual language of appreciation that ultimately honors the Creator. As we keep this in mind, we need also to have not just our minds but our hearts unlocked, to know that responding to beauty and even to make it are not diversions from "the task"; they are part of the Creator's loving plan for what he made.

So how, then, would we try to answer Ruskin today? That there is such a thing as a legalistic, loveless, bad-news gospel sometimes to be encountered in our churches, we can agree (though I would not know where to find it); and such would of course be hostile to all art. But we might also gently point out that when the loveless Mr. Ruskin encountered the loveless Waldensian preacher, we really do not know which of them had the best of it. The great critic may have missed something and seen what he expected to see. There is a case for arguing, and many churches would, that spiritual encounters are not conditioned by culture and that there is a mysterious cut-off point between our cultural ambitions, whether generous and artistic or mean and crude, and the transforming life of God.

---

4. See Matt 26:6–13, Mark 14:3–9, Luke 7:36–50, and John 12:1–8. There are variations in the accounts.

However, we have also seen that culture cannot be avoided. While its signals can be ambiguous or misleading, and its reception impossible to control, we are in culture whether we like it or not and have a choice as to whether our manner of life, in our homes or in our worship, is gracious and inviting or standoffish and unwelcoming. Here we have some sympathy for the young Ruskin. He did not want to hear everything he believed in, the best of art and music, evangelical or not, hammered from the pulpit. Would it not have done him good to enter a space with visible signs of the "abundant life" Jesus promised, and which celebrated human culture, for all its failings, as signs of how life was intended to be?

10

Art and the Church[1]

The question I want to discuss is why it is that the evangelical church is willing to employ art as something useful to the gospel, but is reluctant to embrace art as art. I realize a lot, perhaps too much, is assumed in that sentence and will try to define my terms.

By "evangelical church" I mean that body of Christians striving to read Scripture with an open mind and as far as possible follow its precepts. It is a body that does not, of course, come to Scripture without presuppositions. But within its tradition and society there is freedom to try to correct what has been passed down. For evidence of this, we need look no further than the huge reevaluation of art that has occurred particularly since Francis Schaeffer and Hans Rookmaaker in the 1960s and 1970s. Artists are now openly supported and encouraged in the churches and their gifts are no longer treated with suspicion. However it still seems true that for a "culture of art" within the church we would have to look more to the liberals. Evangelicals are not natural aesthetes. (I do not attempt to speculate here why liberals are empathetic with art. But if it is recent art, then the liberal culture of tolerance does make liberals vulnerable to cultural pressure. One wishes there were some clear criteria rather than openness to whatever is pushing at the door.)

Next, we need to look at the contrast between seeing art as useful to the gospel and treating art as art. This distinction begs many questions, but if we peel away the layers, I hope we will see a real issue. It is not that art has to be "use-less." The church historically always patronized art when it was useful. The pages of the Bible were translated into stained glass pictures,

---

1. The original version of this essay was written in February 2011.

carvings, and altarpieces, all of which reminded worshippers of the body of truth to which they belonged. Today the idea that we look at these things as "works of art" seems quite detached and artificial, a bit like looking at food as something to admire but not to eat. The way we usually see art, and even produce it, has much to do with museums and the way we have learned to relate to the objects in them. So one can hardly criticise the evangelical church for wanting art that serves the message it proclaims. Any art (including film, fiction, poetry) it promotes must sit within the gospel of the lordship of Christ and allow God's Spirit to speak through it.

"Art for art's sake" is a comparatively recent concept and has always risked cutting art off from the connections—particularly with power and money—that have done most historically to make it happen. It also risks covering up the ambition of the artist who wants to make a name or at least express the vision of his or her art; so that, in fact, art is seldom just for art's sake. So why is it that we still need to claim something for art that is beyond the merely useful?

The distinction I think we need to make is not between useful art and art for art's sake. We have agreed that you can have good art that is useful. It is more between art that is allowed to be what art is and art that is limited by being seen only in an operational sense. The most obviously useful art form is advertising. Sometimes it reaches a high degree of creativity, excellence, and sheer delight in originality. Yet essentially it has a purpose, to communicate an idea from mind A to public B. The success of the advertisement is measurable by the correspondence between what A wishes to be understood and what B receives. Many of us look at art like that. Possibly this is a model for how art is seen in the churches. And there is truth in this view. It is a poor artist who is unable to say what they want to say or show what she has seen.

However there is a difference between art and advertising. In advertising, the message is permanently linked to the item advertised. If there is no Marmite, there is no message. The advertisement has nothing to say about anything else. There is little else to feed on in the advert if you cannot buy the product. But art is multivalent. It is not just one idea from the mind of the artist, but it is about some thing, a chunk of reality seen in the round that can be understood and approached in different ways. The artist perceives it but does not always understand it. What is conveyed is often bigger than what is known. The artist sends it out into the world, but it is more than a message from his mind, dependent on him for explanations, as if always on hand to back up his checks with cash in the bank. The work of art, if it succeeds, is cash. It contains its own truth, which the artist has put there, laboring until it is complete.

This distinction between art that is a message and art that is truth seen in the round explains some of the historical tensions between the church and artists. The church commissions a "Madonna." The artist's model for Mary looks remarkably like his mistress. The artist has already gone "off message." So perhaps the artist is required to find a model who is chaste and saintly. This would seem controllable by the commissioner. However, if the artist is not to produce mere propaganda, he must enter into personal observation of what it means to be a young woman in the world and this may take him far from anything prescribed. Relationships are free. If his "Mary" is to live as art, she must seem like a rounded human being, someone personally envisioned by the artist, whom no theologian could devise. Once seen, she will have meaning for people as Mary, as a girl, as a mother, and in other, unforeseen ways, according to how much truth of life her image contains.

The relationship between the true artist and the church cannot—which perhaps is obvious—be that of executive and executant. The artist needs to be trusted because he or she has to go beyond what is prescribed. But the artist can rightly be trusted only if he or she is a participator in the truth, fully sharing in its roundedness along with those who commission the work. In other words, the truth itself must not be an instruction or message but must be a wider vision that can be inhabited and shared by both patron and artist.

This brings us full circle to the question of evangelicals and art. How do we read the Bible? Do we see it as a series of messages from God to ourselves, instructions for us to follow "to the letter"? If so, that is what we will want our art to be. Or do we see it more as truth to be "indwelt," a thought world we inhabit from which motivation and obedience come? Probably these are not hard and fast alternatives. In the heat of the battle, one needs to know the mind of the commander, one's position in the army, and have precise instructions to hand. But clearly the artist is more than a dispatch rider. To communicate, he needs the bigger picture and to understand it from the inside. In biblical language, the artist has to operate not so much as a servant, fetching and carrying, but more as a son, knowing the father's heart.

It would take a different sort of study to characterise the ways we use the Bible. At our worst, I believe we detach it from the lips of God our Savior and from the breath of God our Counsellor. As such, it can be impersonal, heartless, and merely legal. This does not create a good atmosphere for art. Art must feel free to see things and say things, all within the context of acceptance. This freedom is provided by the gospel. This does not mean that art strikes off on its own, judging the church or trying to command it. It is within the body that artists receive their truth. But it does mean that art is, in its essence, not susceptible to control. The work of art goes where it will. It has to engage with truth from within. The security of the church is that the artist belongs (and that it does not have to like what the artist does). The church leader is an instructor in truth, but also a sharer in truth, and needs to be willing to receive what the artist gives.

The modern church has been characterized by instrumental language: for example, "That woman has been much used by God," "My gifts are used by God," or, "That church has been used by God to bring revival." More recently we have allowed that God might also take pleasure in his children (Psalm 149:4). When we think, primarily, of the arts being "used," we intend to bless them with our favor. But instead our language and intentions send a chill upon gifts that are not just useful but good in themselves, just as we are not only useful but loved in ourselves. We must not forget that it was Judas who thought that beauty was a waste of money (John 12:3–5). God's dwelling in the desert was designed according to his own instructions as the most beautiful, extravagant tent ever created. So when the evangelical church considers its art, it must know that while it may be useful, to adorn truth and make places appealing, it is much more than that. In accommodating art, and hopefully buying it, the church should be getting more than it has bargained for.

11

The Holy Spirit in Art[1]

When Francis Schaeffer and Hans Rookmaaker[2] began to shake up the way Christians looked at art, some fifty years ago, they provided an invaluable tool: world-view analysis. Instead of feeling intimidated or "got at" by works of art, Christians were now able to adopt a position of detachment. No longer subjected to feelings, or the lack of them, they could interpret works of art as messages that could be expressed in words, representing particular philosophies. For example, Impressionism could be decoded under the label "Positivism," the philosophy that says we can never know what things are, only the sense data that come to us. Something of Impressionism's insubstantiality, combined with its strange confidence in the sufficiency of what we know, seems to have been captured by this reference to a French philosophy of the mid-nineteenth century. And so, the thought goes, "We know where we are with Impressionism." It is "philosophy in paint." Moreover it is philosophy that is (perish the thought) bad theology. It does not trust that we can know, beyond our sense impressions, that the world was created, and is sustained, by God. Therefore, the radical conclusion runs (not that anyone would say it), "Impressionism is wrong." Oddly enough, however, Impressionist pictures are still out there making points of contact with viewers, and Christians are scarcely behind the unbelievers in enjoying them. Clearly the "philosophy" in a work is not the whole story.

For viewers this may be important, but for artists it is even more so, for, while it is true that a worldview or philosophy is manifest in a work,

1. The original version of this essay was written after seeing the Millennium Exhibition in St. Andrew's Church, Oxford, October 2000.

2. Rookmaaker's arrestingly original *Modern Art and the Death of a Culture* was published in 1970.

it is very difficult to work the process the other way around, to start with a worldview and then devise a work of art. And yet we have sometimes given the impression that a Christian artist should operate like this. Find the correct philosophy, then make the work, and, presumably, do not make the work until you have found the philosophy, or perfect theology. This approach could be slightly inhibiting. But there is much more going on in works of art besides their philosophy (as Schaeffer and Rookmaaker would have known well). There is, at the least, a kind of grace operating when the artist, brush in hand, whatever his or her philosophy, is somehow in contact with the life of the world. And there is a point of contact with the viewer that is not attained through a "detached" posture. The direct, emotional point of contact with a painting, the electrical discharge that jumps on you unexpectedly, the impression that crosses your threshold as a guest, uninvited and unnamed, but somehow welcome—these experiences need not be invalid or always "dangerous" for the Christian soul. Indeed, it is at this level that the work of art first starts to function. But here it is appropriate to speak less of a work's philosophy than of its "spirit."

Inevitably, to speak of the "spirit" of a work is going to sound nebulous. However, as Christians we should have a very precise notion of what our spirits are, and of what we can do with them. In Rom 8, St. Paul tells us that our spirits are "alive because of righteousness" (v. 10). That is to say, the true, created, motive force in us, the stream from which flows our enthusiasms, loves, hates, and decision making, has been switched on. And in principle the primal energies that used to motivate us have been switched off and are treated by God as dead, even though they seem to twitch rather vigorously. "Though your bodies are dead because of sin, your spirits are alive because of righteousness" (Rom 8:10 ESV). The appetites which used to drive us, which are doomed along with our physical bodies, have had the plug pulled on them. The art that we do now comes from a new center, an alive spirit.

When writers discuss the spirit of a work of art, outside that alive Christian spirit, I am never quite sure how to place it, as a pre-Christian spirit, in terms of St. Paul's picture. Does all non-Christian art come from dead flesh? When one reads modern art historical accounts of it, where everything is explained away in terms of the artists' and patrons' politics and worldly motivations, it might be quite reasonable to think so! But I like to think that there is a surplus, some point of contact with the world that makes the work endure as art, which has some connection with the human spirit, perhaps enlightened by God in a limited way. Referring again to Impressionism, what lasts, for example, in Monet, is what he saw, not what he failed to see. The paintings go beyond what the painter knew or understood, and that is, in its way, a form of worship. His human spirit must have been involved in this painful and devoted reaching out beyond himself, and yet one might feel that there is a lack of full connectedness to the meaning of what he saw. For Christians there is always the invisible presence of relationship, where there is, not just "the artist and the landscape" as an ever-tense duality, but the sense of the artist as "with" the given creation in the gracious presence of God.

This gives the clue to the essence of the Christian spirit. It is hard to pin down in itself, because it is defined by the relationship that colors it, affects, and empowers it, the relationship to the Holy Spirit. Being defined by relationship, it also has the quality of being unbounded. It is not limited by what a human personality can know and do. If it is open to the Holy Spirit, it is necessarily going to let in and be moved by a Person beyond itself—at the very least, by the wisdom of God.

This might seem slightly unfair, and indeed it is. It is doubly unfair that Christian artists should be able to access a wisdom beyond themselves, in that the gift is completely free and not just given to those artists of particular skill and talent; though we should not assume that the Holy Spirit is not interested in skill and talent (rather the reverse, as in the account in Exodus of Bezalel and Oholiab). But the emphasis, nonetheless, is on what that skill and talent articulates, which is something from God himself. Now how are we to identify this?

I was reflecting on this after an all-too-brief visit to the Millennium Exhibition at St. Andrew's, Oxford, earlier this year. Around a display of some very fine carvings by Nicholas Mynheer were paintings by a trio of artists who have established themselves as among the most confident and integrated exponents of Holy Spirit truth that this country has perhaps seen for many years. Mark Cazalet showed a series of twelve pen and ink drawings of incidents in the life of Christ, set in Provence, as well as a painting of *In the Eden Motel*, in which our first parents were shown in modern dress, or, more correctly, undress, in modern surroundings. I did not altogether understand the meaning, but Mark certainly has a remarkable ability to make a biblical subject substantial and real, as if Adam and Eve were his own relations and he knew, when painting them, what their lives were about. This was particularly true of the Christ scenes, where, in a moment, he seemed to have traveled through pen-work of trees, hills, and light and shade into the peaceful presence of the Lord, seen reading a book under a tree or walking with his disciples amid the beehives. Roger Wagner displayed a great triptych of the story of Ruth and Boaz, also hovering somewhere between biblical and modern ages, with oil drums and telegraph posts not seeming out of place in the utterly biblical stillness. This was a picture of meetings and relationships, predestined, momentous in consequence, yet humbly and meekly arrived at.

Let us step back a bit, and ask ourselves what these two artists are doing. They are interpreting the Bible, the book which is our Book, about which we have our own opinions and interpretations. Yet what they are doing is more than just a "view," as when we see a favorite novel interpreted on television, and find the characters, faces, and places do not fit what we have visualized. What they are attempting to do is to get through to the place where the Bible text is itself timeless, speaking out of its own authority to every situation. But to do that they must get beyond a personal view. I believe they do, but one is tempted to ask, where do they get all this stuff from? Is this not presumptuous of them? Well, in theory it could be, and I am sure they would be the first not to claim too much for what they do. But is not the logic of being Christian artists that they should get this "stuff" from the Lord himself? If their works have any authority, I believe we should not be inhibited about accrediting that authority to the Spirit within them.

The third painter, Richard Kenton Webb, displayed a series of abstracts that were vertical strips, painted all over in rhythmical movements and titled with prophetic names, such as *Yoking* and *The Garments*, with the whole entitled *The Time of Preparation*. Alongside the series, a video was shown of Richard painting them, in which it was made clear that his paintings were direct responses not only to his own prophetic insight but to a piece of music written by Helen Graham. One might think that these abstract paintings would make this notion of spiritual authority harder to account for. Yet it was Richard's abstracts that first gave me the clear sense that "there is more than something personal here: this is authority." We must leave on one side the tempting question, Is this great art? We would of course love to know whether one day such paintings will be on display next to Pollock and other precursors. And it is not an irrelevant question, because if there is enough of the mind of God in something, it cannot help being great, because God's thoughts are so high.

But the question for the moment is, What do we mean by authority and what do we gain from such works? And the answer is, returning to Monet, that there is no authoritative interpreter of the world apart from God. The authoritative painting, then, is that which goes beyond the personal, to be impregnated with a strength of vision and understanding that comes from heaven. How can we see this in paintings that are "just" a series of layers of interwoven color? I do not find myself very quick to relate Richard's paintings to the titles that inspired them, but what I do find is that if I take them as visual music, they have an extraordinary power to encompass the length and breadth of life in God's kingdom. Just as, when listening to

Bach, one can find oneself meditating on the cross, or on the fatherhood of God, which seem to be "in" the music, so in these paintings one seems to be in touch with both the love and the toughness of God, both the hardness of the human heart and the joy of the believer. But again one must ask, Where does he get this stuff from? We cannot get "there," to that sort of wisdom, from "here," our ordinary working minds. One can only say that this mind has been tapping in, not self-consciously but as a "normal" thing, to the luxury of the Holy Spirit.

This sort of life in God can easily be made to sound odd, a sort of Christian eccentricity. But if we leave art aside for a second, New Testament Christianity is that and nothing else. There is nothing to recommend in Christianity apart from dependence on God and life in the Spirit. So we should not be unduly surprised to encounter something from God himself in Christian art. But it is, perhaps, not so easily come by. So when we do find it, we should certainly celebrate it.

Sir Hugh Lane, 1875–1915, art dealer, philanthropist, director of the Dublin National Gallery and founder of the Municipal Gallery of Modern Art (now the Hugh Lane Gallery), Dublin, from an original undated photo (c.1915?) in the author's possession

12

Aesthetic Certainty in an Age of Relativism

Sir Hugh Lane and the Legacy of His Beliefs[1]

Since coming to Dublin two things have struck me. On the one hand, there is the tremendous fact that Hugh Lane's vision has been in large measure achieved, so many years after his death. Art, visual art, is now part of the lifeblood of Irish culture, accepted, talked about, and at home; and flourishing in a diversity of styles and galleries. It has its own life; it makes its own decisions in an international context without too much sense of subservience to what is going on elsewhere. The gallery Lane founded has become, as he intended, a point of reference—not a model or law for Irish art but an encouragement and mark of the highest standard, and it is held in affection by Irish painters and sculptors who by no means try to work in the styles favored by Lane and his supporters. The achievement of Lane's vision, which of necessity was long term since it involved such a radical change in the then perceptions of art, does to a large extent place in diminished proportion the complaints, the ruffled feathers, and the gossip about the way in which he did things, which so often miss the point that without very resolute action, even by a flawed and fallible person such as Lane was, much of this might never have happened.

1. The following is a recollection and expansion of a lecture given to the Friends of the Hugh Lane Gallery, Dublin, Oct. 22, 2000, on the occasion of the publication of Robert O'Byrne's new biography of Lane. Sir Hugh Lane was my mother's uncle, and although he perished in the Lusitania when she was only three, his memory, alongside many of his possessions, surrounded me while growing up. Later, I made a study of Lane's papers for my BA dissertation.

On the other hand, one could not fail to be struck also by the fact that the manner in which Lane's vision has been fulfilled has diverged very far from his original purposes. To put it simply, the art that his vision has enabled in Ireland is very different from any definition of art he would have recognized or indeed from the kind of art he actually enjoyed. His conception of art, the love of which aroused such a sacrificial devotion, was centered in clear values, even for contemporary art, deriving from his connoisseur's passion for beauty, form, and fine painting and workmanship. Art, for him, did not just go anywhere but had distinct boundaries and a center from which its value came.

The contrast between Lane's kind of art and that which his vision has enabled to be seen and admired today could not have been more pointedly demonstrated than in the sculptural display in the entrance hall of the Hugh Lane Gallery at the time of this lecture. Placed side by side are a Lane Gift sculpture, Rodin's *Age of Bronze*, and a modern work by Eilis O'Connell. Rodin's work, though revolutionary in its time for its naturalism, is the embodiment of humanist values. The person and the human being are still center stage for any serious statement as to life's meaning. It is true, as contemporaries realized, that we are already seeing the removal of the classical "skin," the idealization of man by which so many achievements, and probably not a few crimes, were legitimated. We are beginning to see the distinctly modern conception of man as left on this planet to fend for himself, his gods gone, but here with his beauty and some of his idealism still intact. But in O'Connell's work, we have reached something like the end of that track, something more like the situation in public religion today where the human has sunk back into nature, technically superb (as nature itself is) but, as far as consciousness goes, no longer feeling able to bear the burden of separation from nature, wanting only to merge with it. Her work, we are told, relates to old standing stones; and she does indeed capture the sense of a mystery beyond, her polished pyramid pointing like an antenna to an unknown world or being in space. Of classical proportion and harmony her work knows nothing, because there is no external world of ideas, no ideal based on transcendent gods or on the transcendent Creator God, to keep them in place. There is a certain uncanny presence in her work, but its form is by necessity somewhat arbitrary.

Lane, however, stood for beauty of form, and it seems deeply ironical that the movement for contemporary art to which he devoted so much of his strength has given rise to an art that has virtually reversed the good he intended. One cannot look at Lane's life, moreover, or come into contact with his personality and beliefs, without seeing the need to face up to questions arising from this. Were Lane's values simply the product of time and place, to be bypassed by the road of history?

In facing this nagging issue, one can, of course, practice historical evasion. One could argue, conveniently, that Lane begot essentially two streams of thought, that of his own personal values based on his love of art, which issued in purchases around his own taste, and a slightly different set of values based on his love of artists, for which he was willing to widen his taste and to be open to the possibility that the future would see things differently. So the two different streams could be labeled the "beauty" stream and the "modernity" stream, and one could say correctly that Lane believed in both. One could then go on to say that the vision for modernity has been the most successful, going far beyond what he himself had planned. The stream of his own taste, the "beauty" stream, one could then label simply as the taste of "a man of his time," a taste that has been outmoded today. In this neat historical relativization, modernity is the convenient and comfortable winner.

Now it is true that Lane, living in a time of artistic ferment, died before ever fully having to face these issues. We do not know what things he was pondering on his way back to England on the ill-fated Lusitania, having talked to John Quinn in New York about modern art. It is hard to imagine someone of his aesthetic delicacy even setting eyes on a Picasso but apparently at that stage he was confident that what Picasso was doing was "rubbish."[2] But he must have been aware of the earthquake beginning to shake the world of art and that his own era of confident aestheticism was about to end. At his death, his library contained books of reproductions of Cézanne and Gauguin, so evidently he was starting to acclimatize himself to the new art. He had been offered a Cézanne to buy but had not yet bitten. Whatever his concerns at the end, what is certain is that the two streams to which he had devoted his life were diverging and that had he lived he would have had to face some very difficult decisions. How far could this Old Master dealer continue to commit himself to the very best of contemporary art? For certainly he was not someone who would have been long satisfied with anything meretricious or second rate, simply because it accorded with the styles he liked.

The assumption that one might make, then, is that had Lane lived, he would have adapted and switched his energies from the prewar Beauty

---

2. Conversation reported in Reid, *John Quinn*, 213–14. Quinn was also arguing, Reid tells us, that Benjamin West's *Death on a White Horse* was "quite cubistic or futuristic." He told "Lane that the whole question turned on how one defined art, and whether one wanted to limit it to what had been art and to keep it in the lines of tradition. His [Lane's] only answer was that painting was too beautiful a thing and too fine a medium to be distorted."

stream into the postwar stream of modernity, which has carried the day. His taste for beautiful objects would then be relativized as the product of period and class and not something of permanent commitment and importance, unlike the stream of contemporaneity, in which a work of art being up to date and authentically of its time is always the priority.

However, to relativize Lane's taste in this way is almost certainly to fail to come to terms with Lane the man, and to assume that his taste had no grounding beyond temporary fashion. We cannot spend very long in his company, whether through Robert O'Byrne's or the earlier biographies, without realizing that taste for him was nothing superficial but was of the integrity of his being, which affected every aspect of his life. My favorite story of him is one O'Byrne quotes from Thomas Bodkin's account, about his visit to the hypnotherapist.

In the last few years of his life, Lane sought treatment for a nervous condition brought about by stress, then known as neurasthenia. On one occasion, Bodkin (a friend and colleague of Lane's) accompanied him to an expensive specialist and sat in the car "while the patient was supposed to be undergoing hypnosis. At the end of the session, his friend emerged and told Bodkin the experience had been 'ineffectual as far as he could judge, and yet rather funny.' It transpired that after talking to Lane for a while, the specialist had left him alone with instructions to count to one thousand. But 'when he went out I just popped up and arranged his beastly mantelpiece for him, and when I heard him coming back, I lay on the couch and pretended to be asleep.'"[3]

This story shows that correcting and redeeming bad taste, bringing order into disorder, was more important for Lane than his own health. Clearly the love of beauty was for him something at the core, not the surface, and it was for this cause that he was prepared to persuade and cajole, give and threaten, and bear notoriety and abuse.

So far we have used phrases like "love of art, of beauty, of good taste" very loosely, hoping that we are indicating an idea that will be familiar to us from Lane's own patronage and activities. However, if we are going to consider what Lane was really about in making this concept of art his cause, we will need to try to be a bit more definite. What was this "art" for which he was prepared to expend his life and fortune and yet which, as we have seen, has not been seen by subsequent generations as in "the true line of descent" that has given us the official sequence of modern art? And to put it even more sharply: if Lane was a man of conviction rather than of fashion, were

---

3. O'Byrne, *Hugh Lane*, 192.

his convictions simply wrong, or was there something in his beliefs that is of importance today?

In considering this issue, I am sure that we are enormously helped by historical distance. For example, it is far easier today to begin again to look at the art of the period on its own terms and without the prejudice of "progressive" and "conservative" party labels. For example, Wilson Steer, a friend and supporter of Lane, was a painter who was not ashamed to paint somewhat in the style of Constable and later to drop historical anchor somewhere in late impressionism. That is to describe his paintings solely in terms of how "advanced" they were. But in terms of the content of the pictures—what they were trying to convey in whatever style—here is a painter who did not lack fresh vision or a certain integrity in relation to nature. In other words, he does not necessarily have to be modern in order to enable us to see. But, it may well be that Steer's beliefs—that is, his conviction that landscape, light, the weather, etc. were worthy of attention—were in his time becoming outmoded and that with this erosion of belief his paintings have started to look different. One of the things we need to learn repeatedly is to see paintings in terms of what they are rather than in terms of what they are not. I have found Steer's paintings, for me, started to look "fresh" again, perhaps as Lane himself once saw them.

For Lane, art was certainly not just a matter of "good taste," or he would never have had such a profound and practical involvement in contemporary art. Good taste thrives on negatives: on not having the "wrong" colors or the "wrong" things in one's house. But Lane was a risk taker, far too interested in what was new and in helping to bring it into being to be stuck into negative thinking as he approached art. Otherwise, we would never have seen him involved with such difficult and quixotic characters as Mancini and Augustus John. You will remember that John was supposed to be painting decorative panels for the entrance hall in Lindsey House, the home Lane restored with old paneling and filled with Old Masters, and could very well have decorated with something far more tasteful than John's family of Gypsies draping themselves along the wall in superhuman scale—a scheme that was never finished.

For Mancini's art Lane also put himself out, taking on enormous social risks and the inconvenience of an eccentric Neapolitan who might prove a loose cannon but who in fact worked with immense diligence under Lane's direction. Mancini's paintings have never passed all the tests of taste; there is something about the thick and apparently careless impasto, erupting into the room like the irrepressible gestures of the voluble Italian himself, that can never be completely contained within notions of high breeding. But Mancini's portraits, even if they are not about staying within the bounds of taste, do, in retrospect, seem to be about something. When we look at them carelessly, they seem, like Annigoni—or early Picasso—to have a rather literal vision, but encased in a crust of modernity. But looked at more closely, we can see a method to the madness. Certainly he turns out to be a colorist, and when we see his juxtapositions of pure and very beautiful tints that contrast and coalesce from a distance, we realize that there is nothing arbitrary about them. Yet it is when we begin to realize his serious engagement with his sitters and their personalities that we see that here is a man who has gone a long way beyond style.

Obviously it makes no sense that an embarrassingly extroverted southern Italian, unable to speak English, let alone to read the nuances of Anglo-Irish culture, could be other than a superficial observer of his too-easily impressed patrons, and if that is so, then of course Lane made a huge mistake in placing such a large number of his works in Dublin, not least because those Irish artists to whom he was attempting to give a lead by importing the best modern continental work, such as Orpen and Yeats senior, were deeply unimpressed by Mancini. And yet if we look again, after ninety or so years, at these paintings that have lain in the dust of disregard (but which have remained in surprisingly good condition), we can see that Mancini was not, after all, an exponent of affectation, but that in all his profusion of paint he was strangely economical—in that all his effects seem to have been ordered by that plain and humble business of the portraitist: character.

In looking at the portrait of my great aunt, Ruth Shine, I was amazed to suddenly recognize the very person, the "scent," of the old lady whom I used to visit as a child. Her almost bony face in the portrait betrays quite a strength of character, which indeed was true of her and of her management of her brother Hugh's effects and his memory in the years following his death. As Lady Gregory recalls in her *Hugh Lane*, Ruth had trained as a horticulturalist, and I remember her with her vegetables and flowers, with that certain decisiveness that makes one realize she had missed much by not having children.[4]

The portrait of her aunt, Augusta Lady Gregory, is also unusual in that Mancini has not been overwhelmed by her "august" personality; by contrast, Orpen seemed to see her too much from the outside, as a figure one had to deal with. J. B. Yeats also had perhaps been too frightened to get close. But Mancini's portrait is the only one that, allowing she could be formidable, also shows she could be a friend. He has not had to belittle her to do this, but he has somehow grasped her humor and that there could be something

---

4. Gregory, *Hugh Lane*, 160.

like being on an equal footing with her—a status she certainly extended to her nephew Hugh.

The portrait that outshines them both, however, is the full length of Lane seated, completed in Rome in 1904, which even Mancini's detractors agreed had caught his sitter's nervous manner and pent-up energy. What I find remarkable too, apart from the striking color essay and the fact that at a distance the whole seems almost three-dimensional, is Mancini's very direct ways with his patron. Sargent had made his fortune in projecting his sitters' ideal or self-image, seldom showing a trace of reserve on his own part and willingly playing along with the imperial or moneyed roles his patrons had adopted. Mancini has not chosen to flatter or indeed to criticise; instead he has taken Lane as he found him, almost seeming to have picked him up bodily and placed him down in a not entirely tasteful studio interior, to see how he would react. Lane not looking at ease seems, probably, to be more generally true of his deportment in the world than any of the more conventional depictions in which his sense of not belonging was covered up. Mancini has also unsettled our expectations by lighting the figure from above, as if Lane is at the bottom of a well, so that his face is in darkness. The sense, slightly, of being trapped, even among furs and luxury, and of being in semidarkness, seems to say quite a lot about a figure who still seems obscure in some of his dealings and motives.

None of this interest in character, of course, seems quite adequate to the intellectual demands of modern art, where the scrambled cubes of Picasso's *Kahnweiler* portrait were soon to set a new standard, a standard by which anyone who appeared to know directly what character was came to be seen as naive about the perceptual difficulties. Anything as simple as doing a job any non-artist could criticise, if a likeness failed, came to seem outmoded, compared to a new portraiture to which only the artist, with a more sophisticated insight than the ordinary man, held the key. And in this sense Mancini was old-fashioned: there is an integrity in his work in which he really seemed to be trying to integrate what he was saying, in terms of character, with the means of saying it. But the way in which he did it, showing so clearly and uninhibitedly the presence of the artist (even leaving his marking threads intact on the canvas), does seem to have foreshadowed some of the concerns of today.

Now if it is true that Mancini is not Lane's unfortunate aberration, as I used to believe, but is in a sense central to the sort of aesthete Lane was, then looking at Mancini will help us understand what it was that Lane meant by art, and why it was such an important cause. It may, I know, seem perverse to take the one modern master that is liked least, when we have the Impressionists and all the Old Masters to choose from to illustrate Lane's taste, and my doing so may result largely from a sense of challenge! However it is also from the unexpected that we may perhaps observe what in other painters we would miss, simply by taking it for granted; for it is something to do with art itself that we are trying to isolate. Everyone these days, after all, admits to liking art, but what we are trying to grasp is what it was that was distinctive in Lane's liking of art, what it was that made it so important to him, not just for himself but as a benefit he was convinced he should provide for others.

So we have established that art, for Lane, meant more than good taste, since we cannot include Mancini within any very tight canon of good taste. Art had to go beyond the negative, or even the positive good taste of "doing things right." The architect Lutyens, a friend of Lane's and designer of his garden, was at this time a very stylish exponent of "doing things right," though for him personality and expression were very soon to burst the bounds of this tidy scheme and he was to invent powerful modernist expressions, albeit still in semiclassical language. But with Mancini we can see Lane as going beyond good form into an art that was prepared to take huge risks, for the sake of an end in view. Robert O'Byrne describes other aspects of Lane the risk-taker: the intrepid rider, the lover of speed, the gambler. Lane was perhaps drawn to an art that sailed close to the wind as Mancini's did. But the main purpose of risk was not just the thrill but the chance to win, and that meant for Lane living life at a heightened level, often by daring to acquire works of art by painters who themselves had done just the same. An aspect of the "art," then, he was after, was probably something like what he experienced in music, where life is lived totally, in an expressive and articulate way, uniting color and form and feeling, as he tried to do in the handling of his own life.

Deriving loosely from Mancini, then, we can identify three aspects of the art that Lane pursued: the element of color and form, or *beauty*; the element of *truth*, as in the meaning of character; and the element of risk or of *life*. Such phrases, of course, could be applied to almost any of the great masters represented by Lane's purchases for the National Gallery in Dublin, and also, in varying degrees, to those "modern" painters whose work he was trying to search out and represent when he formed the Dublin and Johannesburg "modern" collections. What, as phrases, they miss, is perhaps the one quality that unites them and unites them with the idea of taste in general but does so in a way that is difficult to put in modern terms. It is a feeling of things being "right," not, as we've said, in a negative way, but more in a joyful sense of "this is how things are meant to be." Obviously one cannot demand of a picture that its color, for instance, is beautiful and surprising, but with certain passages of color, even in the despised Mancini, there is what seems a gift of something absolutely "right," which, once thought of, "has to be there." Lane's passion could be defined as a passion for an art of this kind, for a rightness that seems both external to the ordinary world and yet, which, once given, seems absolutely essential to it. One could use the rather old-fashioned term, not usually applied to aesthetics, "righteousness." Lane's calling in the world of art was a passion for aesthetic righteousness.

All who knew Lane must have been struck by an "all or nothing" approach in his taste. As Robert O'Byrne points out in his biography, one of Lane's difficulties with his opponents was his insistence, for example, on having complete control in matters of aesthetic choice, as when he wanted to have the final say in the gallery design and site in the plan for the Dublin Municipal Gallery of Modern Art. He could be dictatorial in his opinions, and others could sometimes wonder if their judgments had any validity beside his own. Likewise, in matters of connoisseurship, he believed his own intuitions on, say, a Rembrandt authorship, had final validity. We could, and indeed must, note a weakness in him here, in which the power of his great gift was being abused to exclude other points of view. There is no such thing as a perfect taste nor indeed of an absolutely final word on questions of attribution (and nor is the latest opinion necessarily the best). There must be many who would like to be allowed absolute authority in matters aesthetic and no doubt some who could handle the power better than others.

But what I think we need to focus on, with Lane's "all or nothing" absolutism, is to try to establish in what his authority was based. Because while it is easy to regard it as merely a personal judgment somehow grown totalitarian, a kind of taste the First World War justifiably swept away, along with the social structure which supported it, that does not quite allow for the kind of taste it was. Because what we have seen is that the kind of things that Lane enjoyed in pictures, the things on which his passion was based, are things that are really there. His authority, then, was not an undisciplined extension of his own subjectivity but was based on his life as a "seer," someone who sees what he believes to be there. This was most clearly seen in the way he staked huge sums of money on his own convinced attributions.

We can allow that there were merely social and temporary aspects to his taste. He moved with people who used paintings for self-flattery, who bought eighteenth-century portraits in order to elevate themselves and their diamond-gained fortunes to the kind of gentlemanly innocence that was supposed to reside in land, tradition, and class. We can allow that much of Lane's activities, in dressing drawing rooms and dressing ladies to adorn them, had to do with social image as much as with aesthetics. Yet the common thread to all this activity was the desire always to find the point at which the mundane became beautiful and to elevate and make distinctive every space he was in. In other words, his taste was, as well as a private passion, profoundly objective, concerned usually with objects, and the entirely rational consideration of shape, texture, and color—a passion that took him into very diverse fields, such as oriental porcelain, for his purchases. This meant that disagreeing with Lane, for him, meant not just disagreeing with his personal judgment or opinion, but with his very strong convictions about the way things were, about aesthetic right and wrong in some sort of absolute sense.

In what sort of absolute sense, however, could Lane's kind of aesthetic judgments be considered to have validity? Here we are at the nub of the issue his taste raises, as we confront the extreme divergence between his sort of taste and the art that became dominant after his death. Was he simply wrong, or do his beliefs have a coherence we can, albeit in a less exclusive way, hold onto?

The only way I can see to answer this question is to begin by noting that the divergence we have been describing, between one kind of art and another, also represents a divergence of belief. This is not always seen in the art histories and certainly was not in the histories with which I grew up, where art history was told as a continuum from Giotto to Pollock, in which one movement succeeded another in a natural evolutionary sequence. The main issues were vision, perception, change for its own sake, and progress. Art was supposed to be about art, generating its own concerns from within its own tradition. One could consider color, or form, or texture, or any manner of specialisms, and art had its own boundary within which all these could be explored. Moreover, it could drag more and more of the external world within the "Art" boundary—but art itself remained self-sufficient and self-defining. What we did not see, however, in this view of art, was that in itself it expressed a belief position on the question of ultimates.

This is most easily seen if we consider the question at the heart of our discussion, that of beauty. Beauty *matters*. That is the heart of the perception of beauty: not only that it is enjoyable but that in some sense it is valuable and important. In other words, the perception of beauty includes some kind of "understood" external referent. But this is where we see the divergence in modern art. For what is there externally for beauty to refer to? On the one hand, in the history of modern art, almost all the description tends to relate to art internally, or to human psychology. Color, for example, is described in terms of its effects on our emotions, as if works of art were therapeutic tools. Form is described as if relationships were important for their own sake, or in terms of relationships with other works of art. But what we do not hear is anything of the ideal of form or beauty as having an intrinsic value or importance. The reason for this is more than obvious if we take account of history. Beauty is no longer considered *true*. It can only be considered as a "leisure asset," a consumer durable since, after civilization's self-image came apart in two world wars, beauty is no longer considered to have any meaning. During the Great War, artists, like their fellow soldiers, were propelled straight from the drawing rooms of polite society where they collected their sitters, to the front line, and for many, what they had taken for granted of the meaning of art ceased to make sense. Orpen was one of those who found himself completely unprepared, intellectually, for the horrors into which he was thrown. His whole artistic language had developed in a tradition in which man continually looked towards an ideal, developed in the sculpture of Greece and Rome and in the classical art which derived from it. And yet, here, that ideal was exposed as completely inadequate to the remaking of helpless humanity in the machinery of a modern war, that no one had desired or designed. Lavery, we learn from a picture label in the Hugh Lane Gallery, carried on with scenes of sybarite leisure, regardless of the guns overseas: but which was more true? In some ways, they were both crazy. The beauty of a lazy afternoon on the river at home could have been something that the war was being fought for, but was it "true" enough to be worth the price? Such were the questions the mere love of feeling, of pleasure, were unable to answer.

Therefore it is not surprising that a divergence began to take place between an art of traditional naturalism that seemed to have to subsist on its own without external explanation or validation, and a kind of devotion to taste, good living, which was cut adrift from any serious reference to truth. Thus in our own time, instead of a unity of the arts, as in the way Chardin, or Snyders before him, might paint the elements of a gourmet meal, linking together art, beauty, and appetite, there is now a schizoid split between say, Delia Smith's cheerful view of meat, on one side, and Damien Hirst's sermonic approach to flesh, on the other. There is still a serious approach to beauty in life, but it is disguised in something we take very seriously, food, but not intellectually seriously or in relation to truth.

To liken art to food, however, is not good enough, not least when our subject is Lane, for whom food had no importance whatever when compared to art. The question we need to consider is whether there is not after all something in beauty that has an intrinsic importance and authority. This can only be considered from the point of view of faith.

The proposition is this. One cannot really explain beauty, the sheer goodness of art, in a gustatory way. It diminishes art, beyond its own nature, to regard it only as a form of re-creation or as a kind of caffeine for the soul. It makes Lane out to be a mere addict and his gallery founding achievements little more than the building of coffee houses—pleasant, good, useful, but hardly worth the pain and sweat. On the other hand, the history of the last century has firmly rejected beauty as true. As an ideal, it has seemed too far away from humanity's real condition. Art, drama, and film have concentrated far more on the devil within than on the ideal to which civilization has sought to attain. But where, then, does that leave the beauty of art? It must be a hope that is false—a brief truce at Christmas for "good feelings" before normal hostilities resume at new year. It is on this ground that architecture has been able to espouse the "brutal" as more authentic, more real, than the civic virtues of the classical style. But here we have two contradictory statements: on the one hand, beauty has an intrinsic authority and sense of worth and, on the other, when we look at history today, hope and joy seem to many a lie. What is the solution?

The solution seems to me clear if one accepts this paradoxical statement: "the meaning of art is not in the art." There is nothing strange about this, but it does mean that very often we have been looking for meaning in the wrong place. Meaning is to do with mind, with thought, with value, and these things we do not find *in* nature. The meaning of a sunset is not in the dust particles illuminated by light; it is in something external to it, something like the sheer surprise and welcome of beauty and color as gift in the middle of predictable daily existence. For its meaning, its surface offers little help; we need to see its place in the whole existential mix. In the same way, one can take a great picture, like the National Gallery of Ireland's Vermeer, and, if you look too close, not only does the surface dissolve into blobs but its meaning too becomes flat and incoherent, for the meaning it coordinates on its frail surface is all to do with assumptions we may share in common about the world outside: the value of humanity and domesticity, the majesty of light, the beauty of things. If none of these things had meaning, the picture itself would fail.

So it is with beauty. The "righteousness," the "way things should be," that describes Lane's kind of fine art taste is dependent on a belief about the world that is really external to art. It follows a belief that "the way things should be" is worth pursuing because it is, intrinsically, *more true*, than the ugliness and disorder in which the world commonly finds itself. It depends ultimately on belief in God, the Creator of a good world, and in Jesus, whose life showed the authenticity of goodness in the world and hence the inauthenticity of evil, which had assumed the right to this world's high places. It depends on a belief that things like goodness are worth fighting for, even when they do not appear to succeed, because their authority is transcendent and will, in the end, be vindicated. The beauty that keeps appearing in art, then, is both something given, that cannot be fully accounted for by nature, and something worth striving for, because it represents a "wager" on how things really are.

The consequence of this theological view is that we do not need to confine our truth to what we see, or rather, we do not need to consider ugliness and the bestiality of human behavior to be the only or true account of the world. The rationale for beauty may seem to have been undercut, but that is only the case if it is linked to an unattainable ideal, which a sober estimate of human nature shows we are better without. But if beauty is linked to the nature of the God who made us, then it is more like a call into the kind of life we are made to have and which God intends should be restored to us, if we are willing.

This is very far from saying that art itself is redemptive. Art gives a taste of redemption, it gives a sense of how things might be, but it is not in itself any sort of elixir of life. It may be that for Lane, perhaps trying to feed his inner self from the masterpieces he owned, art seemed to have the power to redeem, though the picture we have of him in his later years was of someone empty and spent. The sarcasm and bitterness that, we are told, came to characterise his speech tells of someone whom neither ownership nor friendship could renew. Nor, however, could hostility to his cause diminish his burning inner conviction about the value of art.

Was Lane himself religious? Can we situate his love of art in a personal theological framework? Lane's parents had been drawn to each other out of a shared concern for faith, his mother inheriting her mother's firm Protestant convictions, so it seems, and his father turning from law to ordination, as would one of Lane's brothers. Lane's diaries as a young man reveal that he continued to attend church. The plaque placed in his memory by Sarah Harrison recalls his "sincere and devout faith." Alongside this one must set his gambling, his dabbling in the occult, and his superstition. We do not know how influenced he was by Yeats, who seemed to have cast him in the role of a Nietzschean aristocratic hero, a superior person continually under threat from lesser mortals—an identity not particularly helpful for Christian humility. We can see that his most obvious form of religion was art; that it was art that gave him his own sense of worth, and art that he felt most profoundly had saving power for others. But, as Christ said, "Man shall not live by bread alone"[5] (something Lane would most heartily have concurred with, as he starved himself for art), meaning that this physical world itself is not sufficient to sustain life; what we need is "every word which comes from the mouth of God," that is to say, personal contact renewing us from God; and this, it seems likely, Lane lacked.

However, the point about beauty is that it is a gift, a free gift. It does not need a theological framework to be enjoyed. It is part of the experience

---

5. Luke 4:4, ESV.

of art in every culture of the world, whatever its belief, just as is good cooking. But it does thrive in cultures where goodness as gift, as "the real thing," is believed in, and this certainly has been true of Western culture over its many centuries. Many have been content to cash checks on that inherited bank account of common faith in goodness without the associated belief in and fear of God. Where the theological framework is needed, however, is when scepticism comes in.

When philosophy and science become deliberately sceptical about God, the soil of art is eroded, and creative form and beauty cannot easily flourish. But that is the time when religion has to become self-conscious again and when we need to consider afresh who we believe in and what public beliefs are likely to sustain a true and good art in the future. The same is true in the political arena. Everything good that the state is supposed to do has to have, in the end, some basis in ultimate beliefs about what is good and who we are responsible to. Otherwise, as we have seen with fascist and communist regimes, the public definition of what is good begins to slide, until the "good people" cease to be able to tell good from evil.

Finally, where does this leave those with charge of galleries today? We began by looking at two streams of art curating deriving from Lane's ideas: the "beauty" stream, and the "contemporaneity" stream, and we considered that had he lived, he might have observed the divergence of those two and had to face some hard choices. If beauty actually has a transcendent importance, what is a gallery director to do? Make this a rule of exclusion?

We are really looking at two kinds of truth here. The best of contemporary art is "true," true to an authentic sense of how the world seems to be to moderns living their lives without a sense of God and believing in a lonely and unfathered planet in which we have to make our own meanings. As a Christian I question whether that actually is "true truth," and whether a view of the world that ignores revelation from its Maker can actually make good sense of it. So for me, this contemporary art that sidelines the traditional qualities of form and beauty as inauthentic and untrue has begun to seem not so much exciting and relevant as predictable and lacking in life. I have little doubt that Lane would have thought the same.

We do have a difficulty here. It is important for voices to be heard, and it is not good for galleries to act as censors, trying to control taste. The art we have is the art we have. However, it is also important that when we try to be "inclusive," we do so sincerely, not thinking merely of the margins, but warmly giving space to the center. And we do need to know that we have choices. We are not, as we sometimes think, helpless riders on the runaway horse of culture. Each one of us affects the direction in which culture goes. The choices we make, in the art we do or the art we sponsor, will affect one another and generations to come. Our choices reflect our commitments. Goodness is a discipline; it is far easier to go along with the current or mediocre, to continually say yes, and never no, or not give support to the thing that is good. So we should make a definite commitment to be "inclusive towards goodness."

Art, then, is a strange thing—if expected to generate meaning and value out of itself, it dries up; if too much is expected of it in terms of perfection or redemption, it is apt to cause quarrels, pain, and stress; but if held on a light hand, seeing its meaning as coming from the Giver who made it, is pure pleasure and delight, a tangible hint of the hope to come, with the weight of something that will, in God's good time, become ever more solid and real.

Bibliography

Clarkson, Jonathan. *Constable*. New York: Phaidon, 2010.
Constable, John. *John Constable's Correspondence: The Fishers*. Vol. 6. Edited by R. B. Beckett. Suffolk Records Society 12. Suffolk, UK: Boydell, 1968.
———. *John Constable's Discourses*. Compiled by R. B. Beckett. Suffolk Records Society 14. Suffolk, UK: Boydell, 1970.
"Docklands' Lincoln Plaza Luxury Flats Win Carbuncle Cup." *BBC News*, Sept. 7, 2016. https://www.bbc.com/news/uk-37294090.
Fry, Roger. *Transformations: Critical and Speculative Essays on Art*. London: Chatto and Windus, 1927.
———. *Vision and Design*. London: Chatto and Windus, 1920.
Gibbert, Matt, and Albert Hill. *Ornament Is Crime: Modernist Architecture* New York: Phaidon, 2017.
Gombrich, E. H. *Art and Illusion*. 2nd ed. London: Phaidon, 1961.
———. *In Search of Cultural History*. Oxford: Oxford University Press, 1969.
Gregory, Lady. *Hugh Lane: Life and Achievement*. London: John Murray, 1921.
Loos, Adolf. *Ornament and crime, a lecture of 1910, published in German in 1929, and republished in Trotzdem,* Innsbruck: Brenner Verlag, 1931.
Mascall, E. L. *Words and Images: A Study in Theological Discourse*. London: Longmans Green, 1957.
Newbigin, Lesslie. *The Gospel in a Pluralist Society*. London: SPCK, 1989.
———. *Truth to Tell: The Gospel as Public Truth*. Grand Rapids: Eerdmans, 1991.
O'Byrne, Robert. *Hugh Lane, 1875–1915*. Dublin: Lilliput, 2000.
Pevsner, Nikolaus. *The Outline of European Architecture*. 7th ed. London: Pelican, 1960.
———. *Pioneers of Modern Design: From William Morris to Walter Gropius*. London: Penguin, 1960.
Polanyi, Michael. *Personal Knowledge: Towards a Post-critical Philosophy*. Rev. ed. London: Routledge & Kegan Paul, 1962.
Reid, B. L. *The Man from New York: John Quinn and His Friends*. New York: Oxford University Press, 1968.
Richter, Paul. "On Professor Gombrich's Model of Schema and Correction." *The British Journal of Aesthetics* 16.4 (Autumn 1976) 338–46.
Ruskin, John. *Modern Painters, Vol. 1*. 3rd ed. London: George Allen, 1900.
———. *Praeterita*. Vol. 3. London: George Allen, 1899.
Sayers, Dorothy L. *The Mind of the Maker*. London: Methuen, 1941.

Scott, Drusilla. *Everyman Revived: The Common Sense of Michael Polanyi*. Lewes, UK: Book Guild, 1985.
Tate Gallery. *Mark Rothko, 1903–1970*. London: Tate Gallery, 1987.
Taylor, Basil. *Constable, Paintings, Drawings and Watercolours*. 2nd ed. London: Phaidon, 1975.
Thistlethwaite, David. *The Art of God and the Religions of Art*. Carlisle, UK: Solway, 1998.
Torrance, Thomas F. *The Ground and Grammar of Theology*. Charlottesville: The University Press of Virginia, 1980.
———. *Incarnation: The Person and Life of Christ*. Edited by Robert T. Walker. Downer's Grove, IL: IVP Academic, 2008.
———. *Theological Science*. New York: Oxford University Press, 1969.
Watkin, David. *Morality and Architecture: The Development of a Theme in Architectural History and Theory from the Gothic Revival to the Modern Movement*. Oxford: Clarendon, 1977.
Wittgenstein, Ludwig. *Tractatus Logico-Philosophicus*. 2nd ed. London: Kegan Paul, Trench, Trübner & Co., 1933.

www.ingramcontent.com/pod-product-compliance
Lightning Source LLC
Chambersburg PA
CBHW071447150426
43191CB00008B/1265